Innovative and evidence based, this introduction to the main concepts and issues in language teaching uses a "key questions" structure, enabling the reader to understand how these questions have been addressed by researchers previously, and how the findings inform language teaching practices. Grounded in research, theory, and empirical evidence, the textbook provides students, practitioners, and teachers with a complete introductory course in language teaching. Written in a clear and user-friendly style, and avoiding use of jargon, the book draws upon real-life teaching experiences and scenarios to provide practical advice. A glossary of key terms, questions for discussion, and further reading suggestions are included. The book is perfectly suited to language teaching modules on English Language, TESOL, and Applied Linguistics courses.

Alessandro G. Benati is Head of the English Department and Professor of English and Applied Linguistics at the American University of Sharjah. He is visiting and honorary professor at the University of York St. John and the University of Portsmouth.

Key Questions in Language Teaching

An Introduction

Alessandro G. Benati

American University of Sharjah

CAMBRIDGE
UNIVERSITY PRESS

CAMBRIDGE
UNIVERSITY PRESS

University Printing House, Cambridge CB2 8BS, United Kingdom

One Liberty Plaza, 20th Floor, New York, NY 10006, USA

477 Williamstown Road, Port Melbourne, VIC 3207, Australia

314–321, 3rd Floor, Plot 3, Splendor Forum, Jasola District Centre, New Delhi – 110025, India

79 Anson Road, #06-04/06, Singapore 079906

Cambridge University Press is part of the University of Cambridge.

It furthers the University's mission by disseminating knowledge in the pursuit of education, learning, and research at the highest international levels of excellence.

www.cambridge.org
Information on this title: www.cambridge.org/9781108425247
DOI: 10.1017/9781108676588

First published 2020

Printed in the United Kingdom by TJ International Ltd. Padstow Cornwall

A catalogue record for this publication is available from the British Library.

ISBN 978-1-108-42524-7 Hardback
ISBN 978-1-108-44140-7 Paperback

Cambridge University Press has no responsibility for the persistence or accuracy of URLs for external or third-party internet websites referred to in this publication and does not guarantee that any content on such websites is, or will remain, accurate or appropriate.

This book is dedicated to my dear wife
Bernadette, my daughter Grace, and
my son Francesco.

Contents

Acknowledgments

I would like to thank my students and colleagues at the American University of Sharjah for their support, feedback, and encouragement without which this book would have not been possible. A special gratitude to my colleagues in SLA who have read this book and two anonymous reviewers who have provided me with priceless advice on how to improve its content. I would also like to express my gratitude to Rebecca, Stephanie, Victoria, and all the colleagues at Cambridge University Press for supporting me and ensuring publication of the present book. I am grateful to Karthik, Charlie and Christine for their work on the production of the book and to Najat Alabdullah for producing the index.

Prologue

This book is composed of six main chapters (and one final evaluation chapter) raising questions about language teaching. (Chapter 1) What do we know about second language acquisition and what are the implications for language teaching? (Chapter 2) How has second language teaching methodology evolved over the years? (Chapter 3) What is the nature and role of communication and interactive tasks (speaking and writing)? (Chapter 4) What is the nature and role of listening, reading comprehension, and writing tasks? (Chapter 5) What is the nature and role of grammar, vocabulary, and corrective feedback? (Chapter 6) How do we carry out second language research? (Chapter 7) The book ends with an overall evaluation of the questions raised.

These main questions and other related questions are examined from the point of view that a good definition of communication is the expression, interpretation and negotiation of meaning for a purpose in a given context, and that language is abstract and complex and it is not learned like any other mental phenomenon. There is a difference between acquisition and language skills. There is a difference between acquiring a second language and developing a language-like behavior.

- In chapter one, some of the key and relevant questions addressed in second language research to investigate how acquisition happens will be presented with the main aim to extrapolate useful implications for language teaching and teachers. Some of the findings obtained in second language research have provided important insights in determining the key elements responsible for language acquisition. A better understanding of how acquisition happens and a better knowledge of the main second language acquisition constructs would push language teachers to question the prevailing methods and approaches in language teaching. A brief account of main contemporary theories in second language acquisition is also provided in this chapter.

- In chapter two, the reader is provided with a brief examination of the main current and past teaching methods and approaches in language teaching. For each of them, *the main principles* and *pedagogical procedures* will be presented. The chapter concludes with a discussion on the importance to go beyond specific language teaching methodologies and the necessity to develop an evidence and principle-based approach to language teaching. One that provides language teachers with a variety of "effective options" all grounded in theory and empirical evidence from second language research.

- In chapter three, it is argued that the main goal in language teaching is to ensure that language learners develop their communicative skills in the target language.

Communication is the expression, interpretation, and negotiation of meaning for a purpose in a given context. The use of language tasks promotes acquisition and provides a purpose for language use. A task can also be used to achieve a specific lesson objective. Tasks (and not mechanical exercises or activities lacking meaning) should form the backbone of the language teaching curriculum. The nature and role of interactive speaking tasks (exchange-information tasks) is examined. The nature and role of language writing in second language teaching from a communicative perspective is also examined. Writing, like any other aspects of second language development, is about communication. In real life we write e-mails, notes, letters, grocery lists, reports, and essays, and these different tasks have a communicative purpose and a specific audience. A more communicative and task-based approach to the development of writing skills is proposed. In order to develop more effective tasks for developing writing skills, language instructors must clarify the communicative purpose of a written task and the target audience. Language teachers must integrate writing with other language skills and use more meaningful, realistic, and relevant writing tasks based on L2 learners' needs.

- In chapter four, input is defined as the language that L2 learners hear or see in a communicative context. Input is language that learners try to comprehend for the message contained in it. Language acquisition is input-dependent. The key issue in developing effective listening and reading comprehension tasks is to understand the nature and role of listening and reading in another language. General guidelines as to how to construct effective listening and reading comprehension tasks in the language classroom are presented. An interactive and communicative approach to teaching listening and reading skills is explained and proposed.

- In chapter five, the nature and role of grammar, vocabulary, and corrective feedback in second language learning and teaching are examined. Traditional grammar instruction (paradigms) and grammar practice (drills) are not an effective way to teach languages. Research and theory in second language acquisition provide valuable information about how grammar is learned and how different factors may impact on the effectiveness of different pedagogical interventions. These pedagogical interventions move from input (e.g., input enhancement, consciousness-raising tasks, input flood, structured input tasks) to output-based options (e.g. collaborative tasks, dictogloss, structured output tasks). The role of vocabulary is explored. Some vocabulary tasks are presented and an effective way to teach vocabulary is examined. In this chapter, the nature, types, and role of interactional modifications and corrective feedback in language learning and teaching is discussed. It is through negotiation of meaning that L2 learners not only resolve breakdown in communication and clarify somebody else's message, but also receive corrective feedback on the erroneous sentences. Corrective feedback is provided through different conversational techniques and negotiation strategies (e.g. clarification requests, confirmation checks, prompts, elicitation, repetition, recasts) during interaction and classroom tasks. In the past thirty years, the key issues addressed by teachers and scholars, as far as error correction is concerned, are: Should errors be corrected? How should we correct errors? Is the difference in effectiveness of corrective feedback depending on the nature of the feedback itself?

- In chapter six, a minimal definition of second language research is provided. The main designs (e.g., Action Research, Experimental, Observation, Case Study, Psycholinguistics Methods) and procedures used in second language research are briefly presented. Research findings from classroom-based research could lead to a revision of how best we teach languages. The purpose of the chapter is to provide the novice readers and teachers with basic research tools to carry out their own research in the classroom.
- In chapter seven, an overall evaluation of the following key questions is provided:

What do we know about second language acquisition that is useful for language teachers and teaching?
Is there a particular language teaching method or approach better than others?
Is there a particular type of speaking task better than others?
Is there a particular type of writing interactive task better than others?
Is there a particular type of listening comprehension task better than others?
Is there a particular type of reading comprehension task better than others?
Is there a particular type of explicit information (rules explanation) better than others?
Is there a particular pedagogical intervention to grammar instruction more effective than others?
Is there a particular type of error correction better than others?

It is impossible for an introductory book of this kind to be exhaustive. The pedagogical interventions and language teaching options presented in this book are some of the options available to language teachers. The main objective of this book is to provide suggestions for language teaching which are grounded on research, theory, and empirical evidence.

The chapters are written for the novice reader, avoiding a scholarly style and tone and using a reader-friendly approach. The book is written for students and practitioners with no or little background in language teaching or language acquisition theory and research. Each chapter has the following common sections: Chapter overview; Exemplary Study; Recap; References and Readings; Discussion and Questions. The hope is that the book will serve as a basic introduction for the novice student and language teacher who is willing to reflect on some of the key issues in language learning and teaching.

What Do We Know About Second Language Acquisition and What Are the Implications for Second Language Teaching?

Overview

In this chapter, some of the most relevant questions addressed by second language research and theory will be presented with the main aim to extrapolate useful information for language teaching and teachers. Findings from empirical research have provided a shift in the way we understand and conceptualize second language acquisition and language teaching. We begin with explaining second language acquisition (SLA) with a brief overview of the key theories and a description of the nature of language.

The study of second language acquisition is the study of how L2 learners come to create a new language system with often a limited exposure to the second language. It is the study of how they can make use of that system during comprehension and speech production. For the purpose of clarification, a second language (L2) refers to a language that is acquired after the first language (L1) has been established in early childhood.

Theory and research in second language acquisition have emphasized the cognitive (mental) process involved in the acquisition of another language, how learners process language, and how they create "intake" from language input (i.e., what gets processed and what doesn't). Research and theory in second language acquisition also looks into how L2 learners accommodate language into their internal new system, and how they access the information for speech production.

Second language acquisition scholars are mainly interested in exploring the key processes and factors involved in language acquisition. Research carried out within this context is often about learners and learning (e.g., researchers are interested in finding out how particular groups process a certain grammatical feature, or how a particular syntactic structure develops in a learner's mind/brain). However, the main findings from second language research often have implications for teachers and teaching. For example, based on the research findings and theory in instructed second language acquisition research, teachers can develop effective pedagogical interventions to teach grammar.

Consider this ...

Name three main findings from second language research that you might already know and think of possible implications for language teaching.

1.
2.
3.

What Is Second Language Acquisition?

Second language acquisition consists of a series of theories, theoretical views, hypotheses, and frameworks about the way L2 learners create and develop a new language system. Bill VanPatten (2003) has equated second language acquisition research to the construction of a building. When we build a house, we need to take care of the foundation, the frame, the electrical system, the plumbing, the heat and the air system, and so on. All these are necessary steps and one alone is insufficient. Very much like those who work in house construction and are electrical contractors or plumbing contractors, in second language acquisition scholars are often dealing with different matters: the roles of input and output; how the internal language system develops; and so on.

Second language acquisition is a complex phenomenon as it entails the acquisition of different systems (e.g., the phonological system, the lexical system, the morphological system, the syntactical system). It also consists of a number of mechanisms that are responsible for how L2 learners are able to process language input, internalize language, and tap into the system for language production (output).

The field of second language acquisition research addresses two fundamental issues:

- How L2 learners come to internalize the linguistic system of another language; and
- How L2 learners make use of that linguistic system during comprehension and speech production.

Within these two fundamental and overarching issues, there have been a number of related and significant questions raised by scholars in this field and addressed by second language acquisition research and theory. The ones that have more relevance and direct implications for language teaching and will be presented and discussed in this chapter are:

- What are the similarities and differences between first and second language acquisition?
- What is the nature of language?
- How does the internal language system develop?
- What is the role of input?
- What is the role of output?
- What is the role of instruction?

Please look at the following statements about second language acquisition and indicate whether you agree or disagree.

	Agree	Disagree
Languages are acquired through imitation		
Language acquisition is like learning any other skills		
People acquire grammar rules		
The acquisition of L1 and L2 is different		
Language acquisition is largely implicit		
Input and interaction are key factors		
Output plays a limited role		
Instruction makes the difference		

Please look at your choices again once you finished reading the chapter!

Scholars in second language acquisition believe that input is a necessary ingredient for the acquisition of a second language. However, there is considerable debate over the nature and design of the internal mechanisms that create our so-called internal language system (mental representation). There are two competing accounts (domain general and language specific) as highlighted by Gregory Keating (2016: 3):

(a) some scholars and researchers argue that language is like any other complex mental tasks such as reading, playing chess, and in general solving problems. Like any other complex mental phenomenon is learned via the same domain-general mechanisms that enable us to learn how to program a computer or solve difficult puzzles;

(b) other scholars and researchers instead contend that language is special and it is not learned in the same way as other complex mental phenomenon. Their claim is that humans are hardwired to learn language and have cognitive mechanisms specifically designed to deal with language. These are separate mechanisms from the domain-general one.

This distinction made here will be useful to understand some contrasting views about second language acquisition and proposing effective options and solutions for language teaching.

What Are the Key Theories in Second Language Acquisition?

Theories in second language acquisition have been developed and proposed in the attempt to understand how language learners come to develop and use their internal language system. Theories in second language acquisition are not mutually exclusive. In the next paragraphs we examine the main ones.

Behaviorism

Behaviorism that prevailed in the 1940s and 1950s made a number of claims:

- There is no innate knowledge.
- All behavior is viewed as a response to stimuli.

According to this theory, language acquisition was seen as a progressive accumulation of habits and the ultimate goal was error-free production. The L1 was seen as a major obstacle to L2 acquisition because it caused interference errors (caused by habits in the L1) and negative transfer (from L1 to L2) of habits. The concept of positive and negative transfer was central to behaviorism. Positive transfer is when learners transfer a structure from their first language to their second language. Negative transfer is when learners inappropriately use an L1 structure in the L2.

Transfer was seen as the process used by learners to rely on the L1 system to construct the L2 system.

Within the behaviorist framework, theorists believed that language acquisition involves acquiring good habits. Learners proceed from form to meaning; that is, first master the grammatical forms and then move on to express meaning. Certain conditions were applied for acquiring these habits:

- The learner imitates and repeats the language heard;
- The imitation has to be rewarded; and
- As a result of this, the behavior is reinforced and eventually becomes habitual.

This theory was translated into the Audio-Lingual Method (see Chapter 2), which emphasized the teaching of languages through memorization and pattern practice (drills).

The Universal Grammar Theory

The Universal Grammar Theory claims that a language is a complex and abstract system that develops in the human mind. Language learning cannot be treated as a process of mechanical habit formation. The actual verbal behavior is only the "tip of the iceberg." Noam Chomsky (1965) argued that all humans possess innate knowledge of language universals and principles that regulate the acquisition of languages. These universal principles are modified in the light of the input to which humans are exposed. In other words, humans start with a knowledge of

> Poverty of the stimulus is a key concept in the Universal Grammar Theory. It suggests that people are born with an innate specification for language.

language universals and generate from that knowledge a series of hypotheses about the particular language they are learning, at the same time modifying and correcting them in the light of the data available. We are all born with some kind of special language processing ability called "language acquisition device." The presence of an innate hypothesis-making device emphasizes the active role played by the language learner. This is in antithesis with behaviorism, which views the growing mastery of the language as a "passive" response to pattern practice.

Researchers within this theoretical framework have been concerned with how languages are represented in the mind and how learners come to know more about a language than what they have been exposed to (poverty of the stimulus). There are many aspects of language that are universal and built in prior to exposure to the input language. Given that, humans have an innate knowledge of what is allowed and what is disallowed in a language. For example, first language speakers of English know (without being taught) the following:

(a) *I've done* (contraction of *I've* is allowed)
(b) **Should I've done it?* (contraction here is disallowed)

How does a person come to know that *I've* (and contractions more generally) is allowed in some instances and disallowed in others? Despite the fact that we are not taught this, every native speaker of English comes to know what is disallowed with contractions. This is what we call a universal feature that is available to humans from the start.

The Universal Grammar Theory makes a number of key claims:

- Learners have their own internal syllabus (abstract principles) to follow that constrains language acquisition. The information contained in our mind (innate knowledge) influences the development of mental representation. Our mental representation of language is complex, abstract, and implicit.
- Universal grammar consists of a variety of features that regulates how the language operates. Languages have different characteristics as they select different features. For example, Japanese is "head final" (*Alessandro Japanese speaks*). This means that the "head" (in this case the verb) comes after the complement (the object).
- Learners make projections about the language they learn, which is often beyond the information they are supposed to know. In other words, they sometimes know how a linguistic feature works, what is grammatical or ungrammatical, without having been exposed to that particular feature.

This theory was translated into the view that learning should be allowed to take place naturally in the course of using the second language for communication. The goal of language teaching is to reproduce these natural conditions.

The Monitor Theory

The Monitor Theory suggests that L2 learners acquire language mainly through exposure to comprehensible input in a similar fashion as they acquire their first language. The main requisite for this to happen is that learners are exposed to comprehensible and message-oriented input.

Input is the key ingredient in language acquisition.

The key claims of the Monitor Theory are:

- Grammatical features are acquired by L2 learners in a specific order (order of acquisition) no matter the learner's L1. Morphological features such as the progressive -*ing* in English is acquired before the regular past tense -*ed*, or irregular past tense forms, which is acquired before third-person singular -*s*. Instruction is therefore constrained by universal and predictable order of acquisition.
- When learners acquire a second language they develop two systems that are independent from each other. The "acquisition system" (unconscious and implicit) is activated when we are engaged in communication. The "learning system" (conscious and explicit) functions as a monitor of the language we produce upon producing it.
- It is paramount that L2 learners are exposed to input (comprehensible) that is slightly above their proficiency level (i+1) and learn a second language in a very relaxed environment that enhances L2 learners' motivation.
- Learners who are comfortable and have a positive attitude toward languages will have their affective filters low and will have access to comprehensible input. Stressful environments in which learners are forced to produce before they feel ready will raise their filters blocking learners' processing of input.

According to this theory, there is a need for the creation of a kind of environment in the language classroom that resembles the condition where L1 learning takes place. There are certain practical implications for classroom practice consistent with the Monitor Theory that form the basis for the Natural Approach (see Chapter 2).

The Interaction Hypothesis

The Interaction Hypothesis focuses on how interactions affect acquisition with the view that input is a key ingredient for the acquisition of a second language. Interactional input refers to input received during interaction where there is some kind of communicative exchange (and negotiation) involving the learner and at least one other person.

NATIVE SPEAKER: How are you, Alessandro?

ALESSANDRO: Fine, thanks.

NATIVE SPEAKER: How was your weekend?

ALESSANDRO: Sorry?

NATIVE SPEAKER: Saturday, Sunday ... did you enjoy?

ALESSANDRO: Ah, Yes.

The Interaction Hypothesis explores how such interactions affect acquisition in essentially two ways: (1) by modifying input and (2) by providing feedback related to the linking of form and meaning. A form-meaning connection is the mapping of a form and the meaning that the form encodes. For example, the word *car* is a lexical form that corresponds to the meaning of a "vehicle with four wheels."

Through interactions, learners have the advantage of being able to negotiate meaning and make some conversational adjustments. Input modifications happen when the other speakers adjust their speech due to perceived difficulties in learner comprehension or they provide corrective feedback.

This theoretical framework makes the following claims:

- Input is an essential element in language acquisition. It consists of two types: interactional and noninteractional. Interactional input is that received during interactions where there is some kind of communicative exchange involving the learner and at least another person (e.g., conversation, classroom interactions); noninteractional input occurs in the context of nonreciprocal discourse and learners are not part of an interaction (e.g., announcements).
- Interaction plays an important role in second language acquisition. It gives learners the opportunity to be exposed to input, notice language they wouldn't notice otherwise, and produce target language.
- Negotiation of meaning in conversations or interactions occurs when there is communication breakdown between two speakers and an adjustment is made to facilitate comprehension (see previous example).
- Corrective feedback (see Chapter 5 for more information about the types and role of corrective feedback) is used when speakers indicate to other speakers that what they have produced is nonnative like. Interactions that elicit feedback (implicit and form focused) can have a facilitative role in acquisition.
- Output refers to the language learners need to produce the target language to express meaning. It can play a number of roles: it might cause noticing through interactions; it might help the formulation of hypotheses about the target language that learners can test during language production.

> Noticing refers to the fact that learners would need to notice linguistic elements in the input for those elements to be learned. This implies that learning requires some level of awareness.

The Interaction Hypothesis provides some clear implications for language pedagogy. It suggests a new classroom dynamic in which instructors and learners take new roles and responsibilities in the language classroom. Teachers are playing the role of "architects" as they are planning a language task and learners must take more responsibilities in completing the task. Learning is becoming more learner centered. Comprehensible and message-oriented input and interactions play key roles in the acquisition of a second language. Learners and instructors are engaged in a number of interactions (clarification requests, confirmation checks, and comprehension checks), which facilitates language acquisition. Output practice should help learners use the target language to accomplish a task (see Chapter 3) and language production should not be simply mechanical practice void of meaning. Grammar instruction (see Chapter 5) might be beneficial if it is provided by enhancing the input through the use of different pedagogical intervention (e.g., input enhancement, textual enhancement). It might have a facilitative role in helping learners pay attention to the formal properties of a target language without the need of metalinguistic discussion.

The main concepts of this theoretical framework can be associated to teaching approaches such as the Communicative Language Teaching and Task-Based Language Teaching.

The Processability Theory

The Processability Theory is a theory of language development that accounts for how learners develop and use certain output processing procedures to string words together in speech production. These procedures emerge over time in a particular order and cannot be skipped by learners. For example, in English question formation, L2 learners, no matter their L1s, would initially produce sentences without the "copula inversion" (*Where she is?*) before they produce the correct sentence (*Where is she?*). Learners acquire single structures (i.e., negation, question formation) through predictable stages.

The Processability Theory makes two main claims:

- The theory supports the view that second language acquisition can be broken down in stages. L2 learners can only produce linguistic forms for which they have acquired the necessary processing capacities. If a learner is at stage 3, he or she cannot produce – in a creative fashion – grammatical structures that require the procedures at stages 4 and above;

  Language acquisition is stagelike.

- Learners follow a very rigid route in the acquisition of grammatical structures. Structures become learnable only when the previous steps on this acquisition path have been reached.
- Learners might display individual variation with regard to the extent they apply developmental rules and they acquire and use grammatical structures.

The main claims of the theory are translated in the so-called teachability hypothesis. This hypothesis argues that learners would only acquire language features in a predictable order. Language teachers must take into consideration that L2 learners will not be able to produce forms or structures for which they are not ready.

The Input Processing Theory

The Input Processing Theory explains how learners perceive and detect formal features in language input. When learners are exposed to target language input, only a small portion of that input is processed (this reduced portion of input is called "intake"). This is due to two main factors: (1) humans' limited capacity for processing information; and (2) use of processing strategies to cope with the amount and type of information that the mind has to process. For example, when the same meaning is encoded both lexically and grammatically, L2 learners might not process the grammatical item, as they prefer to extract the meaning of the sentence from the lexical item (see following examples).

He talks
He won two prizes

In the first sentence, both the subject pronoun (He) and the verbal marker (-s) encode the same meaning (third-person singular). In the second sentence, both the adjective (two) and the noun inflection (-s) express the concept "more than one." Learners tend to process information economically and efficiently by processing words before grammatical forms (e.g., verb forms, noun inflections). What we mean by this is that learners would skip in both cases the processing of the grammatical features.

Processing strategies seem to provide an explanation of what learners are doing with input when they are asked to comprehend it, either in aural or written forms.

The Input Processing Theory makes two main claims:

- Learners process input for meaning (words) before they process it for form (grammatical features). In a sentence such as "Yesterday I watched my son playing in the park," which contains a lexical feature encoding a particular meaning (temporal reference "yesterday"), learners will tend to process the lexical item (Yesterday) before the grammatical form (-ed) as they both encode the same meaning. This is due to the use of processing strategies, which causes learners to skip grammatical features in the input and failure in mapping one form to one meaning;

> Form-meaning mapping is when a connection is made between a form and the meaning that the form encodes.

- Learners parse sentences as they need to figure out who did what to whom. When they do that, they parse sentences relying on word order and employ a first noun processing strategy that assigns subject or agent status to the first noun or pronoun they encounter in a sentence. In the sentence "Paul was kissed by Mary," learners erroneously assign the role of agent to the first noun or noun phrase in the sentence and therefore misinterpret the sentence as it was "Paul who kissed Mary." This can cause delay in the acquisition of syntax.

This theory has particular relevance in relation to its pedagogical model called "processing instruction." Manipulating the input might help learners to process language grammar features more efficiently and accurately (see processing instruction and structured input tasks in Chapter 5 in this book).

The Skill Acquisition Theory

The Skill Acquisition Theory relates to a cognitive and information processing model centered on the following stages of development: cognitive, associative, and autonomous. According to this theory, second language acquisition results from exposure to input and the ability for L2 learners to process information and to build networks of associations. Second language acquisition would entail going from controlled mode of operation (declarative knowledge) to automatic mode (procedural knowledge) through repeated practice.

> Second language acquisition entails to go from declarative to procedural knowledge.

This theory addresses issues related to the way language learners develop fluency and accuracy.

The three main claims in the Skill Acquisition Theory are:

- Learning begins with declarative knowledge (information is gathered and stored) and slowly becomes procedural (people move toward the ability to perform with that knowledge). Declarative knowledge involves acquisition of isolated facts and rules (e.g., *knowing that a car can be driven*). Procedural knowledge requires practice and involves processing of longer units and increasing automatization *(e.g., knowing how to drive a car)*.
- The theory is only applicable to learning situations in which the following four criteria are met: adult learners are of high aptitude; structures are simple for learning; learners are at fairly early stages of learning; and the context is instructional.

In relation to language teaching, this theory views second language acquisition as a process that entails going from controlled mode (declarative knowledge) to automatic mode (procedural knowledge) through repeated practice. Learners need to be taught explicitly and need to practice the various grammatical features and skills until they are well established, thereby reaching increased level of fluency.

Emergentism

Emergentism is a cognitive theory that accounts for how learners develop language abilities and competencies. According to this theory, second language acquisition is governed by similar processes and principles that underpin everything else in human knowledge. Language acquisition is a dynamic process in which a number of elements (e.g., regularities, frequencies, associations, L1, interactions, brain, society, and cultures) operate and are responsible for the emergence and development of the second language.

> Frequency and regularity are key factors in second language acquisition.

The theory makes two main claims:

- Language acquisition is an implicit process where frequency in the input is a key factor. Acquisition is the result of a learner's interaction with the surrounding environment. Language and its properties emerge over time and are the result of cognitive mechanisms interacting with input.
- Language and its properties emerge over time and are not the product of an innate mechanism constraining language learning. What is meant by this is that language elements and properties are not universals as argued by the Universal Grammar Theory. A second language develops as a result of the interaction between cognitive learning mechanisms and input from the environment. Language instructors should therefore provide learners with exposure to form to help them to develop their new language system.

According to this theory, frequency and regularity are key factors in language acquisition. Acquisition is the result of a learner's interaction with the surrounding environment. Language and its properties emerge over time and are the result of cognitive mechanisms interacting with input. The implication for teaching is that it is better for the language instructor to expose L2 learners to the real and natural settings so that they could have a better perception of the world and thus increase their knowledge. The more knowledge about the language, the more interaction is initiated and carried out by the learners. Although the role of grammar instruction is limited and it is not always effective, it can have a facilitative role in developing "noticing" of target forms that might not be salient in the input language and speeds up the rate of acquisition.

The Complexity Theory

The Complexity Theory is mainly concerned with the behavior of dynamic systems that change in time and evolve with disorder (chaos leads to order). According to this theory, second language acquisition is a complex model in open interaction with its environment, and always susceptible to change. It is complex as it comprises of many elements, which interact with each other.

The main claims of this theory are:

- Second language acquisition is not characterized by simply processing and internalizing data. The system is more complex than the acquisition of a set of rules and features.
- Interaction with the environment, the context, and the variability of learning outcomes across L2 learners are key features in this theory. What gets strengthened and what gets weakened within the dynamic system depends on who L2 learners interact with and on the environment in which they find themselves.

The Complexity Theory supports the importance of a learner's exposure to input and a social participation view of second language acquisition, without excluding the psycholinguistic perspective, and therefore providing us with a wider perspective toward research, theory, and pedagogy, but not offering any explanation about how the system emerges.

The Sociocultural Theory

The Sociocultural Theory argues that the development of human cognitive functions derives from social interactions. It is the participation of individuals in social activities that draws them into the use of these functions. The theory focuses not only on how adults and peers influence individual learning but also on how cultural beliefs and attitudes impact instruction and learning.

The Sociocultural Theory makes the following claims:

- All learning or development take place as people participate in culturally formed settings. These settings include schools, family life, peer groups, and workplaces. These environments shape the most important cognitive activities in which people engage. Thus, all learning is situated and context bound. Social interaction plays a crucial role in the process of cognitive development. In this context, social learning precedes development.
- Learners use tools such as speech and writing to mediate their social environments. These tools mediate between individuals and the situations in which they find themselves. At the same time, these tools have certain limits, such that people use them in only certain ways.

A clear application of the Sociocultural Theory principles to language instruction is in the form of the Task-Based Language Teaching. This approach emphasizes the importance of social and collaborative aspects of language acquisition and how the interaction between learners can scaffold and assist in the L2 acquisition process.

In the following table, the main claim of each of the contemporary theories in second language acquisition is provided. These claims had a direct impact in language teaching approaches and methods, as it will be discussed in the next chapter.

Second Language Acquisition Theories	Main Claim
Behaviorism	Acquisition happens through imitation of good habits
Monitor Theory	Acquisition happens through exposure to comprehensible and message-oriented language input
The Universal Grammar Theory	Acquisition happens through the interaction of innate knowledge and exposure to language input
The Interaction Hypothesis	Acquisition happens through interactions, corrective feedback, pushed output, and negotiating of meaning opportunities
Input Processing Theory	Acquisition is facilitated through appropriate form-meaning connections
Processability Theory	Acquisition is characterized by developmental stages
Skill-Acquisition Theory	Acquisition is facilitated through exposure and practice, which would entail going from controlled mode of operation (declarative knowledge) to automatic mode (procedural knowledge) through repeated practice.
The Complexity Theory	Acquisition is facilitated by the behavior of dynamic systems that create their own conditions of development in open interaction with the environment
Emergentism	Acquisition is facilitated by frequency in the input and the ability to make formal associations
Socio-cultural Theory	Acquisition is facilitated through social interaction and a supportive interactive environment

What Are the Similarities and Differences Between L1 and L2 Acquisition?

The underlying question in the field of second language acquisition is whether or not L1 and L2 acquisition are similar or different processes. Two of the key questions generated from this line of research are: (1) to what extent are first language (L1) and second language (L2) acquisition similar or different? and (2) to what extent do learners transfer the L1 system into the new L2 system?

Scholars have investigated the nature of L1 and L2 and overall their findings have indicated that there are similarities and some differences between L1 and L2 acquisition. In the development of both L1 and L2, learners need input to develop an internal language system. Input is the main ingredient for successful L1 and L2 acquisition. Effective language input must have two requisites: language learners must comprehend it, and it must contain a message.

To What Extent Are First Language (L1) and Second Language (L2) Acquisition Similar or Different?

Similarities

1. In both L1 and L2 acquisition, learners follow predictable stages and natural orders in the acquisition of formal features of the target language. Findings from research have indicated that there is a specific and similar order in the acquisition of grammatical morphemes such as inflectional features, in all languages.
2. L1 and L2 acquisition require extensive exposure of input.
3. L1 and L2 acquisition are fundamentally similar in terms of the internal processes and mechanisms responsible for language acquisition. Potential differences between L1 and L2 acquisition can be attributed to external factors such as availability and type of exposure to language input and interaction. Children are consistently exposed to adequate quantity and quality of simplified input. Adults typically don't have the same opportunity.

Differences

1. In acquiring the L1, children might have full access to the innate and internal language system. Adults, however, might not have access to the same innate ability when learning the L2, and therefore they might resort to using problem-solving skills to acquire the target language.
2. Adults are not exposed to the same quantity and quality of input.
3. The different context of L1 and L2 acquisition plays an important role. While it is possible to acquire an L2 in various contexts, L1 acquisition takes place only in a natural context where the child is growing up. In this context, the child gets sufficient quality L1 input.

L1 and L2 acquisition follow similar processes. However, context and circumstances are different.

To What Extent Do Learners Transfer the L1 System into the New L2 System?

The role of L1 transfer is still very much debated in second language acquisition. However, the debate has moved away from the idea that learners automatically transfer the L1 into the L2 and all errors are simply the results of L1 interference.

Current findings from research have demonstrated the following:

- L1 does not seem to influence acquisition orders and sequences. No matter the L1 of the learner, L2 learners seem to go through similar orders and

stages in acquiring grammatical forms and structures (e.g., "*ing*" is processed before -*ed*);
- L1 does not seem to be the main cause of learners' errors in the L2. For example, English native speakers can use L1 speech procedures to cope with L2 production (The say *sono venti anni* instead of *ho venti anni* – I am twenty years old instead of I have twenty years old). This type of error is a communicative strategy used by L2 learners (English native speakers learning Italian) to produce a sentence by dressing up their own L1 utterance in L2 vocabulary. There are more complex linguistic and cognitive constraints and processes responsible for learners' errors;
- L1 transfer is constrained by universal aspects of language and internal language processing. For instance, L2 learners make use of implicit and universal processing strategies when they process grammar in the input (see Input Processing Theory).

Overall, L1 and L2 acquisition, to a certain extent, share the same processes and mechanisms for the development of an internal language system.

What Is the Nature of Language?

Before we discuss how the language system develops, we should define the nature of language. The lack of knowledge about what language is and how it works can cause a number of misconceptions.

> ### Consider this ...
>
> What is language?
> Please provide a definition

The main misconception is the belief that what it is in a language textbook (e.g., explanation of rules, paradigms) is what winds up in our mind/head. What we mean by this is the conception that language is a list of rules and they can be learned through paradigms (summaries and explanations about grammatical rules). The reality is that there is no mechanism in the mind that can turn explicit knowledge into implicit knowledge. This misconception derives from a lack of understanding of what language really is.

Language is not subject matter in the typical or traditional sense. Languages are not learned in the same way we learn history, English literature, and any other disciplines. In fact, language is not something to be learned the way a person learns anything else (e.g., playing tennis, driving a car, playing cards). Language is a complex, abstract, and an implicit system.

Language is not subject matter, but a complex, abstract, and implicit system.

Complex

Language can be described as multicomponential and a complex system. Learning a language means acquiring a number of elements:

- The total stock of words (lexicon), word elements, and their meanings;
- The sounds (phonology) that make up words (pronunciation), and the way they come together to form speech and words;
- The patterns (morphology) of word formation (e.g., inflections on verbs and nouns) and how new words are made from other words (e.g., prefixes and suffixes);
- The rules of sentence structure (syntax) to explain what is permissible and what is not in a language;
- The use of sentences to intend something specific (pragmatics). The role of context in language and how people rely on it for successful communication;
- The study of the language (sociolinguistics) and how it functions in society. The study of the interaction between linguistic and social variables, such as when it is appropriate to use different types of language; and
- The way sentences are connected (discourse). How coherent and cohesive linguistic elements are in sentences.

Learning a language means acquiring all these elements all at the same time. Each person, no matter whether it is a first, second, or third language, creates an internal language system we call language. This system is abstract in nature as its features are difficult to describe with exact words.

Abstract

This abstract representation bears no resemblance to rules found in language textbooks. Much of the grammatical information is stored in lexical entries with embedded features (see following examples).

For example, *Does* [<Q>, <T><+V><-V> + <present ><-past>3rd person sing].

Does, for example, stores the feature <Q> (Question) and <+V> (Verb) and encodes the semantic meaning <present> and third-person singular.

This complex and abstract system is also implicit as we know we have language in our heads, but we don't really know what the contents are.

There are many aspects of language that are universal and built in prior to exposure to the input language. We have an innate knowledge of what is allowed and what is disallowed in a language. For example, first language speakers of English know (without being taught) the following:

(c) *I've done* (contraction of *I've* is allowed)
(d) **Should I've done it?* (contraction here is disallowed)

How does a person come to know that *I've* (and contractions more generally) is allowed in some instances and disallowed in others? No one teaches a child. And yet every speaker of English comes to know what is disallowed with contractions.

Sentences have underlying hierarchical structure consisting of phrases (e.g., noun phrase [NP, verb phrase (VP), prepositional phrase (PP)] that requires a "head" and a "complement" [see following example]).

- noun phrase (NP) = noun (head) + complement = Alessandro *is professor*
- verb phrase (VP) = verb (head) + complement = *teaches Italian*
- prepositional phrase (PP) = preposition (head) + complement = *at the University of Greenwich*

Language as mental representation builds up over time due to consistent and constant exposure to input data. It needs input to know whether there are variations between two languages. English is a head-first language whereas Japanese is a head final language. Thus, for verb phrases, English follows verb (head) + complement (*Ahmad crashed the car*) while Japanese follows complement + verb (*Ahmad the car crashed*). This gives English its characteristic subject-verb-object word order while giving Japanese its characteristic subject-object-verb word order. For learners of English to build a language system with head final if they learn Japanese, they need exposure to input in the target language. This will allow them to reset from head-first to head final language.

Implicit

This complex and abstract language system is also implicit as we know we have language in our heads, but we don't really know what the contents are. This implicit system is a vast network of forms and lexical items in the brain. A network is a map of grammatical and lexical items linked to each other through connections demonstrating semantic (relation based on meaning such as between *boring* and *interesting*), lexical (root word relationship such as *interest* and *interesting*), and formal relationships (a relationship between grammatical form that does not change the meaning of the root but when added produces a new word such as *boring* and *bored*). The network grows in our head as we process more language and make the right connections.

Language as mental representation refers to the abstract, implicit, and underlying linguistic system in a speaker's mind/brain. It is implicit because we are not aware of it and we cannot describe its content with exact words. A rather different understanding and definition of language is the concept of language as a skill. Skill is the ability to use language in real time (speaking, writing, listening, and reading). It does involve the intersection of accuracy and fluency (speed in using the target language). Language learners acquire skills by participating in skill-based activities.

What are some of the implications of our discussion on the nature of language for language teaching?

So, what are the implications of this view about language for teachers and teaching?

Language as mental representation is too abstract and complex to teach and learn explicitly. In short, language as mental representation is not the rules and paradigms that appear on textbook pages. Learners don't acquire rules but abstract properties.

Explicit rules and paradigm lists can't become the abstract and complex system because the two things are completely different. This implication stems from the fact that there is no internal mechanism that can convert explicit textbook rules into implicit mental representation. Comprehension-based approaches are the only ones that foster acquisition. More discussion about this matter appears in Chapter 5 of this book.

The internal language system (mental representation) gets in our head not through practice, but through consistent exposure to input. Input is a crucial ingredient in language acquisition and language teaching. All aspects of language are input dependent (e.g., lexicon, morphology, phonology, syntax, pragmatics). The only exception is for those aspects of language that are universal and built in prior to exposure, these universal aspects of language that cannot be learned (are innate or derived from universal properties).

How Does the Language System Develop?

L2 learners develop an internal linguistic system in a similar fashion as L1 learners. This system is neither the first language nor the second language, but something in between that learners build from environmental data (input). The internal language system refers to a dynamic and changing system that is an implicit and an unconscious representation of the language (e.g., morphology, phonology, syntax).

It is a complex unit continuously evolving and made of networks of forms and lexical items linked to each other via semantic relationships (e.g., sad and funny); formal relationships (e.g., interesting and interested); lexical relationships (e.g., interesting and interest); and syntax (e.g., Subject-Verb-Object) that governs sentence structure that informs learners of what is possible and what is not possible in a target language. How the system develops and what factors affect its growth have been discussed over the years.

Language acquisition processes are characterized by orders and stages of acquisition that are fixed and cannot be changed (although a degree of variation can occur).

> The language acquisition system is abstract, complex, dynamic, implicit, and continuously changing.

There are two different types of developmental sequences in second language acquisition: stagelike (specifically sentence structure); and orderlike (i.e., A precedes B, B precedes C).

Stagelike

Developmental stages (or sequences) have been documented for a number of features (e.g., English negation, see following table). L2 learners (no matter their L1s) seem to follow this order in the acquisition of particular structures.

Stage	Description	Example
1	"No" is in front of (not attached to) verbs or nouns, sentence initial	*No eat that*
2	"No" moves after the subject of the sentence, and in front of (not attached to) verbs or nouns; "don't" appears as an alternative to "no"	*I no eat that*
3	Negation is attached to verbs, modals negated	*I can't eat that*
4	"Do" with attached negation	*I don't eat that*

Orderlike

L2 learners follow a particular order in the acquisition of language morphemes. For English verbal inflections, the following acquisition orders have been established:

1. progressive -*ing*
2. regular past tense -*ed*
3. irregular past tense
4. third-person singular -*s*

Both stagelike and ordered second language development offer clear evidence that learners must possess internal mechanisms that process and organize language material over time in a systematic manner.

What are some of the implications of our discussion on the internal language system for language teaching?

Knowing how the system develops would help language teachers to evaluate their teaching methods. The rules and structures presented in textbooks do not resemble the organization of the linguistic knowledge in L2 learners' minds. L2 learners need to be exposed to sufficient quality and quality input (comprehensible, easy to process, meaningful) to ensure their internal system is fed with the right information to develop mental representation. This clearly has an impact on the type of activities language teachers should develop and should use in their teaching.

There are activities that promote development of mental representation (internal language system) and others that promote development of communicative ability. Overall, input-oriented activities help to develop mental representation. Interactive activities help to develop communicative competence.

Input-oriented activities help to develop mental representation. Interactive activities help to develop communicative competence.

L2 learners develop linguistic systems in an organized way that seem little affected by external forces such as instruction and correction. Most researchers view second language acquisition as an implicit process, principally guided by the learner's interaction with L2 input (see the Interaction Hypothesis in this chapter).

Stephen Krashen (see "The Monitor Theory" in this chapter) distinguishes between two autonomous and separate processes in second language acquisition: the learned system (conscious process) used by L2 learners to construct rules in a pedagogical context; and the acquired system (subconscious and intuitive process) used when L2 learners are involved in using language in actual communication. This position is consistent with nativist perspectives drawn from theories on linguistic universals. These universals can't be taught using rule explanations and paradigms in the traditional sense.

Robert DeKeyser (see "The Skill Acquisition Theory" in this chapter) argues that explicit L2 knowledge, attained through explicit learning, can become implicit L2 knowledge. This is generally achieved through practice in which learners deliberately focus their attention on L2 form as it encodes message meaning and work toward both understanding and internalization. Within this perspective, second language acquisition is viewed as a skill, and its acquisition as a linguistic system is assumed to be built up gradually through processes of attention, conscious awareness, and practice.

Nick Ellis (see "Emergentism" in this chapter) has questioned how much explicit learning and explicit instruction might influence implicit learning and has identified possible limitations for instruction. Supporters of this position assume that acquisition is predominantly implicit. However, the linguistic system can be also built up through a number of instructional interventions that enable learners to notice crucial relationships of L2 form and meaning in the language input and eventually process these form-meaning connections. Teachers should consider incorporating classroom tasks that focus both on form and meaning. This type of task, for instance in the teaching of grammar and language skills, would be very beneficial to most L2 learners.

What Is the Role of Input?

Input refers to the language that L2 learners hear or read and has a communicative intent. In second language acquisition, learners hear or read the language that contains certain linguistic features (e.g., vocabulary, grammar, pronunciation) and other information about the L2. These features make their way into the learner's language system only if they are linked to some kind of meaning and are comprehensible to the learner.

Input must be comprehensible as learners must be able to extract the meaning of the message contained in the input. Input is language that learners try to comprehend for the message contained in it. When somebody says, "How old are you?," the listener would focus on what the person would like to know and the response will focus on the meaning contained in what this person is asking ("I am twenty years old, and you?").

To fully understand the nature of input, it is also important to clarify what input is not.

Input is meaning-oriented language that learners hear or see. It is not what they produce as what language learners produce is called output. Another important distinction to make is between input and explicit information. Explicit information (e.g., grammar explanations about the target language L2 learners are often exposed in the language classroom or in textbooks) is not input for acquisition. Explicit information is not input for acquisition because in that information provided to L2 learners there is not an attempt/intention to communicate a message that learners need to attend to. Input is also not explicit error correction to learners.

Consider this ...

Which of the following examples is input for acquisition?

My friend loves Italian cinema. He likes the films of Fellini, Rosi, and Amelio. Tomorrow we will see Sorrentino's latest film….

Or …

The past tense consists of two elements: the present of an auxiliary verb (*avere* [to have] or *essere* [to be]), followed by the past participle….

Input for acquisition is therefore the language that is embedded in a communicative context that learners attend to for its meaning.

What we mean by this is that L2 learners acquire language mainly through exposure to comprehensible input in a similar fashion as they

> Input refers to the language (in both spoken and written forms) the learner is exposed to and carries a message.

acquire their first language. The input that L2 learners receive should be simplified with the use of contextual and extra linguistics clues such as drawings or pictures.

Language learners should be exposed to comprehensible input and they should be provided with opportunities to focus on meaning rather than grammatical forms. As the reader will recall, in order for the input to be effective and useful for L2 learners, it must have two main characteristics: (1) it must be comprehensible, and (2) it must have a communicative intent.

The most important consideration for language acquisition to happen is that the language learner can easily understand the input (more in Chapter 4). We need to ensure that the language L2 learners are exposed to is clearly and easily understood. Secondly, to be effective input must contain a message that learners must attend to for meaning. Learners have to be involved in an activity that has a communicative purpose for it to be effective.

Consider this ...

If input must be comprehensible and message oriented to play a crucial role in the acquisition of a target language, what would "'good input" look like?

Think about some common activities in language classrooms, such as memorizing vocabulary lists and learning the rules of grammar. Do these constitute input? Why or why not? In your experience, is rich input usually available in language classrooms?

Language is a tool for human communication, and the formal features of language – lexical items, morphology, syntax, etc. – all work together to encode meaning. So, as learners work out the meaning of the input they are exposed to, they are also making connections between the meaning of the input linguistic forms.

Several elements can facilitate this process. L2 learners benefit from simplified input and modified input. Simplified input is language input that is less complex so as to be more comprehensible. The language that native speakers (NSs) normally use to talk to young children is generally a simpler language as adults adjust their vocabulary to make the speech easier for the child to understand. In the context of L1 acquisition, children are continuously exposed to simplified input that contains a message and must be comprehended (e.g., Are you thirsty? Would you like a drink of milk? Do you like this game?). This kind of child-directed speech makes it easier for children to learn their native language. In addition, the language is highly contextualized within communicative events. What this means is that children at the age of two, for example, are hearing language that is embedded in concrete here and now situations – even during story telling when they are looking at pictures. Lexical simplifications, despite syntactic complexity, facilitate comprehension.

In the second language acquisition context, we also find that simplified input is effective. Evelyn Hatch noted that simplified input to L2 learners consists of a variety of characteristics when compared to native-to-native speech: slower speech rate (and thus clearer articulation), use of high-frequency vocabulary, pausing at appropriate places with pauses often longer and more frequent, rephrasing, and the use of shorter and simpler sentences.

The use of shorter sentences, for example, reduces the information-processing burden on the L2 learner. Additional pausing does the same thing: pauses give learners "processing time" before the next round of information comes in. These modifications result in greater likelihood of comprehension, which in turn facilitate the necessary conditions for acquisition.

Michael Long investigated how the structure of an interaction can be modified to make input more comprehensible for nonnative speakers (NNSs). Through these interactions, L2 learners have the advantage of being able to negotiate meaning and make some conversational adjustments. Negotiation of meaning refers to the efforts made by both NSs and NNSs to modify the interaction to ensure comprehension along the lines of what Evelyne Hatch has described. Learners sometimes request clarifications or repetitions if they do not understand the input they receive. In short, negotiation of meaning leads to input modification by the other speaker, and this leads to greater overall comprehension for the L2 learner. When learners comprehend more, they "process" more of the input and this facilitates second language acquisition.

> Interactions are crucial for language development. Interaction modifications make input more comprehensible, and comprehensible input promotes acquisition.

Rhonda Oliver has identified three of the most common types of interactional modifications to negotiate meaning: comprehension checks, confirmation checks, and clarification requests. Comprehension checks are used when one speaker is not convinced that the other speaker has understood what has been said (e.g., *Do you understand? Do you follow me*?). Clarification requests are expressions used to clarify speakers' utterances (e.g., *What did you say? Huh?*). Confirmation checks are used to ensure that one speaker has clearly understood what is said by another speaker (e.g., Is this what you mean?). These types of interactions provide L2 learners with comprehensible input and opportunities for acquisition. The role and effects of corrective feedback will be discussed in Chapter 5.

Consider this ...

Were you exposed to comprehensible modified input?

Have you had any experience in negotiating meaning with another interlocutor?

If so, what type of techniques did you or you interlocutor use?

How were the breakdowns in communication repaired?

L2 learners are exposed to a vast amount of input; however, not all the input learners are exposed to is processed. Pit Corder made an important distinction between input and intake. Input refers to what is available to the learner, and intake is the part of the input internalized by the language learner. Intake is the portion of the input that is "taken in" by the learner. It is often the case that when acquiring another language, we are exposed to language that is totally incomprehensible (e.g., an example is sometimes the announcements made at train stations). The language is fast and sometimes it is not clear. Learners don't understand the input and therefore that input is not integrated into the current learner's internal language system.

For that input to make its way into the language internal system it must first be comprehensible. Despite this important feature, it is not possible for learners to take in all the input they are exposed to as humans have limited capacity to process and store information. There are a number of positions/theoretical views about the fact that for input to be usable for acquisition it must be attended to and noticed in some ways.

> Attention is a cognitive process involving the ability to focus on certain stimuli rather than others.

> Awareness refers to the fact that learners are conscious of what they are learning.

Richard Schmidt argued that L2 learners require attention to successfully process forms in the input. Learners must pay attention to a form in the input and notice that form for that form to be acquired. A degree of awareness is also crucial for L2 learners to incorporate the new language into their internal system.

> Detection is an element of attention and refers to the registration of stimuli in our memory.

However, for Russell Tomlin and Victor Villa input must be detected and this process does not involve awareness. Whether awareness plays a role, input must be noticed. L2 learners must pay attention to the input to which they are exposed.

Bill VanPatten assigns a crucial role to input and argues that language acquisition happens as a by-product of language comprehension. His model of input processing focuses on what learners process and don't process in the input and why. He argues that when L2 learners attend to or notice input to comprehend a message, a form-meaning connection is made. When learners process input, they filter the input, which is reduced and modified into a new entity (intake). Only part of the input L2 learners receive is processed and becomes intake. This is mainly due to processing limitations (memory capacity) and processing strategies.

Bill VanPatten has identified a series of processing strategies (see "The Input Processing Theory" in this chapter) used by L2 learners when they process and filter linguistic data at the level of input. These strategies/principles allow learners to selectively attend to incoming stimuli without being overloaded with information.

These two main strategies are:

- The Primacy of Meaning Principle. Learners process input for meaning before they process it for form;
- The First Noun Principle. Learners tend to process the first noun or pronoun they encounter in a sentence as the subject/agent.

According to the Primacy of Meaning Principle, during input processing, L2 learners initially direct their attention toward the detection of content words to understand the meaning of an utterance. Learners tend to focus their attention onto content words to understand the message of the input to which they are exposed. In doing so, they do not process grammatical forms, and consequently they fail to make form-meaning connections. This is the case for forms that are redundant in the input, for example. Redundancy is when, in a sentence or discourse, both a grammatical form and a word encode the same semantic information. For example, when learners try to make moment-by-moment connections between surface forms and meaning for the sentence *Yesterday, I played tennis with John in the park*, they need to tag *played* as a verb (<+V>, <-N>), that its meaning refers to playing a sport, that it is past tense, not present (<+present><-past>), and so on. However, because learners process the first element (the lexical item *Yesterday*) before they encounter the verb, they already know to interpret the sentence as a past time event. Thus, they can skip the form *-ed* in *played* as it encodes the same semantic information. The presence of a lexical item encoding the same referential meaning as the linguistic form makes the form redundant in this sentence and prevents learners from making an immediate form-meaning connection. This processing strategy is called the Lexical Preference Principle and it is a subprinciple of VanPatten's Primacy of Meaning Principle. To make these connections successfully, L2 learners must not only notice the form but also comprehend and accurately process the meaning encoded by the form.

According to the First Noun Principle, L2 learners also tend to process the first noun or pronoun they encounter in a sentence as the subject or agent. This processing strategy leads them to misinterpret the meaning of an utterance and may cause delays in acquisition. L2 learners must be able to determine which is the subject and which is the object in a sentence they hear or read. Linked to this processing principle is the concept of parsing. One of the main functions of parsing is to figure out who did what to whom in a sentence. In the sentence *The police officer was killed by the robber*, learners, in the attempt to make moment-by-moment computation of sentence structure during comprehension, would process the first element they encounter in the sentence as the subject of the sentence. So, L2 learners would, as predicted by the First Noun Principle, interpret the sentence as if it were the police officer who killed the robber. This will cause a delay in interpreting the meaning of the sentence and therefore a subsequent delay in the acquisition of syntactic structures that don't follow the expected word order, such as passive constructions and causative forms.

Consider this ...

Can you think of some examples of a form-meaning connection L2 learners might have to make in language input?

Can you think of some examples of structure affected by the two processing principles described in this section?

Brian Machinery (see "Emergentism" in this chapter) has pointed out that all linguistic performance requires making connections between language forms and functions. The forms are morphological inflections and word order patterns. The functions are grammatical functions with specific semantic properties. The mapping of one form and one function is part of first language (L1) acquisition, and, according to this model, second language acquisition involves adjusting the existing mapping system in the L1 acquisition so that it is appropriate for the second language system.

Within this framework, input plays a key role in terms of providing multiple cues for the learners. According to this model, the acquisition of appropriate form-meaning mappings is driven by a number of factors mainly related to how reliable a particular cue is. Three main factors contribute to the reliability of a given cue:

- Frequency. This factor relates to how often a form-meaning connection occurs in the input. If it is frequent, then the cue is strengthened and L2 learners can rely on the particular cue;
- Contrastive availability. This factor relates to whether the cue is important for interpreting meaning. If it does not (this is the case of forms made redundant by a lexical item, for example), the cue will tell learners nothing about form-meaning connections;
- Reliability. This factor refers to how cues can be more reliable than others in helping learners to make a correct interpretation.

Second language acquisition is intake dependent because only input that has been noticed and processed is usable for acquisition. Exposure to input is both necessary and sufficient for children L1 learners to acquire all the components of their native language. In other words, without input, children will not learn the L1. At the same time, access to input is the only thing that children need to learn the L1. The question for L2 learners is whether input is also both a necessary and sufficient condition for L2 acquisition. All L2 researchers agree that L2 acquisition will not happen without access to input. They disagree, however, on whether input is the only thing learners need. The debate is around whether output and interaction also play central roles in L2 development.

Because L2 learners have a wider variety of outcomes than L1 learners, some researchers believe that input alone is not enough for L2 learners to acquire a second language. Other researchers have pointed out that a key difference between L1 and L2 acquisition is that L1 learners are exposed to a wide variety and different quality of input in comparison to learners learning an L2 in a foreign-language learning context. Indeed, there is evidence that quantity and quality of input matter for L2 learners. L2 learners who are immersed in the target language, either because they live in the country where the language is spoken or because they are studying subjects such as business or arts using the target second language, have access to more and better input than students in traditional foreign language classes. Findings from immersion studies clearly indicate that immersion-language learning is superior to the foreign-language learning experience. Learners are exposed to a higher quantity of input and a better quality as the input learners are exposed to is communicative input. This is also the case of the study-abroad experience. Learners who develop advanced proficiency in an L2 usually have some immersion experience.

Input is a necessary and vital factor for second language acquisition as it provides the primary linguistic data for the creation of an implicit unconscious linguistic system. Different perspectives may differ on what happens to the input as the learner interacts with it and what winds up in the head but they all concur that the data for language acquisition are in the input.

> Input is a key and vital ingredient in second language acquisition.

What are some of the implications of our discussion on input and interaction for language teaching?

Although exposure to input is necessary and vital for second language acquisition, mere exposure to input might not be sufficient and sometimes input might need to be enhanced through some kind of formal instruction. Input can be enhanced to increase the possibility that L2 learners might notice particular forms in the input to which they are exposed. Textual enhancement is an instructional intervention carried out to enhance the saliency of input in written or oral texts with a view to facilitating learners' noticing of targeted forms and thereby enhancing their acquisition. Textual enhancement makes use of typographical cues (e.g., boldfacing, italicizing, underlining, coloring, enlarging the font size) to draw learners' attention to particular forms in a text. Overall, research on input and textual enhancement has indicated that it is an effective input manipulation pedagogical intervention to increase frequency about a target form in the input and foster noticing (see Chapter 5 in this book).

Input can be restructured so that form-meaning connections can be facilitated. Processing instruction is a pedagogical intervention to grammar instruction that exposes L2 learners to a particular type of input to push learners away from non-optimal processing strategies mentioned earlier so that they are more likely to make correct form-meaning connections or parse sentences appropriately (compute basic structure in real time) during comprehension. Processing instruction relies on structured input tasks to push learners away from inefficient processing strategies so that they are more likely to process the relevant forms in the input. Overall, the research into the effects of processing instruction on the interpretation and processing of target structures has revealed that it is an effective input-based pedagogical intervention.

Interactional input refers to input received during interaction where there is some kind of communicative exchange involving the learner and at least another person (e.g., conversation, classroom interactions). In these exchanges, L2 learners negotiate meaning and make some conversational adjustments. This means that conversation and interaction may make linguistic features salient to the learner and the process of negotiating meaning can facilitate acquisition. Learners sometimes request clarifications or repetitions if they do not understand the input they receive. In the attempt to facilitate communication, one person can request the other to modify his/her utterances or the person modifies their own utterances to be understood. This kind of negotiation of meaning may trigger interactional adjustments by the NS or more competent interlocutor. Negotiation of meaning may facilitate language acquisition because it connects input, learner-internal capacities, particularly selective attention, and output in productive ways. Research into the relative effectiveness of modified input on acquisition has shown it might have an impact on learners' ability to negotiate the input they need at a particular stage of development.

Corrective feedback can provide learners with additional input and indicate that utterances are not targetlike (more in Chapter 5). This can take several forms in conversational interaction, such as puzzled looks, confirmation checks, clarifications requests, and corrective recasts. A recast is where learners are provided with a correct form in the input, in response to an error. The interlocutor will reformulate a learner's nontargetlike utterance so that it is targetlike in the hopes that the learner becomes aware that something is wrong in their output. Research on the effects of recasts has provided mixed results. Some researchers have argued that corrective feedback is more effective when L2 learners are actively engaged in negotiating a form, or when they have to think about and respond to the other speaker's feedback in some way.

What Is the Role of Output?

Output refers to the language that learners produce in communicative contexts. It is language that learners use to express their own meaning. For output to have a communicative purpose, it must be linked to specific intents, and the meaning of the language produced must be central to the task (e.g., making a grocery list, planning a holiday, attending an interview, and talking about your education and experience).

The kind of output practice often used by teachers in the language classroom is not language that L2 learners would produce in communicative contexts. Learners are asked to repeat a sentence, transform a sentence (e.g., present tense sentence into the past tense), or engage in practice where the focus is grammar (e.g., tell me your daily routine to practice reflexive verbs in Italian, or tell me what you did last night to practice basic present tense).

> Output is the language that learners produce with a communicative intent in communicative contexts.

Output as part of interaction is not merely practice but communication with a purpose. In output as part of meaningful interaction, L2 learners do not use language for the sake of using language. They use language to get something done or to let someone know something.

Consider this ...

Output is the language that L2 learners produce and carries some kind of meaning.

Is the language that L2 learners produce through mechanical exercises the kind of good output for acquisition?

Please think of an example of output produced for a communicative purpose.

Stephen Krashen assigns a limited role to output in second language acquisition. If L2 learners are exposed to a great amount of comprehensible input in a non-stressful environment, they will acquire the new language. For Stephen Krashen, output is the result of acquisition and only serves to prove that it has occurred. As said in the previous section, input plays a fundamental role in second language acquisition. What about output? Output does not play the same role as input. It does not provide the raw material (as input) for the development of learners' implicit system. However, output can facilitate the development of language skill. Skill, in this context, is the ability for learners to use language fluently.

The idea that output might have a beneficial role in language acquisition comes from studies of French immersion programs in Canada. Native English speakers in these programs, despite the abundant comprehensible input received, failed to acquire full grammatical competence in the target language. In particular, although learners had good receptive skills (listening and reading skills), their production was marked by persistent nontargetlike forms, especially when it came to morphological marking.

One of the scholars who has been working on the nature and role of output is Merrill Swain. She argues that, although output does not have the same key role as input, it may have beneficial effects on L2 learners and acquisition. Merrill Swain introduced the notion of comprehensible output or pushed output and assigned a more beneficial role to output in the acquisition process of a second language.

Alison Mackey has provided a very good example of pushed output through an interaction between a NS and a NNS.

> NNS: And in hand in hand have a bigger glass to see.
> NS: It' err. You mean, something in his hand?
> NNS: Like spectacle. For older person.
> NS: Mmmm, sorry I don't follow, it's what?
> NNS: In hand have he have has a glass for looking through for make the print bigger to see, to see the print, for magnify.
> NS: He has some glasses?
> NNS: Magnify glasses he has magnifying glasses.
> NS: Oh aha I see a magnifying glass, right that's a good one, ok.

Pushed output refers to speech or writing that forces learners to produce language correctly, precisely, and appropriately. Producing target language might trigger learners to pay attention to the language needs and convey their own intended meanings in speech production. Merrill Swain argued that output may stimulate learners to move from semantic, open-ended, nondeterministic, strategic processing prevalent in comprehension to the complete grammatical processing needed for accurate production (see "Interaction Hypothesis" in this chapter).

Consider this ...

Think about your experience as a learner. Can you provide an example of pushed output in a conversation/exchange between a native and nonnative speaker?

What Are Some of the Implications of Our Discussion on Output for Language Teaching?

Output might have the following beneficial roles:

- Output might help learners to improve fluency
- Output might help learners to notice a gap
- Output might trigger input modifications
- Output might help learners to test hypotheses

Each of these possible beneficial roles for output will be discussed in the text that follows.

- Output creates greater automaticity and helps to develop fluency in L2 learners. The more you practice, the more automatic a skill becomes. Little effort is required to execute an automatic process involved when the learner carries out an activity that requires them to complete a task without awareness or attention. It becomes routinized and automatized just as the steps involved in walking toward a bike, getting out the key, unlocking it, pushing it, getting on it, and riding it, require little thought.

- Output (oral and written) might help L2 learners to consolidate and to modify their existing linguistic knowledge. A possible beneficial function for output is to push L2 learners to notice existing gaps in their linguistic knowledge. In the Comprehensible Output Hypothesis, output is seen as an opportunity for learners to "notice" the gap between what they want to say and what they can say when interacting with others. As L2 learners are trying to make their speech comprehensible, they might become more aware of what they still need to learn about the target language and become more receptive about certain structures/forms in the input. Producing speech might draw learners' attention to form and structures they need to learn.

- Output in the form of interaction with other interlocutors might also have beneficial effects. Michael Long introduced the concept that the structure of the interaction between speakers can be modified and these modifications, called negotiation of meaning, can facilitate acquisition. Negotiation of meaning refers to the efforts, including comprehension checks, confirmation checks, and clarification requests, that native and nonnative speakers make to modify or restructure the interaction to overcome difficulties in comprehension. One outcome of negotiating meaning is that learner output may trigger better input from other speakers. These discourse strategies provide L2 learners with input adequately suited to their development needs. Output causes changes in the input learners receive, and this has a direct effect on the learner development. Interacting with others is about getting qualitatively better input. In other words, interaction gets learners more comprehensible or communicatively embedded modified input.

- Output might help L2 learners to test hypotheses. For example, if they are not sure about the use of a form they might try out sentences with another speaker (native speaker) and/or receive some feedback. This feedback refers to the incorrectness of their utterances from an interlocutor (e.g., confirmation checks, recast) when learners produce output. In this way L2 learners might proceed to test a hypothesis about what the correct form is or ask the other speaker for the word. The feedback received by L2 learners about the fact that they are doing "something wrong" should help them to pay attention to the input to modify their output. In this case, feedback might positively stimulate the learner's attention.

Scholars in this field agree that input is a necessary element in second language acquisition. Output has a different role than input but might have a facilitative role in developing a skill. Existing empirical evidence seems to suggest that output, especially as part of interaction, may facilitate the acquisition of certain features (e.g., lexical items, verb inflections). However, current empirical evidence has not demonstrated that output and interaction assist in the development of syntax.

Consider this ...

Output is the language that L2 learners produce and carries some kind of meaning.

Is the language that L2 learners produce through mechanical exercises the kind of output necessary for acquisition?

Is it output produced for a communicative purpose?

What Is the Role of Instruction?

L2 learners come to the task of language acquisition with some internal mechanisms that operate on language data. Linguistics and processing constraints limit the effects of instruction. Let's look at two of these constraints:

1. The consistency of the results obtained in the morpheme studies has led to the view that L2 learners follow an order in the acquisition of morphemes. They acquire morphological inflections in a consistent order (like L1 learners). For example, in English the order is: Present continuous forms (-*ing*) > Past Tense forms (-*ed*) > Third-Person singular forms (-*s*).
2. L2 learners follow a sequence in the acquisition of syntactic structures:
   (a) Words access: words are processed without any particular grammatical information;
   (b) Category procedure: access words and put inflection on them (e.g., number and gender, verbal inflection);
   (c) Phrasal procedure: use of inflections at phrase level. Learners can do operations such as the agreement for number and gender between adjective and noun within the noun phrase;
   (d) S-procedure: exchange grammatical information across phrase boundaries. Learners develop the competence in exchanging information between noun phrases and verb phrases. They are able to produce subject-verb agreement;
   (e) Subordinate clause procedure: exchange information across clauses. Learners develop the ability to carry grammatical and semantic information from the main clause to the subordinate clause as in the case of the use of "subjunctive," for example.

There is a hierarchy of output processing procedures (see "Processability Theory" in this chapter), which means that if L2 learners are at stage 3 of output processing, they have acquired stages 1 and 2, but not necessarily 4 and 5. As the reader may recall, a basic claim of the theory is that learners can't skip stages and therefore instruction can't teach learners to do something they are not ready to acquire.

There are two main views around the role of instruction in second language acquisition research: (1) instruction has a limited and constrained role; and (2) instruction might have a beneficial role under certain conditions. Instruction might in certain conditions speed up the rate of acquisition and develop greater language proficiency. What are the conditions that might facilitate the speed in which languages are learned?

The first condition is that L2 learners must be exposed to sufficient input. A second condition is that L2 learners must be psycholinguistic ready for instruction to be effective. A third condition is that instruction must take into consideration how L2 learners process the input.

> There are two positions on the role of instruction in second language acquisition: (1) instruction has a limited role; and (2) instruction has a facilitative role.

Second language acquisition is an unconscious and implicit process, and learners acquire a second language through exposure to comprehensible and message-oriented input rather than acquiring grammar consciously through explicit grammatical rules.

L2 learners acquire single structures through predictable stages. Instruction is therefore constrained by these developmental stages, and L2 learners follow a very rigid route in the acquisition of grammatical features that cannot be skipped. If instruction is targeted at grammatical features for which L2 learners are developmentally ready, then instruction can be beneficial in helping them to move faster along their natural route of development. If learners are instructed and they are not ready, instruction can be detrimental for learning.

> Second language acquisition is an unconscious and implicit process, and learners acquire a second language through exposure to comprehensible and message-oriented input.

What are some of the implications of our discussion on instruction for language teaching?

Instruction helps L2 learners to develop a good level of attainment particularly if opportunities to natural exposure are given. Instruction has a facilitative role when it is used for linguistic features, which are not too distant from the learner's current level of language development. Instruction might have a facilitative role in helping learners to pay selective attention to form and form-meaning connections in the input.

Learners make form-meaning connections from the input they receive as they connect particular meanings to particular forms (grammatical or lexical). For example, they tend to connect a form with its meaning in the input they receive (the morpheme –*ato* – on the end of the verb in Italian refers to an event in the past). L2 learners do not necessarily attend to form and meaning simultaneously with the input they receive.

Therefore, they must be trained on how to process input more effectively and efficiently so that they are in a better position to process grammatical forms and connect them with their meanings.

Instruction might be more facilitative if it is less about the teaching of rules and more about exposure to forms. It would have a facilitative role if it were less about manipulating output and more about processing input. The focus of instruction should be on processing and not on production, at least at the beginning of learning. We will have a dedicated chapter (Chapter 7) to discuss grammar instruction.

> Instruction has a limited but facilitative role in second language acquisition.

Consider this ...

Knowing the limited role of instruction. What is the role of grammar instruction in your view?

Recap

Theory and research in second language acquisition has emphasized the complexity of acquisition processes. How learners process language, how they intake it and the new language system develops, and how they access the information to communicate are key areas in this field of enquiry. The following are the main findings with implications for language teachers and teaching:

- Language can be defined as mental representation or a skill. The two are different constructs and imply different processes. However, in both cases input is the key ingredient in the process of acquisition;
- Input-oriented activities help to develop mental representation. Interactive activities help to develop communicative competence;
- Second language acquisition is primarily a matter of developing implicit knowledge. Our internal system is an abstract, complex, and implicit system;
- L2 learners require extensive input exposure to build their internal language systems apart from some universal exceptions. Input need to be easily comprehended and message-oriented to be processed effectively by L2 learners;
- L2 learners focus primarily on meaning when they process elements of the new language. Acquisition requires learners to make appropriate and efficient form-function connections (the relation between a particular form and its meaning/s);

- Interaction with other speakers, negotiation of meaning, and corrective feed-back are one of the factors to facilitate acquisition;
- L2 learners process linguistic features following a natural order and a specific sequence (i.e., they master different grammatical structures in a relatively fixed and universal order, and they pass through a sequence of stages to master grammatical structure). However, instruction might have a facilitative role through input enhancement/s;
- Language acquisition requires opportunities for output practice. Production serves to generate better input for L2 learners.

What emerges from second language theory and research is a model of acquisition that goes from input to output. Input is not processed in its entirety and it is reduced (intake) due to a number of processing constraints. L2 learners have access to the new language system to produce the language (output) but this access is also constrained by processability problems (see the following model of second language acquisition).

Input →Intake →Language System →Output →

Overall Implications for Teachers and Teaching

Based on the theory and research in second language acquisition briefly reviewed in this chapter, here are some of the takeaways for language teachers: First of all, input provides the primary linguistic data that the internal language system needs to make acquisition of a language possible. Input is the main ingredient in second language acquisition, but acquisition cannot happen unless the input is processed. To be processed successfully it must be comprehensible and it must carry a message. Learners' internal mechanism can't use data that is not message oriented. L2 learners should be exposed to comprehensible and meaningful input to increase the amount and quality of the input they can intake and to ensure that they can make connections between meanings and the forms. Interactions are crucial for language development. Interaction modifications make input more comprehensible, and comprehensible input in turn promotes acquisition.

Secondly, L2 learners do not process all of the input they are exposed to at any given time. This is because there are limits to the amount of input they can process at any given time. One of the key processes in second language acquisition is initially to convert input into intake (e.g., making correct form-meaning connections). Acquisition is directly dependent on the intake (the amount of input that is processed by learners), which is the actual and only usable input for acquisition.

On the whole, input is an absolutely necessary element for acquisition and there is no theory, view, or hypothesis in second language acquisition theory and research that does not recognize the importance of input. However, the question is: Is input sufficient for second language acquisition? Learners must have the opportunity to create language. The emphasis on interactions and negotiation of meaning derives from the concept of communication (see Chapter 3) and how best to create opportunities for L2 learners to produce language.

Thirdly, forms or structures are more difficult to be acquired through exposure to input alone. There are suggestions that there are a number of factors that affect the acquisition of linguistic constructions: the frequency and saliency of features of forms in oral input; their functional interpretations; and the reliabilities of their form–function mappings. Therefore, one of the possible conclusions here is that input is vital for acquisition but exposure to input might not be sufficient. In some cases, it might be necessary to provide some kind of formal instruction to help learners to attend and process input. For example, L2 learners should acquire grammar through the use of a variety of input enhancement techniques. Traditional grammar instruction can only foster a language-like behavior in L2 learners but it does not lead to acquisition. Input grammar practice should precede output practice.

Fourthly, language is not simply a list of rules such as those found in textbooks. Language learners do not have paradigms in their heads. Explicit traditional grammar teaching (including drill practice) is not necessary.

Fifthly, L2 learners should be provided with opportunities for output practice. They should be exposed to tasks that encourage interaction and negotiation of meaning. Language teaching must create opportunities for L2 learners to communicate by performing communicative functions (output). Whenever L2 learners produce language it should be for the purpose of expressing some kind of meaning. L2 learners should engage in speaking, listening, reading, and writing activities through the completion of communicative tasks that promote interpretation, interaction, negotiation of meaning (nature of communication), and meaningful language production.

Sixthly, language teachers should use a more learner-centered teaching approach as opposed to a teacher-centered approach. They must consider the use of corrective feedback in the form of recast and other forms of feedback ensuring that the amount of error correction is kept to a minimum, and learners are encouraged to self-repair.

In the next five chapters we will address these issues with the intention to provide some effective suggestions, options, and solutions for language teachers and language teaching.

REFERENCES AND READINGS

- Benati, A., Angelovska, T. (2016). *Second Language Acquisition: A Theoretical Introduction to Real World Application*. London: Bloomsbury.
- Benati, A., Rastelli, S. (2018). Special Issue: Perspectives in the Neurocognition of the Second Language Teaching-Acquisition Interface. *Second Language Research*, 34 (1).
- Chomsky, N. (1965). *Aspects of the Theory of Syntax*. Cambridge, MA: MIT Press.
- Corder, S. Pit. (1981). *Error Analysis and Interlanguage*. Oxford: Oxford University Press.
- DeKeyser, R.M. (ed.) (2007). *Practice in a Second Language: Perspectives from Applied Linguistics and Cognitive Psychology*. Cambridge: Cambridge University Press.
- Ellis, N. (2007). The associative-cognitive CREED. In B. VanPatten & J. Williams (eds.), *Theories in Second Language Acquisition* (77–95). Mahwah, NJ: Lawrence Erlbaum.
- Gass, S. M., Behney, J., Plonsky, L. (2013). *Second Language Acquisition: An Introductory Course*. New York: Routledge.
- Keating, G. (2018). *Second Language Acquisition: The Basics*. New York: Routledge.
- Krashen, S. (1982). *Principles and Practice in Second Language Acquisition*. Oxford: Pergamon.
- Lightbown, P., Spada, N. (2013). *How Languages Are Learned* (4th ed.). Oxford: Oxford University Press.
- Long, M. (2007). *Problems in SLA*. Mahwah, NJ: Erlbaum.
- Mackey, A. (2002). Beyond Production: Learners' Perceptions about Interactional Processes. *IRAL*, 37, 379–394.
- Mackey, A., Philp, J. (1998). Conversational Interaction on Second Language Development: Recasts, Responses, and Red Herrings? *Modern Language Journal*, 82, 338–356.
- MacWhinney, B., Bates, E. (eds.) (1989). *The Cross-Linguistic Study of Sentence Processing*. Cambridge: Cambridge University Press.
- Pienemann, M. (1998). *Language Processing and L2 Development*. Amsterdam: John Benjamins.
- Robinson, P. (ed.) (2012). *Routledge Encyclopedia of Second Language Acquisition*. New York: Routledge.
- Selinker, L. (1972). Interlanguage. *International Review of Applied Linguistics*, 10, 209–231.
- Schmidt, R. (ed.) (1995). *Attention and Awareness in Foreign Language Learning*. Honolulu: University of Hawai'i, National Foreign Language Center.
- Schwieter, J., Benati, A. (2019). *The Cambridge Handbook of Language Learning*. Cambridge: Cambridge University Press.
- Swain, M. (1995). Three functions of output in second language learning. In G. Cook & B. Seidlhofer (eds.), *Principles and Practice in Applied Linguistics* (125–144). Oxford: Oxford University Press.
- VanPatten, B. (2003). *From Input to Output*. Hightstown, NJ: McGraw-Hill.
- VanPatten, B., Smith, M., Benati, A. (2019). *Key Questions in Second Language Acquisition: An Introduction*. Cambridge: Cambridge University Press.
- VanPatten, B., Benati, A. (2015). *Key Terms in Second Language Acquisition*. London: Bloomsbury.
- VanPatten, B., Rothman, J. (2014). Against rules. In A. Benati, C. Laval, and M. Arche (eds.). *The Grammar Dimension in Instructed Second Language Learning* (15–35). London: Bloomsbury.

DISCUSSION AND QUESTIONS

1. Read the following study on the role of grammar instruction in language teaching: VanPatten, B., Cadierno, T. (1993) Explicit Instruction and Input Processing. *Studies in Second Language Acquisition,* 15, 225–243. Please complete the following table.

Purpose
Questions
Design
Results
Interpretation
Implications, Limitations and further research

2. Think about your own learning experience and provide some examples on the following:

   a. Examples of comprehensible input
   b. Examples of noncomprehensible input
   c. Examples of simplified input
   d. Examples of pushed output
   e. Examples of corrective feedback

3. Please <u>look again</u> at the following statements about second language acquisition and indicate whether you agree or disagree.

	Agree	Disagree
Languages are acquired through imitation		
Language acquisition is like learning any other skills		
People acquire grammar rules		
The acquisition of L1 and L2 is different		
Language acquisition is largely implicit		
Input and interaction are key factors		
Output plays a limited role		
Instruction makes the difference		

2 How Has Second Language Teaching Methodology Evolved over the Years?

Overview

Over the last many years, language teaching has been directly and indirectly influenced by theory and research in disciplines such as linguistics, education, psychology, and second language acquisition. In particular, second language acquisition research has focused on three main areas: (1) how L2 learners come to develop a new language system with often a limited exposure to the second language; (2) how that new system develops in the mind; and (3) how L2 learners can make use of that system during comprehension and speech production. The findings of this research have had direct implications for second language teaching and language teachers. The principles derived from research have been translated in a number of teaching methods or language teaching approaches, from the grammar translation method through the audio-lingual method to the communicative language teaching approach. In this chapter a brief examination of these teaching methods and approaches will be provided. For each of them *the main principles* and *pedagogical procedures* will be briefly presented. The chapter concludes with a discussion on the importance to go beyond specific methodologies and the necessity to develop a more evidence-based approach to language teaching. Before we start, a distinction must be made between the concept of method and the one of approach in language teaching. A method is like a prepackaged set of specifications of how the teacher should teach and how the learner should learn the second language. For the teacher, methods prescribe what materials and activities should be used, how they should be used, and what the role of the teacher should be. For learners, methods prescribe what approach to learning the learner should take and what roles the learner should adopt in the classroom.

An approach is represented by a specific theory on the nature of language and a theory on the nature of language learning. Approaches in language teaching are developed and derived from theoretical areas of linguistics, sociolinguistics, and psycholinguistics. Different theories about the nature of language and how languages are learned (the approach) imply different ways of teaching language (the method) and different methods make use of different kinds of classroom activities (techniques).

The Grammar Translation Method

The Main Principles

The Grammar Translation Method was the teaching method used in many European countries between the 1840s and 1940s. Originally, it was used to teach Latin and Greek languages and to help L2 learners to study foreign language literature. The main principle of this methodology was that L2 learners need to develop the ability to read a text in another language and to translate that text from one language into another. Through the study of the grammar of the target language, the learner also became more familiar with the grammar of their mother tongue.

This familiarity would help learners speak and write their native language better. At the beginning of the nineteenth century, the grammar translation method was the standard way of studying second languages in schools.

> The Grammar Translation Method assumes that language acquisition develops as L2 learners develop the ability to read a text in another language and to translate that text from one language into another

This method was based on the following main principles:

- The goal of learning another language is to acquire it to read its literature. The focus of teaching is to develop the learner's ability to read, to write, and to translate;
- The role of the teacher is very authoritative and the learner's native language is the medium for instruction;
- Learning a language consists of first going through detailed analysis of grammar rules, followed by application of this knowledge to the task of translating sentences and texts into and out of the target language;
- The grammar is taught systematically (following a sequencing grammar syllabus) through explicit teaching of grammatical rules. The main assumption is that a second language is learned through the deduction of the grammatical properties of a target L2. This would then allow L2 learners to develop a conscious and explicit representation of that language; and
- Vocabulary is taught through bilingual word lists, dictionary study, and memorization.

The main goal for this method was to ensure that L2 learners attain a high-proficiency standard in translation and accuracy. The ability to communicate using the target language was not the main goal for language instruction.

Pedagogical Procedures

A typical grammar translation textbook consisted of chapters organized around grammatical points. Each grammar point was listed, rules on its use were explained, and it was illustrated by example sentences. A variety of techniques were developed to help learners to translate, to practice, and to memorize the new language:

- Read and translate a literary passage
- Reading and comprehension activities
- Deductive grammar practice
- Fill in the blanks
- Memorization practice
- Composition

A typical reading and comprehension activity in the Grammar Translation Method consists of the following steps:

1. The class begins with a reading passage from the target language literature;
2. Each learner is asked to read part of the passage and then translate into their mother tongue what they have just read;
3. The teacher helps them with suitable translations in case they lack the required vocabulary;
4. After finishing reading and translating the passage, the teacher asks L2 learners in their mother tongue if they have any questions. Questions and answers are communicated using the mother tongue;
5. The teacher asks learners to write down answers to the comprehension questions at the end of the passage. The questions are the mother tongue and answers should be in the mother tongue as well;
6. After answering the questions, the teacher asks each individual learner to read the question and their answer to that question. If the answer is not correct, the teacher selects another student to supply the correct answer, or the teacher gives the right answer.

Consider this ...

The main goal of the Grammar Translation Method is to develop in L2 learners the ability to read literature in L2. This method focuses on providing learners with a list of grammar rules and words to learn. Accurate translation of L2 into L1 is the outcome desired.

Do you think that this method is still used in language teaching? If so, does it still have a key role to play?

The Direct Method

The Main Principles

The Direct Method was proposed as a reaction to the Grammar Translation Method in terms of its approach to grammar teaching, vocabulary learning, teacher and learner's attitude, and language skills. While in the Grammar Translation Method the primary skills to improve were reading and writing, in the Direct Method the main emphasis was on listening and oral communication skills. In the Direct Method the role of the language teacher became more active.

The teacher asked questions, engaged learners to participate in speaking activities, and encouraged self-correction. L2 learners had to speak a great deal as they were engaged in developing oral communicative skills.

> The Direct Method emphasizes the importance for L2 learners to have the opportunity to use the target language to express meaning.

The Direct Method was developed by Maximilian Berlitz at the turn of the nineteenth century and its principles were based on the attempt to make second language acquisition similar to first language acquisition. It was named "direct" because meaning should be connected to the target language without translation into the native language. According to the Direct Method, language instructors should provide learners with opportunities to convey meaning through the use of the new language. L2 learners should use the target language without translating and without using their native language to communicate. At the beginning of the nineteenth century, the Direct Method was introduced in France and Germany before becoming popular in the United States. It was known as the "Berlitz Method" and became popular in private schools and colleges. The Direct Method was the object of criticism in the 1920s as the emphasis on second/foreign language teaching became the development of reading skills. The emphasis on developing speaking skills, emphasized by the Direct Method, was considered impractical for two main reasons: (1) scarce time available for second language teaching; (2) and limited skills in language teachers.

The popularity of the Direct Method declined toward the beginning of the 1930s leading to the development of new methodologies in language teaching such as the Audio-Lingual Method and other language teaching methodology.

Pedagogical Procedures

The Direct Method consists of a number of main principles that represent the building blocks of this language teaching methodology. These main principles are:

– Language instruction is exclusively conducted in the target language. Language teachers should demonstrate the use of the target language and should not explain or translate. Language teachers and learners are more like partners. Learners are given opportunities to interact with other learners. In this sense, the Direct Method is less teacher centered. The target language is always used in the classroom. Learners are continuously exposed to the target language and teachers do not use the native language as a means of instruction;
– Basic vocabulary is introduced first. Students are encouraged to make links between meaning and the target language. The emphasis is on spoken language and vocabulary is emphasized over grammar;

– Grammar is taught inductively. Rules are not given and learners need to figure them out. L2 learners need to discover rules of grammar. Language errors are not corrected as teachers should provide opportunities for self-correction. According to the Direct Method, instructors should approach the teaching of grammar inductively. This is on the assumption that L2 learners should learn grammar by interpreting contextual and situational cues rather than receiving long explanations.

The Direct Method was characterized by the following:

– Correct pronunciation is emphasized
– Emphasis is on speaking and listening
– Vocabulary is taught through known words, authentic objects, pictures, and miming
– Self-correction is encouraged
– Curriculum is structured on situations/topics, not on linguistic structures
– Communication is at the center
– Purpose of language acquisition is to communicate

Some of the typical activities used in the Direct Method were:

– Read text aloud
– Question and answer tasks
– Fill in the blanks
– Conversation tasks/practice
– Dictation
– Self-correction

A typical activity in this method is the "map drawing." Learners are given a map without labels and then they are asked to label it by using the directions the teacher gives.

The Audio-Lingual Method

The Main Principles

In the late 1950s and beginning of the 1960s, a new method in second language teaching, called the Audio-Lingual Method, was developed. This method was underpinned by a second language acquisition theory called Behaviorism (see also the next chapter). The behaviorist's view was in strong opposition to Noam Chomsky's view of language and language acquisition that argued that humans have an innate language knowledge (see also Universal Grammar Theory in the next chapter) and that they are genetically programmed to develop their linguistic system in specific ways. Behaviorism maintained that it is the learner's experience that is largely responsible for language acquisition and this is more important than any innate capacity.

This theory argued that the child's mind is a *tabula rasa* and good language habits are learned through the process of repetition, imitation, and reinforcement. According to this view second language acquisition is a progressive accumulation of habits and the ultimate goal is to produce language that is error free. The first language was seen as a major obstacle to the acquisition of a second language because it caused interference errors (caused by habits in the L1) and negative transfer (from L1 to L2) of habits. It was believed that language acquisition proceeded from form to meaning, that is, first master the grammatical forms and then move to express meaning. Supporters of this theory saw second language acquisition as a process of acquiring verbal habits. The main conditions for acquiring these habits were:

> The Audio-Lingual Method emphasizes the use of mechanical and pattern drills practice to acquire languages.

– The learner imitated the language heard;
– The imitation has to be rewarded; and
– The behavior is repeated and becomes habitual.

This theory was translated into the Audio-Lingual Method, which emphasized the use of memorization, mechanical, and pattern drills practice. The main principles of the Audio-Lingual Method were:

– Language instructors play the role of leaders and are responsible for providing a good language model. Learners must imitate this model by imitating and following instructions;
– Learners should always be exposed to the target language;
– Learners are exposed to correct models/patterns of the target L2. Practice consists of a type of exercise called "drills practice" (e.g., repetition and substitution/transformation drills). L2 learners have to repeat, manipulate, or transform a particular form or structure to complete a task;
– Learners follow a very structural syllabus;
– Learners engage in activities that focus on structure and form rather than meaning and are corrected for inaccurate imitations/errors; and
– Learners must become accurate in the target L2. Linguistic competence is the main goal of instruction.

Pedagogical Procedures

The main activities that dominated a classroom lesson in the Audio-Lingual Method were:

- Dialog memorization
- Repetition drills
- Transformation drills
- Chain drills
- Question-and-answer drills

Typical example in the Audio-Lingual Method in relation to drills practice is:

(1) The teacher says models (the word or phrases) and the students repeat them.

Example

TEACHER: I was tired, so I went to bed.
STUDENTS: I was tired, so I went to bed.

(2) The teacher asks the students to substitute one word or more to practice different structures or vocabulary items.

Example:

TEACHER: I watch TV, She?
STUDENTS: She watches TV.
TEACHER: They?
STUDENTS: They watch TV.

(3) The teacher gives students a certain kind of sentence pattern. Students are asked to transform this sentence.

Example: (positive into negative)

TEACHER: I like watching football.
STUDENTS: I don't like watching football.

Repetition drills (when no change is made and learners have to repeat after the teacher's model) and transformation drills (when learners are required to make some minimal change, reinforced afterward by the teacher) are accompanied by so-called application activities where, working with memorized materials, learners have to repeat, manipulate, and transform the material presented to meet minimal communicative needs.

Consider this …

Some teachers have argued that drills have a role in language teaching (at least a psychological role in helping learners to become more confident about the acquisition of a second language). Research has shown that drills have no real value in language acquisition. What is your view?

Is drill practice an effective pedagogical technique in language teaching?

The Total Physical Response Method

The Main Principles

In late 1970s an innovative method called the Total Physical Response emerged. James Asher's Total Physical Response Method is a comprehension-based method to language teaching. The method assumes that language acquisition should start with understanding the language we hear or read before we proceed to production. It is a method of language teaching that makes use of physical movements to react to verbal input.

The Total Physical Response Method assumes that understanding language input plays a key and primary role in language acquisition.

A set of principles were set to help L2 learners to increase their understanding of the language to which they are exposed:

–   Instructors provide L2 learners with a nonverbal model that they need to imitate. Only after an initial period of comprehension of the target language, learners will be able to speak;
–   Initially, language instructors issue commands and then perform the actions with students. Later on, students demonstrate an understanding of the commands by performing them alone;
–   Vocabulary and grammar learning are the skills emphasized. Understanding should precede producing. When ready to speak, instructors should let students make errors and should be tolerant; and
–   Language instructors create a relaxed and stress-free environment where students focus on meaning interpreted by movement.

The main characteristic of this method is that it focuses on meaning and comprehension. Verbal response is not necessary and students become performers. Verbal response is not necessary as the main focus is listening and acting.

Pedagogical Procedures

The main activities used in the Total Physical Response Method are:

–   Using commands to direct behavior
–   Role reversal
–   Action sequence

A typical Total Physical Response activity consists of the following steps:

(1) Students learn new material, vocabulary, and verbs that will pertain to the commands;
(2) Teacher develops a set of commands that are related to a specific theme. For example, the theme might be "identifying body parts" and the language instructor runs through body parts to touch.

(3) Let's say the command is, for example, "touch your head with your right hand." L2 learners process the command and physically complete the task as fast as possible. The gauge for success is how rapid the response is.

The Natural Approach

The Main Principles

A comprehension-based approach to second language teaching is the so-called Natural Approach. It was developed by Tracy Terrell and supported by Stephen Krashen in the late 1970s or early 1980s. This approach is based on the Monitor Theory (see next chapter for a brief description of this theory) developed by Stephen Krashen in the late 1970s. According to Stephen Krashen, there is a need for the creation of a kind of environment in the L2 classroom that resembles the condition where L1 learning takes place. He hypothesized that if L2 learners were exposed to "comprehensible" input and were provided with opportunities to focus on meaning and messages rather than grammatical forms and accuracy, they would be able to acquire the L2 in much the same way as L1 learners acquire their first language.

The main principles of this approach are:

> The Natural Approach indicates that L2 learners should be exposed to comprehensible input, and that lessons should not be built around grammatical or vocabulary units but instead be built around themes or topics.

- Language instructors should provide comprehensible and message-oriented input for acquisition. They should create a classroom atmosphere in which there is low filter for learning and they should use a wide range of classroom activities.
- Error correction has a negative effect on motivation, has a positive attitude, and causes embarrassment;
- Language instruction should focus on communicative competence (see definition of communicative competence in Chapter 3 of this book) rather than on grammatical competence only. The main function of language teaching is to provide comprehensible input;
- Language instruction has to aim at the modification and improvement of the student's developing grammar rather than at building up that grammar. Most, if not all, classroom activities should be designed to evoke communication and not be wasted in grammatical lectures or manipulative exercises;
- Language instructors should create the opportunity for students to acquire rather than force them to learn language. Affective rather than cognitive factors are primary in language learning; and
- The key to comprehension and oral production is the acquisition of vocabulary.

Three types of activities dominate the classroom lesson in the Natural Approach:

- Comprehension activities
- Commands that involve the use of single words or short phrases
- Role plays and group problem solving

Comprehension (preproduction) activities are a listening comprehension practice, with no requirements for the learner to speak in the target language. They consist of comprehension activities facilitated by the language teacher with the use of gestures and visual aids.

Teaching focuses on developing communicative ability. Early speech production is introduced when the students have a recognition vocabulary of 500 words. Production activities require Question/Answer (Q/A) on the basis of a single-word answer, or a sentence-completion response in which a personalized question is asked and the answer is provided except for one word, which L2 learners must supply.

Speech emergence occurs after the early speech production phase, and it is characterized by activities such as games and problem solving. The goal of these activities is to reduce anxiety and increase motivation by providing interesting language input and by focusing on meaningful communication rather than on the practice of grammatical forms.

Pedagogical Procedures

To maximize opportunities for comprehension experiences, language teachers create activities designed to teach students to recognize the meaning in words used in meaningful contexts, and to teach language learners to guess at the meaning of phrases without knowing all of the words and structures embedded in sentences or discourse.

Language teachers must use visual aids (pictures, gestures), modify their speech to aid comprehension, speak more slowly, emphasize key words, focus on simple and key vocabulary and grammar, use familiar topics, and not talk out of context. Teachers must always provide L2 learners with a meaningful and comprehensible input language.

The following activities can be used in early speech stage:

- Open dialogues
- Guided interviews
- Open-ended sentences
- Charts, tables, graphs, and newspaper ads

Typical activities to foster comprehension and speech by focusing on message and meaning are:

- Preference ranking
- Games

- Problem solving using charts, tables, graphs, maps
- Advertisements and signs
- Music, radio, television, film strips

L2 learners listen to the input and engage in comprehension activities similar to the one used in the Physical Response Method. They use the target language when they are ready. They will begin with yes and no answers, one-word answers, and short phrases.

In the speech emergence stage, speech production will improve in both quantity and quality. The sentences that L2 learners produce would become longer and more complex, and they use a wider range of vocabulary. Students need to be given the opportunity to use oral and written language whenever possible.

A typical natural approach activity consists of the following steps:

- The teacher shows a set of pictures of different sports, repeating the word that goes with each one; language learners simply watch and listen.
- The pictures are displayed and language learners are asked to point at the appropriate picture when the teacher names it.
- The students listen to a tape of the teacher describing what sports he watches and he plays; language learners tick the items they hear on a worksheet.
- The language learners are then given a gapped transcript of the listening activity, and they fill in the gaps from memory, before listening again to check.
- Language learners, in pairs, take turns to read aloud the transcript to one another.
- Language learners, in pairs, tell each other what sports they typically play or watch, using the transcript as a model. Then, they repeat the task with another partner, this time without referring to the model.

The Communicative Language Teaching Approach

The Main Principles

A key development in language teaching was the emergence of the Communicative Language Teaching Approach. The main assumption behind this approach was that communicative language teaching programs will lead to the development of both Linguistic Competence (knowledge of the rules of grammar) and Communicative Competence (knowledge of the rules of language use). The development of a new communicative approach to language teaching is a complex one that is related to a number of disciplines. Noam Chomsky's criticism of Behaviorism, in undermining the credibility of the Audio-Lingual Method, sets the framework for a more child-centered approach that favors a highly inductive approach.

The Communicative Language Teaching Approach represents a philosophy of teaching that is based on communicative language use.

In the 1980s one could talk of a "fever" for the Communicative Language Teaching Approach. Communicative Language Teaching was considered to be a type of instruction, an approach to language teaching rather than a method. It was the growing discontent on the part of language teachers with the previous methods, together with the need for a new method, that led methodologists to find a way that would essentially bring the learner into closer contact with the target language community. Communicative Language Teaching makes us consider language not only in terms of its structures but also in terms of the communicative functions that it performs. Therefore, this approach aims at understanding what people do with language forms when they communicate. The Communicative Language Teaching Approach is a student-centered type of instruction, a very revolutionary approach to language teaching as it considers findings from both language teaching and second language acquisition theory and empirical research.

If the language classroom can become an area of co-operative negotiation, joint interpretation, and the sharing of expression, then the language teacher is in the position to give the students the opportunity for spontaneous, unpredictable exploratory production of language when involved in classroom language tasks.

The main contribution of this new type of instruction is the shift from attention to the grammatical forms to the communicative properties of the language. The language instructor creates the opportunity and the conditions in the classroom for learners to interact in a communicative way. This is to say that the L2 learner has someone to talk to, something to talk about, and a desire to understand and to make himself/herself understood. If that happens, language acquisition can take place naturally and teaching can be extremely effective.

The Communicative Language Teaching Approach was in direct antithesis with the Presentation–Production–Practice model adopted in the Audio-Lingual Method. The practice stage in this model aimed to provide opportunities for L2 learners to use the grammatical properties of the target language. Criticism of this model suggested that the practice stage was not conducive to communication. Forcing learners to use certain structures in a practice activity does not necessarily mean language learners will use these structures spontaneously later in their speech. Although there are different interpretations and theoretical positions for the Communicative Language Teaching Approach, there are some general principles shared by all professionals:

– This approach encourages the development of communicative competence (e.g., grammatical competence, pragmatic competence, sociolinguistic competence, and strategic competence);
– This approach considers learners' needs a matter of priority;
– This approach suggests that a language syllabus should be based on notional/functional principles and communicative competence; and

– This approach commits to message-orientated use of the target language in the classroom.

The main characteristics of this approach are:

– The meaning is emphasized over form. Genuine questions (ask questions to which students do not know the answer) as opposed to display questions (type of questions asked to make students display knowledge) are used because there is a focus on meaning rather than form;

– Learners should have considerable exposure to the second language speech from the teacher and other learners and instructors should provide opportunities for learners to play an active role. The role of the language instructor is to construct dynamic classroom tasks (architect) and encourage learner's participation and contribution (resource person or cobuilder). To that end, the materials that the instructor uses must permit these new roles. Therefore, the traditional question/answer task should be supplanted by a task-oriented activity. By providing a series of tasks to complete, the tutor plays the role of architect, encouraging learners to take responsibility for generating the information themselves rather than just receiving it;

– Communication is defined by James Lee and Bill VanPatten as the expression, interpretation, and negotiation of meaning. Learners and teachers must make some mutual efforts to understand interactions and negotiate meaning. Negotiation of meaning can be defined as any interactions in which learners and their interlocutors adjust their speech phonologically, lexically, and morpho-syntactically to resolve difficulties in mutual understanding that impede the course of their communication;

– Comprehensible and meaning-bearing input promotes acquisition. Simplifications of the input through the use of contextual props, cues, and gestures also promote acquisition. Comprehension activities should be used without initial requirement for students to speak in the target language. The main function of language teaching is to provide comprehensible input (useful especially for beginners and foreign language learners) that leads to a low filter (high motivation and low anxiety). Little pressure should be exercised for learners to perform at a high level of accuracy and, in the early stages, comprehension is emphasized over production;

– Classroom activities should be designed to evoke communication and not be wasted in grammatical lectures or manipulative and mechanical exercises;

– Learners must be involved in learning tasks that allow them to perform a range of communicative functions with the target L2. Communicative language teaching should encourage the use of a variety of discourse tasks;

– Grammar should be learned communicatively. Learners should be provided with communicative tasks that contain enough samples of the linguistic features that learners are trying to learn. Learners must be engaging in communicative tasks where grammar is enhanced using different techniques (e.g., input enhancement, consciousness raising, input flood, structured input tasks); and

– The amount of correction in the L2 classroom must be kept to a minimum, as the emphasis must be to allow learners to express themselves. In the Communicative Language Teaching Approach, error correction is seen as having a negative effect on learners in terms of lowering their motivation and attitude. An alternative form of correction might be done by the teacher by repeating what the students have said with the correct form (recasting) or using other forms of corrective feedback such as negative enhancement techniques. Negative enhancement techniques would involve providing learners with some information about the incorrectness of the particular use of a form/structure by enhancing the mistake in different ways (e.g., a facial expression or offering a quizzical look).

Pedagogical Procedures

The three main activities proposed in this approach are: (1) activities that involve communication promote second language acquisition; (2) activities that involve completion of real tasks promote second language acquisition; and (3) meaningful activities that make use of authentic language to promote second language acquisition.

The three main features of all communicative activities are:

– One person knows something the other one does not (information gap)
– The speaker has a choice
– The main purpose of the activity is achieved based upon the information that is received from the listener

The main activities used in Communicative Language Teaching are:

– Information gap activities
– Jigsaw activities
– Opinion-sharing activities
– Role plays
– Language games
– Scrambled sentences
– Communicative grammar tasks
– Exchange information tasks
– Discourse type tasks
– Picture strip story

A typical Communicative Language Teaching activity is an information-gap activity. This is an activity where learners are missing the information they need to complete a task successfully. They need to talk to each other to find the information to complete the task. For example, Learner A has a biography of a famous person with all the place names missing, whilst Learner B has the same text with all the dates missing. Together they can complete the text by asking each other the relevant questions to collect the relevant information to complete the task.

Content and Language Integrated Learning

The Main Principles

CLIL stands for Content and Language Integrated Learning. In a nutshell, it is the teaching of subjects to learners through the use of the target language. For example, the teacher will teach drama to a class of ESL students from Japan. Subject matter and target language are therefore integrated and taught at once.

This dual approach has two main aims: (1) one related to a particular subject; (2) and one related to language. If you are teaching Italian you can use as a subject matter "history of art." CLIL has four main components: content (subject aims); communication (oral and written form); cognition (promotes cognitive or thinking skills); and culture (understanding cultures makes the process of communication with other people more effective).

> CLIL is the teaching of subjects to learners through the use of the target language.

The main principles of CLIL are:

- Language is used to learn as well as to communicate
- Subject matter determines the language needed to learn
- Subject matter is taught in simple, easily comprehensible ways, by using illustrations, diagrams, and highlighted terms
- Subject-based vocabulary, tests, and discussion are used by the teacher

The CLIL lesson should combine the following four elements:

- It should not repeat the content learned in other lessons
- It should constitute progression in knowledge
- The focus of the lesson should be the using of the language to learn and learning to use language
- It should encourage the development of thinking skills that link concept formation, understanding, and language
- It should understand culture, community, and global citizenship

The teaching is organized around the content of information that learners will acquire and not around the linguistic characteristics of the language. Subject-matter content is used for teaching purposes and language instructors need to provide learners with assistance in understanding subject matter texts. Learners become highly motivated and are exposed to authentic material and tasks. Language is used to convey specific content. This approach is built on the principles of the Communicative Language Teaching Approach and therefore it emphasizes the importance of real and meaningful communication where information is exchanged between interlocutors.

Pedagogical Procedures

There are specific pedagogical procedures to develop an effective CLIL lesson. Teachers need to ensure that learners understand all the crucial vocabulary and concepts in the lesson. In short, instructors give comprehensible input. They use their whole body to convey nuanced meaning to language learners. Images and pictures are also used to facilitate comprehension. Instead of solely using words in a lesson and letting learners figure out the meanings for themselves, teachers must be more direct about what vocabulary is being featured and needs to be learned. Teachers should preteach vocabulary ahead of the main lesson. Teachers should give language learners plenty of opportunities to engage in activities that offer the chance to practice the target language.

Typical activities in this approach include:

- Language skills tasks
- Vocabulary building
- Discourse organization
- Communicative interaction
- Study skills
- Synthesis of content materials and grammar
- Role plays

In CLIL, a typical task designed for production needs to be subject orientated, so that both content and language are recycled. Typical speaking activities include:

- Question loops – questions and answers, terms and definitions, halves of sentences
- Information-gap activities with a question sheet to support
- Word-guessing games
- Class surveys using questionnaires
- Students present information from a visual using a language support handout

Task-Based Language Teaching

The Main Principles

Task-Based Language Teaching became initially popular in the 1990s. It referred to a type of language teaching that takes "tasks" as its key units for designing and implementing language instruction. The main principles of the Task-Based Language Teaching approach are:

- Learners should be provided with opportunities that make the language input they receive more comprehensible;
- Learners should be engaged in contexts in which they need to produce output which others can understand; and
- Learners should be exposed to real-life language situations in the language classroom.

Task-Based Language Teaching aims at providing L2 learners with a natural context to use the target language. The goal of this approach

> Task-Based Language Teaching is based on the idea that the use of "language tasks" is the most effective way to teach and acquire languages.

is twofold: to promote communication and to develop fluency by attempting to use the L2 in real operating conditions. Learners work to complete a task and have plenty of opportunities for interaction and negotiation of meaning as they have to understand each other and express their own meaning. The essential characteristics of a task in this approach are:

- Meaning must play a key role
- The participants choose the linguistic resources to perform the task
- Learners must resolve a communication-based world problem
- Learners will be assessed in terms of the task outcome

Task-Based Language Teaching aims at integrating all four language skills (speaking, reading, listening, and writing) and providing opportunities for the learners to experiment with and explore both spoken and written language through learning activities that are designed to engage L2 learners in the authentic, practical, and functional use of language for meaningful purposes (i.e., to cultivate the learners' communicative competence).

Pedagogical Procedures

A traditional model (such as the Audio-Lingual Method) for the organization of language lessons, both in the classroom and in coursebooks, has long been the PPP approach (presentation, practice, production). With this model, individual language items are presented by the teacher, then practiced in the form of spoken and written exercises (often pattern drills), and then used by the learners in less controlled speaking or writing activities. A different model is the Test-Teach-Test approach (TTT), in which the production stage comes first and the learners are "thrown in at the deep end" and required to perform a particular task (e.g., a role play).

This is followed by the teacher dealing with some of the grammatical or lexical problems that arose in the first stage and the learner then is being required either to perform the initial task again or to perform a similar task.

Task-Based Language Teaching is an alternative approach that is based on sound theoretical foundations and that takes account of the need for authentic communication. The roles assumed by L2 learners and teachers during Task-Based Language Teaching are very similar with the general roles taken by learners and language instructors in the Communicative Language Teaching Approach and are also influenced by the specific tasks used.

The activities used in Task-Based Language Teaching are:

(1) Jigsaw tasks: they involve L2 learners to combine different pieces of information
(2) Information-gap tasks: they involve L2 learners to find out a set of information to complete the task
(3) Problem-solving tasks: they involve L2 learners to find a solution to "a problem"
(4) Decision-making tasks: they involve L2 learners to identify problems and possible outcomes
(5) Opinion exchange tasks: they involve L2 learners to engage in discussion and exchange ideas

A typical example of a task in Task-Based Language Teaching is described in the following text:

Step 1. Three students – each has one picture and describes it to the rest of the class
Step 2. Students from the rest of the class ask the three students questions about their pictures
Step 3. One student from the class tries to tell the story
Step 4. Steps 2 and 3 are repeated

A similar phase-based procedure is used in Task-Based Language teaching for listening comprehension, reading comprehension, and speaking and writing tasks:

– Pretask phase: L2 learners are involved in pretask activities such as brainstorming, problem-solving tasks to introduce the topic, and the situation of a given task;
– Task phase: L2 learners work in pairs or groups with a task and all the different steps and cues provided to complete the task. During this phase, L2 learners are involved in planning and accomplishing the task. The language teacher is available to provide more information, for advice, and to clear up any possible questions. Report and analysis of the task is conducted by both learners and teachers; and
– Posttask phase: L2 learners are given opportunities to compare how they perform in the task and they engage in posttask activities to build and expand on the work done during the task phase.

Structured input tasks (discussed in Chapter 4) are activities that promote development and are compatible with Task-Based Language Teaching.

> **Consider this ...**
>
> The Task-Based Language Teaching offers the opportunity to be exposed to communicative and meaningful classroom instruction.
>
> What do you think are the main advantages? Name three:
>
> 1.
> 2.
> 3.

Recap

Here is a small recap of the main methods and approaches in language teaching briefly described in this chapter (see following table).

- The Grammar Translation Method focuses on developing the ability for L2 learners to read a text in another language and to translate that text from one language into another.
- The Direct Method focuses on providing L2 learners with the opportunity to use the target language to express meaning.
- The Audio-Lingual Method makes use of memorization and mechanical and pattern drills practice to develop L2 learners' language skills.
- The Total Physical Response Method focuses on developing practices that improve first L2 learners' ability in listening and reading before speaking and writing skills.
- The Natural Approach argues that L2 learners should be exposed to comprehensible and message-oriented input, and that language teaching should not be built around grammatical or vocabulary units but instead themes or topics.
- The Communicative Language Teaching Approach represents a philosophy of teaching that is based on communicative language use. It emphasizes notional-functional concepts and communicative competence, rather than grammatical structures, as central to language teaching.
- The Content and Language Integrated Learning is an approach in language education designed to provide L2 learners instruction in content and language.
- Task-Based Language Teaching focuses on asking students to undertake meaningful tasks using the target language.

A summary of the main claim in each method and approach to language teaching is provided in the following table.

Teaching (methods and approaches)	Main Claim
The Grammar Translation Method	Read and translate texts from one language into another
The Direct Method	Use the target language to express meaning
The Audio-Lingual Method	Memorize, learn, and practice the language mechanically
The Natural Approach	Expose learners to comprehensible and message-oriented input
The Communicative Language Teaching Approach	Develop communicative competence
The Total Physical Response Method	Developing listening and reading skills
The Content and Language Integrated Learning	Provide content language
Task-Based Language Teaching	Use of meaningful tasks

Over the last eighty years a variety of methods (e.g., Grammar Translation, Audio-Lingual Method) and approaches (e.g., Natural Approach, Communicative Language Teaching, Task-Based Language Teaching) have been proposed for the teaching of languages. Language teachers have been interested in finding innovative and more effective ways to teach languages.

To provide teachers with effective options for language teaching, we should consider carefully what we know about how a language is acquired. Based on what is presented and discussed in the first chapter of this book, an effective approach to language teaching is one based on and informed by theories and empirical research in second language acquisition.

Despite the fact that theory and research in second language acquisition mainly focuses on learners and learning, both the theory and the findings from research very often have implications for language teachers and language teaching.

The main implications for language teaching are highlighted in the following text to provide effective options for language teachers and to work toward a more principled and evidence-based approach to language teaching:

- Mental representation cannot be directly manipulated. That is, language can't be taught in the classic sense (e.g., grammar explanations and mechanical drills).
- Traditional practice helps to develop a language-like behavior. Developing a skill is different than second language acquisition.
- Input is indispensable for acquiring a language.
- The language input provided in the classroom must be comprehensible and meaningful to be properly processed by learners.

- Instruction should be less about the teaching of rules and more about exposure to form. We should provide learners with opportunities for form-meaning connections.
- Instruction ought to be less about manipulating output and more about processing input (input manipulations such as structured input and textual enhancement tasks should be used for grammar teaching).
- Output is constrained by processability.
- During language interactive tasks (e.g., information-exchange tasks), learners have the opportunity to interpret input, interact with others, exchange information, negotiate meaning, and eventually produce new language at the appropriate time. The concept of task is crucial for effective language teaching.
- The role of the teacher is the ones of the architect or the resource person. The teacher sets up language tasks and needs to ensure that language learners have considerable exposure to language input and the opportunity to interpret, negotiate meaning, and produce language in a context and for a specific purpose.
- To develop good language practice we need to clarify the role and nature of communication (see Chapter 3).

REFERENCES AND READINGS

- Asher, J. (1977). *Learning Another Language through Actions: The Complete Teacher's Guide Book.* Los Gatos, CA: Sky Oaks Productions.
- Chomsky, N. (1965). *Aspects of the Theory of Syntax.* Cambridge, MA: MIT Press.
- Hinkel, E. (ed.) (2005). *Handbook of Research in Second Language Teaching and Learning.* Mahwah, NJ: Lawrence Erlbaum Associates.
- Krashen, S. (1985). *The Input Hypothesis: Issues and Implications.* New York: Longman.
- Krashen, S., Terrell, T. (1983). *The Natural Approach: Language Acquisition in the Classroom.* Hayward, CA: Alemany Press.
- Larsen-Freeman, D. (2000). *Techniques and Principles in Language Teaching.* Oxford: Oxford University Press.
- Lee, J., VanPatten, B. (2003). *Making Communicative Classroom.* New York: McGraw-Hill.
- Long, M., Doughty, C. (eds.) (2009). *The Handbook of Language Teaching.* Oxford: Wiley-Blackwell.
- Long, H. M. et al. (2018). A Micro Process-Product Study of CLIL Lesson: Linguistic Modifications, Content Dilution and Vocabulary Knowledge. *Instructed Second Language Acquisition*, 2, 3–38.
- Richards, J. C., Rodgers, T. S. (2001). *Approaches and Methods in Language Teaching.* Cambridge: Cambridge University Press.
- Wong, W., VanPatten, B. (2003). The Evidence in IN: Drills Are Out. *Foreign Language Annals*, 36, 403–442.

DISCUSSION AND QUESTIONS

1. Prepare a lesson plan (see following template) according to the main tenets of the Communicative Language Teaching Approach. Be ready to teach it to your fellow colleagues in the next meeting. Use intermediate textbooks for making your lesson plan.

   Objective(s):

   Prelesson:

   Introduction:

   Schedule:

   Speaking/Listening/Reading/Writing:

   Assessments:

2. Read the journal article that follows and write down your critique of CLIL indicating weaknesses and strengths and how to maximize the benefits from using this approach.

   Long, H. M. et al. (2018). A Micro Process-Product Study of CLIL Lesson: Linguistic Modifications, Content Dilution and Vocabulary Knowledge. *Instructed Second Language Acquisition*, 2, 3–38.

Weaknesses	Strengths	Maximizing Benefits

3. What are the advantages of Task-Based Language Teaching compared to the PPP approach?

Task-Based Language Teaching vs. PPP model	Advantages

4. Can you discuss how the same topic/item can be addressed using three different methods/approaches?

Topic

3 What Is the Nature and Role of Communication and Interactive Tasks (Speaking and Writing)?

Overview

In this chapter, the nature and role of interactive speaking tasks (e.g., exchange-information tasks) is examined. Language teachers concentrate most of their efforts in ensuring learners speak in the classroom and interact with others. However, in most cases the practice is still based on the Question/Answer (Q/A) paradigm or the open-ended questions type of activities. Communication cannot be equated with Q/A practice or open-ended questions. Communicative tasks promote acquisition and provide a purpose for language use. A definition and understanding of the nature of communication is crucial for developing effective language tasks. Tasks (and not mechanical exercises or activities lacking meaning) should form the backbone of the language teaching curriculum and can be used to achieve specific lesson objectives.

The nature and role of language writing in second language teaching from a communicative perspective will also be examined in this chapter. Writing, like any other aspects of second language development, is about communication. In real life we write e-mails, notes, letters, grocery lists, reports, and essays, and these different tasks have a communicative purpose and a specific audience. A more communicative and task-based approach to the development of writing skills is proposed. To develop more effective tasks for developing writing skills, language instructors must clarify the communicative purpose of a written task and the target audience. Language teachers must integrate writing with other language skills and use more meaningful, realistic, and relevant writing tasks based on L2 learners' needs.

What Is Communication?

Most language textbooks contain activities that are so-called communicative. For instance, learners are asked to look at some pictures or a dialogue and then produce the target language following a specific pattern. Another example is activities where teachers ask L2 learners to talk about a topic (e.g., describe a friend or a member of your family or talk about your weekend or your summer holiday. See the following example.

Work in pairs and describe what you did last summer and make sure you provide the following information:

– Who you were with
– Where you stayed
– What you did
– What you liked most

The main purpose of these activities is language practice. The real purpose of activities like the ones described is for learners to practice a particular form (past tense in the case of the preceding example) and use specific and relevant vocabulary.

The fact that L2 learners are working together and speaking does not mean they are communicating. In the case of role plays practice, for example, learners have to play a role. They are provided role player cards with concrete information and clear role descriptions so that they could play their roles with confidence following the instructions (see following example).

Cue Card A:

You Are in a Bar

1. Say hello
2. Order a coffee
3. Pay and say goodbye

Cue Card B:

You Are a Barman

1. Greet the client
2. Ask the client what he would like to drink
3. Tell the client how much it costs and say goodbye

Although role plays require L2 learners to express meaning, they fall short of being communicative. The meaning learners have been asked to express is not their own but of imaginary people in an imaginary setting. Very often, learners are playing an unreal role. It would be necessary to clarify what real communication means.

Sandra Sauvignon has defined communication as the expression, interpretation, and negotiation of meaning for a specific purpose in a given context. Let's now define the components of communication.

> Communication is the expression, interpretation, and negotiation of meaning for a specific purpose in a given context.

Expression and Interpretation

In Bill VanPatten's view "expression" refers to any type of production during a communicative event. Expression of meaning can take an oral form and people express meaning without language (e.g., raising eyebrows, smiling, waving, eyes narrowing). In face-to-face interactions, people tend to use both oral and nonoral expression of meaning.

Communication is not one-sided, and there is always someone or some other entity expected to understand the message or the intent of the message we are trying to convey.

Negotiation of Meaning

Negotiation shows up in a variety of ways:

Statement: "I'm sorry, but I don't understand." "Please, say it again."
Comprehension check: "You know what I mean?"
Confirmation check: "Let me see if I got this right. You're saying that...."

All these initial reactions and others are ways in which interlocutors initiate meaning checks, which can then lead to negotiation of meaning. Meaning refers to the information contained in the message we intend to convey. If someone says, for example, "*sono le tre*" (it's three o'clock), the literal message is that it's three o' clock. But meaning can also refer to a speaker's intent. Maybe the person who says "it's three o'clock" is worried that someone else is taking too long to get ready or it could be that he/she is unaware of the time.

Context and Purpose

The construct of "context" refers to two principal aspects of communication: the setting and the participants. When people speak, write, listen, or read, they do so with a purpose. Context is a powerful dimension of any communicative event. Context constrains how people communicate. Being in a classroom, for example, is not the same thing as being at a dinner table at home with friends or family. Interacting with your lawyer is not the same as interacting with your wife. The context would dictate the way we interact and communicate messages.

People communicate for a purpose. We don't use language or gestures or signs or anything else involved in communication without a specific reason. In everyday life, these two major purposes of communication overlap and we often move back and forth between the two during an interaction. People generally use language for the following purposes:

- Psycho-social purpose: to establish and maintain personal relationships, for example (e.g., saying "hello," to invite someone out for dinner, to inquire about members of the family);
- Cognitive-informational purpose: to exchange information with someone and learn something new, to obtain information for a specific purpose.

Communication between two or more people always has some purpose. People use language to accomplish something (e.g., getting directions from a passerby and going from A to B, discussing your birthday to organize a party). The question is: Do language teachers engage L2 learners in communication in the language classroom? Considering the way very often languages are still taught in schools and universities or in other contexts, it would appear that learners are not exposed to appropriate communicative activities in which they are engaged in interpretation, expression, and negotiation of meaning. The activities in the language classroom are often constructed to simply practice language.

> ## Consider this ...
>
> Does the following look familiar to you?
>
> Restate the question using inversion.
>
> *Est-ce que vous parlez espagnol*? (Do you speak Spanish?)
>
> *Est-ce qu'il étudie à Paris*? (Did he study in Paris?)
>
> How about the following activity? Does it look familiar to you?
>
> Interview your partner and find out what he or she did last night.

The preceding activities are not communicative at all. If teachers and learners are not engaged in the expression and interpretation of meaning, what they're doing is not communicative. In the first activity, the learner is simply changing the question from one form to another. We could insert nonsense words and language learners could still perform the activity. And, of course, the activity lacks any communicative purpose. There is no psycho-social or informational-cognitive purpose to what learners and teachers are doing here. The sole purpose is to explicitly practice making questions using inversion. Learners and teachers are not finding out anything about each other. Students and teachers are not building relationships through this interaction. In the second activity, it seems that students are communicating. Imagine the student simply going through the motions. That student says "I studied." The other student says "I watched TV." Neither student is saying much, and we're not even sure they're paying attention to each other. The main characteristics of these activities are:

- There is no focus on the interpretation and expression of meaning.
- The purpose is to practice language.

The concept of communication is at the heart of language acquisition. Communicative language ability develops as learners engage in communication. Communication can be defined as the expression, interpretation, and negotiation of meaning. Mechanical practice does little to foster language development and only fosters a learning-like behavior. Real communication is about language use in context. Learners learn to communicate by practicing communication and negotiating the input (see following example).

NS: *Cosa hai fatto per il fine settimana?* (What did you do last weekend?)
NNS: *Hum ... ?*
NS: *Sabato, Domenica ... Ti sei divertito?* (Saturday, Sunday ... Did you enjoy?)

Interaction fosters acquisition when a communication problem arises and language learners are engaged in resolving it through interaction and negotiation of meaning. Features of language are learned if they have been linked to real-world meaning.

In other words, communication is not simply a matter of questions and answers but involves expression, interpretation, and negotiation of meaning. Negotiation of meaning becomes a key feature and consists of interactions during which learners must resolve problems, reach an agreement, or settle an issue. The main purpose of language use is to accomplish a task and not mechanically practice any particular form.

> The main purpose of language use is to accomplish a task and not mechanically practice any particular form.

Tasks should be used in the language classroom for effective learning. A task is a language-learning endeavor that requires L2 learners to (1) comprehend, (2) manipulate, and (3) produce the target language as they perform some set of work plans. We will discuss the role of interactive tasks in developing language skills and promote learning in the next sections and across the next chapters.

Communicative Competence

Before we discuss the role and nature of language tasks, a brief introduction to the concept of communicative competence is provided. Although grammatical competence is a necessary requirement for somebody who wants to speak in another language, communicative competence is also necessary for L2 learners to be able to communicate competently in a second language. Communicative competence comprises the knowledge of the grammatical system of a second language as well as the knowledge of the social and cultural contexts. Communicative language competence is made up of various components that interact with each other. It is the interaction between knowledge and language use in a specific context that characterizes communicative language use. Language competence involves four main components: grammatical competence, pragmatic competence, sociolinguistic competence, and strategic competence.

Grammatical competence refers to how we organize individual utterances or sentences to form texts. Grammatical knowledge includes knowledge of vocabulary, syntax, phonology, and graphology. It also involves how well we can organize utterances/sentences to form texts (e.g., relationship between sentences in written texts: use of conjunction, lexical cohesion).

Pragmatic knowledge relates to what we really want to say and what our intentions are when we produce sentences.

Sociolinguistic competence enables us to create or interpret language that is appropriate to a particular language use setting (e.g., writing a letter to a friend and writing a letter to a company).

Strategic competence consists of verbal and nonverbal communication strategies that may be called into action to compensate for breakdowns in communication due to performance variables or to insufficient competence.

What are the conditions for the development of communicative competence?

- First, L2 learners must be receptive to the language and have a need and desire to communicate.
- Second, L2 learners require opportunities to take responsibility in communication. They need to ensure they understand language input and they make themselves understood (negotiation of meaning).
- Third, L2 learners need opportunities to communicate by performing communicative tasks. Language teachers must provide learners with opportunities to participate in planned and unplanned discourse similar to outside the classroom.

What Is a Task?

In the previous section, it was argued that an activity is a type of language practice that involves comprehension or production of language with a focus on vocabulary and grammar. Practice should be distinguished from a language task. Tasks are the quintessential communicative event in contemporary language teaching. They are both meaningful and have a communicative purpose. The exact definition of tasks varies somewhat among scholars but at the kernel of all definitions you'll find the following:

- Tasks involve the expression and interpretation of meaning
- Tasks have a purpose that is not language practice

A task is a classroom activity that has an objective attainable only by (1) the interaction among participants, (2) a mechanism for structuring and sequencing interaction, and (3) a focus on meaning exchange.

> Tasks involve the expression and interpretation of meaning and have a purpose that is not language practice.

A task is a language-learning endeavor that requires students to (1) comprehend, (2) manipulate, and (3) produce the target language as they perform some set of work plans. Tasks provide learners with a purpose for language use and make language teaching more communicative. Tasks are activities that involve understanding and processing of the target language. They have specific features:

- Provide a piece of extended discourse
- Have an information gap element
- Have an uncertainty element
- They are goal oriented
- They are real-time processing
- Require two or more autonomous participants
- Privilege the learners' use of the language

To create a communicative and effective message the following criteria should be adopted:

- Identify a desired informational outcome
- Break down the topic into subtopics
- Create and sequence concrete tasks (steps) for learners to do; for example, create lists, fill in charts, or make tables
- Build in linguistic support, either lexical or grammatical or both (the teacher is the resource person and the architect who is planning the task and learners are the executors)

If a language task follows the preceding criteria and is structured in an appropriate way, it can successfully promote communication among L2 learners. Second language research and theory recognizes the importance of comprehensible input but views interactional modifications as important in making input comprehensible. Classroom research has proved that interactional modifications and negotiation take place more successfully in paired group activities than teacher-fronted activities.

As previously mentioned, negotiation of meaning is a form of interaction during which speakers come to terms, reach agreements, make some arrangements, solve a problem, or settle an issue by conferring or discussing. In interaction tasks the main purpose of language use is to accomplish some language tasks and not to practice any particular form. Input will provide learners with the linguistic data necessary to develop the internal language system and output practice will ultimately help learners develop the use of the language for communicative purposes.

Tasks promote communication but the question is whether they also have a beneficial role for second language acquisition. It can be argued that tasks can facilitate language acquisition processes in a number of ways.

Firstly, in interactive tasks, language learners receive and are exposed to meaningful input from a variety of sources: teachers, other learners, and the task. More importantly the input, both aural and written, is made comprehensible and meaningful. The input language to which learners are exposed is simplified and more processable (e.g., short utterances, forms are made salient, the language is simplified). These modifications help language learners to process the target language and it increases the changes for the successful development of their internal language system.

Secondly, in interactive tasks, language learners are not engaged in mechanical output practice (e.g., drills, repetition exercises) where the language they produce is not meaningful. Interactive tasks would instead allow language learners to engage in meaningful production of language that might help them in filling the gaps in their knowledge (forms, words, and structures to convey meaning) and facilitating language acquisition.

Thirdly, in interactive tasks the focus is not just the expression and interpretation of meaning but also the negotiation of meaning. Providing language learners with opportunities to negotiate meaning (e.g., confirmation checks, comprehension checks) would increase the amount of language input that is comprehended and subsequently would facilitate learning.

Rod Ellis has identified the following key features of an effective task:

- A task is a work plan. A task constitutes a plan for learner activity. This work plan takes the form of teaching materials or of ad hoc plans for activities that arise in the course of teaching
- A task involves a primary focus on meaning
- A task involves real-world processes of language use
- A task can involve any of the four language skills
- A task engages cognitive processes. The work plan requires learners to employ cognitive processes such as selecting, classifying, ordering, reasoning, and evaluating information to carry out the task
- A task has clearly defined outcomes

The following exemplary study suggests that (1) a task with a requirement for information exchange is an effective way to teach languages, and (2) interaction is also a key element in language development.

Exemplary Study

Doughty, C., Pica, T. (1986). Information Gap Tasks: Do They Facilitate Second Language Acquisition?, *TESOL Quarterly*, 20, 305–325.

Main aims of the study:

- Compare the effects of tasks and participation patterns (teacher fronted and group interactional) on the modification of interaction
- Examine the total amount of interaction produced by L2 learners during a task

Participants:

- Adult students and teachers from six intermediate ESL classes
- Students from different L1 backgrounds
- Teachers were native speakers of English

Materials and procedure:

- Information exchange task used in three interactional patterns: teacher fronted, small group, and dyad
- Each activity was audiotaped

Results and significance:

- The evidence suggests that a task with a requirement for information exchange is crucial to the generation of conversational modification of classroom interaction
- These findings suggest that conversational modification occurring during interaction is instrumental in second language acquisition
- The main findings from this study suggest that group and dyad interaction patterns produced more modification than did the teacher-fronted situation, suggesting that participation pattern as well as task type have an effect on the conversational modification of interaction

What Is the Nature and Role of Speaking Interactive Tasks?

As we have stated in the previous section, the communication act involves the expression, interpretation, and negotiation of meaning in a given context. Interactive tasks provide language learners with opportunities to interpret and express meaning in a specific context. In addition, tasks have an informational purpose. Speaking is an interactive process of constructing meaning that involves producing, receiving, and processing information. Speaking in another language is not just developing the ability to use grammar correctly, having access to vocabulary, and pronouncing words correctly (linguistic competence). Speaking is also the ability to understand when, why, and in what ways to produce language (communicative competence). L2 learners must be engaged in communicative tasks where they use language that is meaningful and they use it for a specific purpose. All communicative tasks must ensure L2 learners develop their ability to share information, negotiate meaning, and interact with others. Speaking interactive tasks must be developed with the intention to promote communication and communicative language use. As previously said a task is a classroom activity that has (1) an objective attainable only by interaction among participants; (2) a mechanism for structuring and sequencing interaction; and (3) a focus on meaning exchange.

A language task is a learning endeavor that requires L2 learners to comprehend, negotiate, manipulate, and produce the target language as they need to perform some set of work plans. L2 learners must develop their ability to manage interaction as well as engage in the negotiation of meaning. The management of the interaction involves such things as when and how to take the floor, when to introduce a topic or change the subject, how to invite someone else to speak, how to keep a conversation going, and so on. Negotiation of meaning refers to the skill of making sure the person you are speaking to has correctly understood you and that you have correctly understood them. Assuming that our aim is to develop L2 learners' communicative competence, we must create classroom speaking tasks that stimulate communication in the language classroom. In addition to that, we must consider practical needs and possible constraints in developing effective speaking tasks.

Much of the time allocated to speaking tasks must be occupied by L2 learners' talk and not instructors' talk. Classroom discussion must not be dominated by a minority of talkative participants and all learners must contribute evenly (even in the case of a mixed-ability class). Speaking interactive tasks should be developed keeping L2 learners' motivation in mind as learners are eager to speak when they are interested in the topic and have something new to say about it. L2 learners need to use an appropriate, comprehensible, and accurate level of target language. Language instructors must address some of the problems related to getting L2 learners to talk in the classroom.

Speaking interactive tasks requires some degree of real-time exposure to an audience. L2 learners often feel ashamed about what they are trying to say in the target foreign language in the classroom. They are often worried about making mistakes, fearful of criticism or losing face, or simply shy of the attention that their speech attracts. They often think they have nothing to say and often in group work they have very little talking time. In the language classroom, if learners share the same mother tongue, they tend to use it because it is easier and feels unnatural to speak to one another in a foreign language. In traditional oral practice, instructors and learners normally exchange very little real information. Language teachers spend most of their time asking "displayed questions" for which learners already know the answers (e.g., asking "Where is my book?" while showing everybody that the book is on the table). Display questions have clear limitations as, on one hand, they do not offer genuine communication practice and, on the other hand, they take L2 learners away from the use of language for communicative purposes.

How do we develop effective speaking interactive tasks? A series of measures need to be considered to achieve this goal.

First, language teachers should develop group-speaking interactive tasks that increase language learners' talk time and at the same time lower the inhibitions of learners who are unwilling to speak in front of the full class. In group work, learners perform a learning task through small-group interaction. One of the advantages of group interaction is that it can foster learner responsibility and independence, and it can improve motivation and contribute to effective and careful organization/planning.

Second, teachers should base the speaking task on easy and comprehensible language that will help learners to produce target language with the minimum of hesitation.

Third, teachers should keep L2 learners speaking the target language and they should monitor the learners' use of the target language at all times during their tasks. L2 learners should be allowed to initiate communication, and speaking tasks should involve negotiation for meaning. Positive corrective feedback on learners' performance should be carefully provided.

Fourth, language instructors should choose an interesting and familiar topic that would enable learners to use and tap into their ideas from their own experience and knowledge as they perform a speaking task.

Fifth, instructors should provide clear instruction to accomplish the task. In group or pair work everyone in the group contributes to the discussion. A chairperson to each group is appointed to regulate participation. Teachers structure tasks in a certain way but they are not responsible for final accomplishments. Learners must take initiative and full responsibility to complete tasks. Language learners need to take the initiative and make decisions to complete the task successfully.

Sixth, teachers should create a classroom environment where students have real-life authentic communication and meaningful tasks that promote speaking skills. This can occur when students collaborate in groups to achieve a goal or to complete a task. L2 learners must be given a task where they need something to talk about and someone to talk to.

Seventh, teachers should develop a task that is essentially goal oriented and that requires the group or pair to achieve an objective that is usually expressed by an observable result, such as brief notes or lists, a rearrangement of jumbled items, a drawing, or a spoken summary. In designing a speaking interactive task, we must make sure that learners collect data through interaction and production speech tasks designed for a specific purpose. Rod Ellis has identified five components in language tasks that can be applied to the development of effective speaking tasks:

1. Goal: The general purpose of the task.
2. Input: The verbal or nonverbal information supplied by the task (e.g., pictures, a map, written text).
3. Conditions: The way in which the information is presented (e.g., split vs. shared information), or the way in which it is to be used (e.g., converging vs. diverging).
4. Procedures: The methodological procedures to be followed in performing the task (e.g., group vs. pair work).
5. Predicted outcomes: The "product" that results from completing the task (e.g., a route drawn in on a map, a list of differences between two pictures).

Exchange Information Tasks

In structuring the so-called information exchange tasks, language teachers should adopt the following criteria:

- They should identify a desired information outcome
- They should identify information sources
- They should break down the topic into subtopics
- They should create and sequence concrete tasks for learners to complete
- They should build in linguistic support

Information exchange tasks should substitute traditional speaking practice where L2 learners would be asked to talk about a specific topic such as "How do you spend your free time and over the weekend?" In this kind of open-ended question activity type, language learners will have very little to talk about and few opportunities to interact.

Criteria to develop exchange information tasks:
- Identify a desired information outcome
- Identify information sources
- Break down the topic into subtopics
- Create and sequence concrete tasks for L2 learners to complete
- Build in linguistic support

Identify a Desired Information Outcome

This is the first element to consider in developing an effective exchange information task. The main informational goal of the task needs to be determined. In other words, we need to establish what specific questions/activities L2 learners will be able to answer/engage at the end of the task.

Identify Information Sources

Information that L2 learners would need to exchange generates from two main sources: from themselves (e.g., their views, their opinions, their beliefs) and from outside sources (e.g., texts, videos, programs). In developing a task we should consider from which sources learners should tap into to have enough language/ material to complete the task.

Break Down the Topic into Subtopics

To avoid a discussion of Q/A type of activities, it is important to break down the topic into subtopics. For instance, if we ask learners to discuss their view about "smoking" we can set up a number of subtopics (e.g., what is the danger of smoking, what are the possible solutions) that would help them to build knowledge and language necessary to interact with each other and complete the task.

Create and Sequence Concrete Tasks for Learners to Complete

Once goals are established, the interactive task is made of different steps/stages. Steps/stages are set so that language learners can develop and utilize the appropriate vocabulary, grammar, and language to meet the goals of the task.

Build In Linguistic Support

Language learners would need to be provided with the appropriate linguistic support to complete the task (see the following example of an exchange information task). The questions language teachers would need to ask are: Would learners have the sufficient vocabulary to complete the various steps of the task? Would they have the right knowledge about the linguistic properties of the language to complete the task? Would they be able to use the right language functions to be able to express themselves correctly?

Step 1. Using the following chart, fill it in with at least three things that you usually do in your free time during weekdays and over the weekend. Include information about the time when you usually do these things. Use the correct verb forms to speak about yourself.

	Camarade de classe	Camarade de classe
En semaine		
Les weekends		

Step 2. Now interview two people in the class with whom you have not worked much during this lesson. Ask them specific questions to find out if they do the same things. For example, if you wrote for yourself *Je joue au football pour une heure tous les jours après la classe*, ask your partner "Pratiquez-vous tous les sports?" and so on.

The idea is to gather information so that you can write contrasting and comparative statements.

Step 3. Using the information obtained in steps 1 and 2, write a list of three true/false questions and three multiple-choice questions comparing and contrasting you and your classmates.

EXAMPLE: True/False

Je joue au football trois fois par semaine, mais Alessandro joue au basket deux fois par semaine

EXAMPLE: Alessandro joue au tennis le week-end. Je ...
1. joue aussi au tennis
2. vais au cinéma
3. étude

Step 4. Submit your chart and your lists to your language instructor.
Exchange Information Task

Consider this ...

Create a Speaking Information Exchange Task using the following guidelines:

1. Identify the topic
2. Design an appropriate purpose
3. Identify information sources
4. Break down the topic into subtopics
5. Build in linguistic support

The focus in L2 learners' conversational interactions with others (e.g., other learners, native speakers, and teachers) is usually to manipulate the kinds of interactions to which learners are exposed, the kind of feedback they receive during interaction, and the kind of output they produce. The most common way of fostering this is to involve learners in a range of carefully planned tasks:

1. In a one-way task, the information flows from one person to the other. For instance, when a learner describes a picture to his or her partner;
2. In a two-way task, there is an information exchange whereby both parties (or however many participants there are in a task) hold information that is vital to the resolution of the task (see following jigsaw task).

Jigsaw Tasks

In a jigsaw task, learners work in pairs or small groups. They hold different information and they are asked to exchange their information with each other to complete the task. In this "two-way task" both participants or groups must give and receive information. Research has shown that this type of task can lead to the greatest amount of negotiation because both learners and groups must exchange language and they must understand each other correctly to complete the task in a correct and appropriate manner.

An example is a task where two language learners are working in pairs and are given a chart (partially completed) to be filled with different personal information about four people (Paolo, Giovanni, Luisa, Giovanna). The participants are taking turns to ask and answer questions regarding the four people without looking at their partner's chart. They both end up supplying to each other the missing information to complete the task. The information they need to exchange might be about where the four people come from, where they live, how many pets they have, what their favorite sports are, and what music they like best (see following example).

	Paola	Giovanni	Louis	Joanne
Da dove viene? *Where does he/she come from?*				Americana
Dove vive? *Where does he/she live?*			Roma	
Ha animali? *Does he/she have pets?*		4		
Che sport le/gli piace? *What sports does he/she like?*	Tennis			
Che musica le/gli piace? *What music does he/she like?*			Rock	

Jigsaw Task

Information-Gap Tasks

In an information-gap task (see the following example of an information-gap task), one student has the information and the other member of the pair or members of the group must find out about that information. This type of task is called a "one-way task" as the flow of information is likely to be one way. Participation of both learners is required. An example is for a learner to be given a list of questions to use to conduct an interview with a classmate to gather information on the partner (e.g., birthplace, school, work). The second part of the task is for learners to write a paragraph about themselves using similar information.

Step 1. Interview your partner and write down his/her answers to the questions in the chart.

Preguntas	La respuesta de mi socio	Mi respuesta
¿Qué idioma hablas? *What language do you speak?*		
¿Donde naciste? *Where were you born?*		
¿Cuál es tu equipo favorito? *What is your favorite team?*		
¿Cuál es su actividad de tiempo libre favorito? *What do you like to do in your free time?*		
¿Por qué estás estudiando inglés? *Why are you studying English?*		

Step 2. Write down your answers and compare them with your partner to find out differences and similarities and what you have in common.

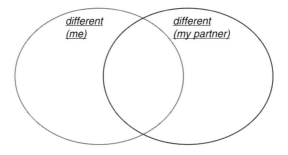

Information gap task

Problem-Solving Tasks

In problem-solving tasks, learners need to take a decision and devise possible solutions to resolve a specific problem. An example is for L2 learners to work out the quickest way to get from one place to another using the various bus route timetables of a big city. This task promotes negotiation of meaning between interlocutors. Problem-solving tasks have several stages. The first stage (1) could be a warm-up activity where the teacher can ask students to answer some questions related to the problem, thus giving a chance to predict what the problem might be and motivate the students. The second stage (2) is reading of the story or watching a video, for example. Find out what words are unfamiliar for the students and discuss them with language learners. The third stage (3) is comprehension check through listening or reading exercises. The fourth stage (4) is discussion. Here the students are encouraged to talk about the issues presented in the reading and also their personal experience. In the next stage (5) language teachers can identify the problems and begin to find/identify possible solutions. When the solutions are ready the language teacher could write them on the blackboard and ask learners about the possible consequences (see following example).

Think of a town where there is too much pollution. In a small group of three, think of four alternative solutions to this particular problem. List the advantages and disadvantages of each alternative. Then decide which alternative would be the cheapest one, the most innovative and effective one, and the most environmentally friendly one. Report your decisions to another group and eventually the whole class. Discuss with them which solution would be the best one to put forward to the local government and write a letter highlighting your suggestions to resolve the problem.

In traditional instruction, the role of the teacher is the one of an authoritative-transmitter of knowledge. The teacher possesses the knowledge about the language and he is willing to transfer that knowledge into the language learners. Learners play the role of note-takers. The following example is a typical one where roles of teachers and language learners are traditional.

1. Students are given ten minutes to individually complete a worksheet containing a multiple-choice activity (filling the blanks with the correct grammatical element).
2. At the end of ten minutes, students are instructed to work in groups of three and come to an agreement on the correct answers.
3. After seven minutes the teacher calls for the class's attention and begins going over the correct answers one by one. The teacher reads each sentence to the class and calls on students to respond. The student provides the correct element to complete the sentence.
4. The teacher offers a lengthy explanation of particular grammatical elements both in the case when the student gives a correct or incorrect answer.

All actions, interactions, and explanations in the preceding example are dictated by the teacher (expert transmitter of knowledge). A learner's role is passive and it is mainly to receive knowledge. Teachers assume full responsibility for all that goes on in the classroom. They supply motivation to study and clear explanations about the language.

They do not provide opportunities for learners to use language in a meaningful and communicative way involving the exchange of messages. A learner's role is to repeat and produce language accurately. Production of language is very restricted. In most cases, learners don't need to know what they are saying, only that it is accurate. Teachers make use of drills and open-ended questions.

In a more interactive and communicative classroom, teachers should play a different role. They should plan and develop language tasks so that language learners become more active/responsible for their own learning (see following example).

Step 1. With a classmate, make a list of actions, attitudes, or qualities that characterize the traditional role played by men in the family structure.

Step 2. Compare your list with those prepared by the rest of the class. Do you all have the same ideas? Do you wish to modify your list?

Step 3. Make a list of actions, attitudes, or qualities that characterize the traditional role played by women in the family structure.

Step 4. Compare your list with those prepared by the rest of the class. Do you all have the same ideas? Do you wish to modify your list?

Step 5. Now, contrast the traditional roles men and women played in the family structure with their contemporary ones. In what ways are their roles in the family changed?

In other interactive language tasks, teachers possess the information and they are willing to supply the information but only if language learners take a more proactive role and gather the information themselves. Their task is not simply to listen and respond but to signal if and where comprehension has not taken place.

Consider this ...

Create one task for language teaching where you plan the steps but you keep in mind that language learners need to play a proactive role.

    In this task you are the consultant/counselor and learners are learning the language by solving tasks!

How Do We Plan a Lesson with Tasks?

In traditional language instruction lesson objectives are often reduced to completing a chapter in a book or covering a particular form, or set of vocabulary. In many cases lesson objectives are equated with the learning and practice of a particular linguistic feature in the target language. The lesson is structured around this feature (e.g., complete the story with the right form; write one sentence for each of the drawings in the story). Language teachers make use of Q/A to measure whether learners are able to use the information and knowledge gained during a lesson. Despite the attempt of the instructor to extract information, Q/A practice very often results in the following:

- Few learners participate
- Native speaker speaks a great deal
- Roles for both instructor and learner are restricted
- Learner speaks very little
- Not much interaction and negotiation of meaning
- Limited exposure to comprehensible and meaningful input

As previously pointed out, communication cannot be equated with Q/A practice and, as also stated, communication is the expression, interpretation, and negotiation of meaning. We know that interaction promotes comprehension and comprehension promotes acquisition. Tasks promote acquisition and provide a purpose for language use. To avoid a discussion of Q/A type of activity, it is important to engage learners in language use to identify the subcomponents of a topic and build them into the framework of the interaction.

A task can also be used to achieve a specific lesson objective. Teachers can build their lesson objectives using an information exchange task approach constructed in a way that encompasses (through the use of subtasks) all the vocabulary, grammar, and language functions that need to be covered by learners in the lesson. Let's assume that our proficiency goal is "to talk about how we spend our spare time." We then decide to use an interactive information exchange task approach (see following task) as our lesson objective. This task will help us to identify the following:

- Vocabulary needed to complete the task
- Grammar needed to complete the task
- Language functions needed to complete the task

> A task can be used to achieve a specific lesson objective. This task will help to identify the following:
> - Vocabulary needed to complete the task
> - Grammar needed to complete the task
> - Language functions needed to complete the task

Let's take the example of an exchange information task provided earlier and try to build a series of subtasks (to complete during the lesson) to ensure language learners develop the relevant vocabulary, grammar, language function, and content necessary to complete the exchange information tasks.

Vocabulary

Once the interactive information exchange task has been set, the question is: What kind of vocabulary do learners need to complete the task? Therefore, we develop a series of subtasks so that we provide the necessary lexical tools for learners to complete the task. We expect learners to become familiar with words such as *reading books*, *watching movies*, *hobbies*, *sports*, *writing poetry/prose*, *learning to play the piano/violin*, etc. Additionally, they will need to know some temporal expressions such as: *in the morning, ... afternoon, ... evening.* They will probably need to know how to say the days of the week (*Monday, Tuesday*) because activities may vary depending on the day. Several lesson subgoals may include work with these lexical items (see Activity A).

Activity A

Step 1. Write three things that one of your classmates does in his/her free time but you do not think your instructor does. Make a list of three things that your classmate does in his or her free time and your instructor does as well.

Step 2. A volunteer reads his/her statements to the class and someone should write them on the board in two columns. Once the volunteer has finished, classmates should continue reading new statements aloud to make the lists on the board as complete as possible.

Subgoal tasks for the days of the week and expression of time can also be planned, as in the following example (see activities B and C).

Activity B

Step 1. Write a few sentences about activities you do in your free time each day of the week. Leave a blank after each one.

EXAMPLE: I go to the gym every Monday. _____

Step 2. Now go about the room telling different classmates about your classes and ask them if they do the same. If so, get that person's signature in the blank. If not, move on to someone else. You must try to obtain five different signatures for the five different days of the week. Be prepared to answer questions that your instructor will ask when you are finished obtaining signatures.

Activity C

Step 1. Using time expressions that you have learned in this lesson, indicate when you do the following activities on a particular day of the week. The last items indicate that you should come up with two activities not on the list.

EXAMPLE: On Sunday afternoon, I watch TV.
           Watch TV
           Go out with friends
           Walk in nature and photograph
           Read a book

Exercise

?_____

?_____

Step 2. Break into groups of three and present your sentences to the two other classmates. They should indicate whether they do the same things. When you have finished, they should add any activities that they do and you did not mention.

EXAMPLE: (you say) I watch TV on Saturdays, but usually in the morning.

(Other person) Me, too.

or

(Other person) I don't. I only watch TV at night.

In each of the activities we see that the tasks require language learners to use language in a manner similar to that which would be required for the final lesson task. In Activity B they use the days of the week to make statements about themselves and to get information from someone else. In Activity C they must choose time expressions to make sentences about themselves. These tasks indicate that learners have achieved a certain lesson subgoal: the ability to use certain words from the vocabulary to exchange information related to daily routines.

Grammar

Likewise in the case of vocabulary, the question we need to ask is: What grammatical features do learners need to complete the lesson's final information exchange task?

They will need to use present-tense verbal morphology. They will need to use first-person singular (*I play football*), second-person singular (*you play football*), and third-person singular (*he/she plays football*). So only these three forms of the verb are needed for the task that requires from them to produce statements about themselves and produce statements and/or ask questions about somebody else. If we look at the Activity A we developed for vocabulary, this activity does double duty as a vocabulary and grammar subtask. Activity D would represent work on second and third person.

Activity D

Step 1. Read the following paragraph. (Note: The teacher gives this passage to only half of the class. The other half would be given a different passage to work with.)

Susanna is a typical sixth grader from London. She spends her spare time doing different things. She has many friends and she spends at least one hour every day with them after school. Every Monday and Wednesday she takes piano lessons. On weekends she usually goes to the cinema or to the theater. Every night before she goes to bed she reads comics. On Tuesdays and Thursdays at 6 PM Susanna plays basketball at school.

If you were to interview someone in class, what kind of questions would you ask to find out whether s/he does the same things as Susanna? Note that the interviewee does not have the text to see what Susanna does, so you will need to ask very specific questions to get all the necessary information.

Step 2. Now interview one of your classmates to find out if that person's day is like Susanna's. Jot down all information because you might need them later.

Functions

In terms of functions, it is clear that for the ultimate task of the lesson the language learners should be able to make simple statements and to ask each other questions. They don't need to connect sentences to make a narrative or to produce an elaborate description. The question that arises here is: What do language learners need to know (and how) to ask the questions they need to ask? For some of the tasks they need to know just few words such as *when* or *how often*. Additionally, they need to know the structure of questions (subject-verb inversion, etc.).

In this task you will prepare a series of quiz items for your instructor to use. You will interview some of your classmates on how they are planning a summer holiday. Then you will make some contrastive and comparative statements.

Step 1. Using the following chart, fill it in with at least three places where you would like to go on holiday this summer and why it is the ideal place. Use the correct verb forms to speak about yourself.

Step 2. Now interview two people in the class. Ask them where they are planning to go and why. The idea is to get enough information so that you can write several contrasting and comparative statements.

Me
My classmate
My classmate

Step 3. Using the information obtained in steps 1 and 2, write a list of three true/false questions and three multiple-choice questions comparing and contrasting you and your classmates' plans for a holiday.

Step 4. Submit your chart and your lists to your teacher.

Information exchange tasks can be effectively used to structure our teaching to accomplish our lesson goals (grammar, vocabulary, language functions). We must remember that language learning requires "good input." Therefore, teachers should make sure that L2 learners are exposed to comprehensible and message-oriented input (see next chapter). We should organize our teaching and our tasks so that learners can move from input practice to output practice. However, we must make sure that we offer learners opportunities to link lexical units or grammatical forms with their meanings before we ask them to produce them.

Recap

The following is a short recap of the main concepts expressed in this chapter:

- Communication can be defined as the expression, interpretation, and negotiation of meaning for a specific purpose in a given context.
- Tasks are the quintessential communicative event in contemporary language teaching. They are both meaningful and have a communicative purpose.
- A task is a classroom activity that has an objective attainable only by (1) the interaction among participants, (2) a mechanism for structuring and sequencing interaction, and (3) a focus on meaning exchange.
- Information-exchange tasks are a good example of interactive tasks and should be a substitute for traditional oral practice.
- Communication cannot be equated with Q/A practice. Tasks promote acquisition and provide a purpose for language use. A task approach should be used to archive a specific lesson objective. Language teachers can build their lesson objectives using an information-exchange task approach constructed in a way that encompasses (using subtasks) all the vocabulary, grammar, and language functions that need to be covered by learners in the lesson.

How Do We Develop Effective Writing Tasks?

One of the major developments in second language pedagogy has been the shift from product-oriented approaches to process-oriented approaches in the teaching of language writing skills. Process-oriented approaches focus on the creation of a text rather than concentrating only on the final product. Writing, like any other aspect of second language development, is about communication. In real life we write e-mails, notes, letters, grocery lists, reports, and essays. All these different tasks have a communicative purpose and a specific targeted audience.

A communicative task-based approach to the development of writing skills is proposed in this section as an effective option in teaching writing. This approach takes into consideration a cognitive-process theory of writing. Writing is a somewhat neglected skill in second language teaching and, very often, writing tasks set up by language teachers might not be motivating for language learners and not properly incorporated into a language lesson. To develop more effective tasks for developing writing skills, language teachers must clarify the communicative purpose of the written task and the target audience. Language teachers must consider the use of a more meaningful, realistic, and relevant writing task based on what L2 learners need.

The Nature and Role of Writing

The development of writing skills will help L2 learners to gain independence, fluency, and creativity in language writing. In developing writing skills, L2 learners improve the way they put their thoughts into words in a meaningful and accurate way to convey a specific message. Writing is a process where language learners explore, consolidate, and develop specific objectives. The same definition used for communication is applicable to the written language. Through writing learners are able to communicate information to a wider audience. What is the main role of writing in language teaching?

First, writing has a role in helping learners to acquire the target language. Teachers might design writing activities to make L2 learners learn new vocabulary, for example. Second, writing can be used to produce a text in a real-life context (e.g., writing an e-mail, producing a poster).

Consider this ...

What is the purpose of writing in another language?

Traditional writing practice is often reduced to practice structures or vocabulary that has just been learned. The role of writing should involve creating content and tailoring this content in relation to writers' needs. Writing involves a complex interaction between a wide range of different processes and L2 learners adopt specific strategies to cope with the task of writing. Before starting to write, L2 learners must define the rhetorical problem:

- The reason/s for writing
- The purpose of the text to be written
- The recipient of the written text
- The topic
- Learner's knowledge about the topic

Furthermore, L2 learners should plan the writing very carefully. Planning writing should involve a number of subprocesses such as planning the composition, generating ideas, organizing ideas, and setting goals. This brief description of the processes involved in writing tells us how dynamic and complex writing is, regardless of whether the learner writes in his/her mother tongue or other languages.

> The act of writing involves three major elements:
> - The task environment
> - The writer's long-term memory
> - The writing processes

A Cognitive-Process Approach

A cognitive and processing second language instruction model emphasizes L2 learner mental processes in writing. Cognitive processes in writing engage L2 learners in exploring, consolidating, and developing rhetorical objectives. The act of writing involves three major elements:

1. The task environment that includes things outside the writer's knowledge such as the rhetorical problem and the text itself;
2. The writer's long-term memory that includes the knowledge that learners might have about the topic, the audience for which the text is going to be written, and its various writing plans;
3. The writing processes that involve three basic processes: planning, translating plans into a text, and reviewing, which includes reading and editing the text produced.

The planning process contains four subprocesses:

(a) Generating ideas that include retrieving information from long-term memory
(b) Searching for ideas
(c) Reaching a specific audience
(d) Setting a goal for the writing

The translating process includes the ability to put ideas into words. It requires the writer to juggle all the various demands of the new language.

The reviewing process depends on two subprocesses:

(a) Evaluating
(b) Revising

The following four main steps are used in developing a composing activity:

Step 1 (generating content) The language teacher assigns one topic to students in groups;
Step 2 (defining audience and content) Each group has an amount of time to make a list of ideas related to that topic;
Step 3 (planning and organizing) Each group should copy the lists from the other groups to be used later in writing;
Step 4 (composing) Take your outline and list of ideas and write your composition.

The following sample provides an example of a task that engages learners and improves their writing (adapted from Lee and VanPatten, 1995: 222). This task allows L2 learners to become aware of the various elements of good writing. In this task, learners have to take into consideration the rhetorical problem; they need to plan well and make appropriate decisions about the ideas they generate and how to organize them; and they need to put ideas on paper and then review them.

Generating Content

Step 1. To each group of three to four students, the teacher assigns one of the two topics:

> Winter holidays of young people in Greece twenty years ago
> Winter holidays of young people in Greece today

Each group will have ten minutes to write as many ideas as possible related to the topic, and for each element of the following:

1. Natural beauties of Greece
2. Sports centers and resorts
3. Recreational and sport habits of youth
4. Economic opportunities for citizens
5. Entertainment

Step 2. Once all the groups draw up lists of ideas, each group will present them to the class, and then the teacher will write a common list on the board and ask them whether they have some other idea to add.

Step 3. Each student will copy the common list so that later s/he can use it to compose the essay. When generating the ideas, the teacher can give additional materials (books, tourist guides, Internet, etc.) as a source of content for the activity to allow supplementary input of formal written language and extra knowledge that students may not possess.

Define Audience and Purpose

Step 1. Using the ideas that students have generated in the previous activity, students should consider the readers of the text/composition. The teacher can suggest them to choose any of the following or propose themselves:

- Friends from abroad you have met during the summer holiday
- Pen friends
- Former friends or neighbors of another ethnic group who have moved to another country and are coming to visit after many years
- Other suggestions: _____

Step 2. Each student should choose one of the two topics and form groups of three students working on the same topic together and write the characteristics of the selected reader (audience). Then, each group will present the characteristics to the whole class, while students are encouraged to help their peers by adding features they may not have thought of.

Planning and Organizing

Step 1. Once the audience; that is, the readers, is defined, the teacher encourages them to think about what they would say. The working groups from the previous exercise continue to work together on this by looking at the list of ideas developed in the first exercise and noting down the information that could be included in their letter.

Step 2. After this step each student individually prepares a summary of the composition that s/he then presents to the others in their group and everyone should note down if the other two in the group thought of something s/he didn't. After that you can offer students the opportunity to present the contents to someone who wrote about the other topic. In doing so, students are encouraged to give each other additional ideas.

Step 3. The three activities (generating ideas, choosing the audience, and planning) engage students to think carefully about the rhetorical problem without having to reduce it to "completing the task." The activities of generating ideas and defining the audience focus on planning and highlight the decisions needed to generate and organize ideas.

Step 4. Once the preparatory work is completed, writing should begin; that is the composing of the text. Previous activities set the stage, and the next activity is transcribing, putting thoughts on paper, and reviewing.

Composing

Step 1. Have the outline and the list of ideas ready while you are writing the text to the selected reader/s. Suggestion: write the initial version of the text and leave it for a couple of days. Don't even think about it, and don't read it. Two days later, take it and read it and answer these two questions:

- Content: Are the ideas you have included still the ones you want to have in the composition?
- Organization: Does the order in which the ideas are presented help convey the message to the reader/s?

Step 2. When you consider your essay to be good enough, review the language you used:

- Verbs: Are forms, spelling, and accent correct?
- Adjectives: What noun do they go with? Are they appropriate?
- Other elements of language you want your students to focus on.

In traditional instruction, writing practice has focused on the texts that writers produce. In doing so, writing is simply reduced to a matter of translating preconceived ideas into a text. In current language textbooks, written activities often focus on production of grammatical and lexical structures. Learners are provided with a list of words that they must use to write a short paragraph or a series of sentences. It can be argued that in this task the rhetorical problem for learners is simply reduced to produce a text using grammatical and lexical items.

The focus of this exercise is only to produce a text that contains particular lexical and grammatical items. The processes involved in traditional writing activities are minimum as the content is not as important as the accurate use of specific linguistic items. Planning consists of constructing and ordering individual sentences. Reviewing focuses on which linguistic items have been used.

> Effective writing tasks include the following phases:
> - Prewriting
> - Writing
> - Focus on language

Traditional approaches to the teaching of L2 writing have mainly focused on linguistic rules and vocabulary.

Process-oriented approaches have shifted the focus on the audience and the purpose of writing. Using communicative composing-oriented written tasks that engage learners in authentic and interactive writing activities is what language teachers should consider. These types of tasks aim at improving learners' writing skills and consist of three main phases:

- Prewriting phase
- Writing phase
- Focus on language phase

In developing and designing writing tasks, language teachers should consider the following questions:

- What is the purpose of the written task?
- Does the task engage learners positively?
- Is the task interesting and familiar?
- Does it focus on a specific genre?
- Does it integrate other skills such as reading and speaking?
- Is there enough support provided to students to be successful in the task?

Writing Interactive Tasks

In developing writing tasks, teachers should consider the following:

- Writing tasks would need to reflect authentic purposes.
- Writing tasks should have clear guidance and a scaffolding approach.

There are different types of tasks that can be used to enhance students' writing skills:

- Matching: listening and writing, matching phrases/description to pictures, matching directions to maps
- Comparing: finding similarities or differences
- Problem solving: real-life situations, case studies, incomplete texts
- Projects and creative tasks: doing and reporting a survey, producing a class newspaper, planning a radio show, designing a brochure
- Sharing personal experiences: storytelling, anecdotes, memories, opinions, reactions
- Ordering and sorting: sequencing, ranking, classifying
- Listing: brainstorming and/or fact finding

A three-stage approach in designing a written task should therefore be adopted to teach how to write in a second language: prewriting, writing, language focus. This approach would improve L2 learners' writing skills as they will become better at formulating their ideas in a coherent way, using correct syntax, grammar, and vocabulary.

- Prewriting phase in which L2 learners are given different options so that they can make choices and decide in which direction to develop their composition;
- Writing stage that begins immediately after the previous phase and during which L2 learners become aware of the elements of good writing; and
- Language focus.

The Prewriting Phase

In the prewriting phase the topic and the specific task are introduced. L2 learners have a chance to recall things that they know. The teacher might decide to show a picture, audio, or video in relation to the topic. The teacher can also elicit appropriate vocabulary or phrases that students might find useful. During this time, L2 learners are expected to work in pairs to decide the nature of their writing task and the composition. Then, they begin drafting. During this period, the teacher should urge them to let their ideas flow onto the paper without concern for accuracy in producing the target language (e.g., forms, structures).

The Writing Phase

The language teacher should be merely a facilitator in the writing process and ensure language learners are supported in their effort to become good writers in a second language. Once the teacher knows that L2 learners have developed an interest in writing, they can provide them with meaningful opportunities to write for different audiences and for different purposes using a variety of genres (e.g., stories, biographical pieces, essays). The writing phase is divided into three stages: (1) the task, (2) the planning stage, (3) and the report stage.

(1) The task phase should not be repetitive and must have a communicative goal for the writer to achieve. For example, making an important decision about buying a car, writing a list of items that may be needed to organize a picnic, or writing a plan for a party. The main purpose of the task is to allow writers to use their own ideas without worrying about grammar, spellings, and other mechanics in a target language. There should be no restriction on the language to be used. The focus is on communicating meaning rather than using forms at this stage.

(2) The planning stage involves language writers to work with the teacher to improve their writing skills. Here, there is a heavy emphasis on form-focused instruction as learners attempt to improve the overall correctness of their writing.

(3) At the report stage, language writers present their findings and the teacher's role is to act as a chairperson to summarize each writer's work and make comments about the written text.

Language Focus

This is the final stage of the writing task and it allows a closer look at some of the specific features occurring in the language used during the writing phase. By this time, learners will have already worked with the language and processed it for meaning, so that they are ready to concentrate more closely on formal properties of the language.

The following example (in French) makes use of this three-phase approach.

Étape 1 (contenu Génération) instructeur assigne un sujet pour les étudiants dans les groups.

Étape 2 (Définition public et le contenu) Chaque groupe dispose d'un laps de temps de faire une liste d'idées liées à ce sujet.

Étape 3 (Planification et organisation) Chaque groupe devrait copier les listes des autres groupes pour être utilisé plus tard par écrit.

Étape 4 (Composer) Prenez votre plan et la liste des idées et écrire votre composition. Vous devez écrire un projet de travail et laisser reposer quelque temps. Vous devez vous poser deux questions: Sont-elles toujours les idées que je veux incorporer?; Est-ce que l'ordre dans lequel les idées sont présentées aide faire passer mon message? Si la réponse est non, vous devriez réécrire la composition.

A different example for a writing task is to ask L2 learners to rewrite a story recalling the story from a listening passage. This task helps students clarify their understanding of the story and gives them more practice in using the language. See the following guidelines used to prepare such a task:

- The teacher should consider a short story that is easy to understand. The teacher need to ensure that learners understand the meaning of the key words.
- The teacher should select key words from the story that the writer can use later (cues) to reconstruct the story.
- The teacher may first listen to the story and ask learners to focus on the main ideas and the key words.
- The teacher should ask learners to take turns (after they listen to the story) with another learner in the class to tell each other the story using their own words.
- The teacher should encourage learners to make use of the key words.
- The teacher should ask learners to write down what they remember from the listening, using key words from the story.
- The teacher may collect the written work of learners for comments and improvement.

Developing writing is a key component in developing learners' ability to communicate in a second language. A composing-oriented approach challenges the way written tasks are practiced in a traditional approach. Likewise, in the listening and reading task, a similar step-by step approach is proposed for developing learners' writing skills.

The exemplary study briefly described in the following text provides evidence of the effectiveness of the task-based approach to develop writing skills.

Exemplary Study:

Ahmed, R. Z., Bidin, S. J. B. (2016). The Effect of Task Based Language Teaching on Writing Skills of EFL Learners in Malaysia. *Open Journal of Modern Linguistics*, 6, 207–218.

Participants:

- Participants from different countries having different ethnographic backgrounds. All students were in their first semester and new to university education.
- All the participants were enrolled in different undergraduate programs at a tertiary level institution and registered in the Intensive English Language program.
- The age group was from nineteen to twenty-two years old.

Materials and procedure:

- Quasi-experimental study with pretest and posttest.
- The experimental group comprised a total of fourteen participants (n = 14) and the control group was sixteen (n = 16).
- The topic of the lesson was "Kinds of Essays" and the main focus of the experimental teaching was on improving learners' descriptive writing skills.
- The pretest and the posttest were administered in the experimental (task-based treatment) and control group (without any task-based treatment).
- Data of learners' writing skill during pretest and posttest of the experimental and control group were collected to determine any improvement in writing skill.
- Accuracy, complexity, and fluency were the quantitative measures used in the tests administered to the groups. Qualitative measures (questionnaire) were used to collect participants' feedback after the instructional period.

Results:

- Most of the participants' feedback was in the favor of the effectiveness of a task-based approach in developing writing skills.
- The statistical analysis (the Eta squared statistics measures effect sizes of L2 complexity, fluency, and accuracy) showed that the experimental group performed statistically better than the control group in their L2 writing skill.

Conclusion:

- Overall this study indicated that there was an improvement in L2 performance indicators in terms of L2 complexity, fluency, and accuracy measures of the research participants from the experimental group as compared to the language learners from the control group.

Recap

- Developing writing is a key component in developing learners' ability to communicate in a second language.
- Communicative composing-oriented tasks can enhance writing skills and provide L2 learners with various options about the content of what they can write.
- The task-based approach considers the various cognitive processes and principles responsible for developing writing skills.

- Defining the rhetorical problem (goal/purpose and audience);
- Planning (generating ideas, organizing them, setting goals);
- Reviewing (evaluation and review).

Using communicative composing-oriented written tasks that engage learners in authentic and interactive writing activities is desirable. These types of tasks aim at improving learners' writing skills and consist of three phases:

- Prewriting phase
- Writing phase
- Focus on language phase

REFERENCES AND READINGS

- Benati, A. (2013). *Issues in Second Language Teaching.* London: Equinox.
- Ellis, R. (2003). *Task-Based Language Learning and Teaching.* Oxford: Oxford University Press.
- Lee, J. (2000). *Tasks and Communicating in Language Classrooms.* New York: McGraw-Hill.
- Lee, J., VanPatten, B. (2003). *Making Communicative Classroom Happens.* New York: McGraw-Hill.
- Long, M. (2015). *Second Language Acquisition and Task-Based Language Teaching.* Malden, MA: Wiley-Blackwell.
- Nunan, D. (2004). *Task-Based Language Teaching.* Cambridge: Cambridge University Press.
- Ortega, L. (2010). Exploring interfaces between second language writing and second language acquisition. Paper presented at the Symposium on Second Language Writing, Murcia, Spain.
- Polio, C. (2018). *Teaching Second Language Writing.* New York: Routledge.
- Savignon, S. (2005). *Communicative Competence: Theory and Classroom Practice.* New York: McGraw-Hill.
- VanPatten, B. (2003). *From Input to Output.* NJ: McGraw-Hill.
- VanPatten, B. (2007). *While We're on the Topic: BVP on Language, Acquisition and Classroom Practice.* Alexandria, VA: American Council on the Teaching of Foreign Languages.
- Williams, J. (2005). *Teaching Writing in Second and Foreign Language Classrooms.* Hightstown, NJ: McGraw-Hill.
- Willis, D., Willis, J. (2007). *Doing Task-Based Teaching.* Oxford: Oxford University Press.

DISCUSSION AND QUESTIONS

1. List at least five things that you learned in this chapter that you did not know before. If you are taking a class, compare your list with someone else. Do your two lists reveal anything?

2. What did you do last summer? Did you go to the seaside? Did you play sports? Did you enjoy it? What were you doing when on holiday? What did you visit?

Now recast this set of "discussion questions" in a task-based format based on the principle of communication and interactive tasks.

3. Look at the following task and develop a new task for your language classroom.

What Did You Do Last Summer?

Step 1. Working with a partner, indicate if each activity typically takes place at the seaside or in the mountains. You and your partner must agree on the categorization.

	SEASIDE	MOUNTAINS
1. Riding a bike	❑	❑
2. Skiing	❑	❑
3. Swimming	❑	❑
4. Sailing	❑	❑
5. Walking	❑	❑

(Does your partner agree with your categorization of these activities?)

Step 2. Add three activities to the list, preferably three that you or your partner have engaged in and indicate whether they are sedentary.

	SEASIDE	MOUNTAINS
_____	❑	❑
_____	❑	❑
_____	❑	❑

Compare your activities with those of your classmate. Do you engage in similar activities?

Step 3. Interview your partner about what he or she did last summer. Keep track of the answers because you will need them in Step 4.

Model: Did you play any sports on your vacation last summer?

Step 4. Compare your partner's responses to the categorization you made in Step 1 and Step 2.

Step 5. Using your evaluations of each other's level of activity, draw a profile of the ideal holiday.

4. Select one of the tasks presented in this chapter and adapt it for the language you teach or will teach. Then do an analysis of what students need to know and know how to do to perform that task. Once you have done this, see if you

can find a "natural spot" in a textbook for the language you are working with to drop it in (assuming that text does not have a task already in that spot).

5. Which elements in a traditional approach to teaching writing might be beneficial for learners? Which one should be abandoned?

6. Following the three main guidelines for a task-based approach to developing writing skills, develop a writing task for your class.

7. Design a written task considering the following questions:

   – What is the purpose of the written task?
   – Does the task engage learners positively?
   – Is the task interesting and familiar?
   – Does it focus on a specific genre?
   – Does it integrate other skills such as reading and speaking?
   – Is there enough support provided to students to be successful in the task?

   If you need more help in completing this task, please read chapter 3 in the following book: Williams, J. (2005). *Teaching Writing in Second and Foreign Language Classrooms*. Hightstown, NJ: McGraw-Hill.

What Is the Nature and Role of Listening and Reading Comprehension Tasks?

Overview

In this chapter, an effective approach to the teaching of listening will be presented. This description will help the reader to understand the nature of listening in another language and to develop listening tasks in which L2 learners are actively involved in listening to a passage in a specific context and for a specific purpose. A more interactive approach to reading comprehension will also be discussed in this chapter. This approach is centered on the idea that L2 learners need reading to extract specific information and not to translate texts. It is vital to train learners in developing the ability to understand written passages without understanding every single word. L2 learners are often asked to read slowly and worry about the meaning of each particular word. Traditionally, the purpose of learning to read in a language has been to have access to the literature written in that language and develop in language learners the ability to translate literary texts. This approach assumes that learners learn to read a language by studying its vocabulary, grammar, and sentence structure. The reading of authentic materials is totally absent in this practice. In the approach to reading comprehension presented in this chapter, developing reading skills is seen as developing the ability to read in another language. L2 learners read texts in another language for a specific purpose. They read to gain specific information. The purpose(s) for reading must guide the language instructor's selection of texts. In addition to that, authentic material should be used. When the goal of instruction is communicative competence, everyday materials such as train schedules, newspaper articles, and travel and touristic brochures become appropriate classroom materials to use with L2 learners. The approach is based on the understanding that the ability to read and comprehend a text is based not only on the reader's linguistic knowledge but also on general knowledge of the world and the learner's ability to activate that knowledge during reading. But before we start, let's talk again about input.

What Is the Role of Input in the Classroom?

What is input in the context of acquiring languages? Input is the language that L2 learners hear or see in a communicative context. Input is language that learners try to comprehend for the message contained in it. When somebody says "Where are you from?," we focus on what (input) the person would like to know and the answer will be "I am from ...." We are responding to the interlocutor by focusing on the meaning contained in what this person is saying or asking. In contrast to this, we often hear language teachers asking an individual or the entire classroom to repeat or memorize some target language. In most cases, language learners can repeat the language they hear without knowing what teachers are saying and understand the meaning of the words used.

It is important to reiterate here that input for acquisition is the language that is embedded in a communicative context that learners attend to for its meaning. L2 learners acquire language mainly through exposure to comprehensible input, in a similar fashion as they acquire their first language. The input that L2 learners receive should be therefore simplified with the use of contextual and extra linguistics clues (e.g., drawings, pictures) to make it comprehensible and processable for language learners. Language learners should be provided with opportunities to focus on meaning rather than grammatical forms.

Simplified input is language input that it is easy to process. A teacher can for example use high-frequency vocabulary to ensure learners can understand the meaning of language they are exposed to more easily. They can also make use of gestures, pictures, or drawings to make input simpler and easier to comprehend. The use of short sentences can also reduce the burden of processing and increase comprehension.

Effective language input for learning is not the explanation about grammar, presentation of vocabulary, followed by mechanical practice. Effective input language is about creating opportunities for language learners to hear or read language in a communicative context that they need to process for meaning. Engaging language learners in communication means creating opportunities for them to interpret, negotiate, and express meaning in a specific context. Language teaching should focus on providing learners with a rich variety of comprehensible input and opportunities to use language spontaneously and meaningfully. Interaction offers opportunities for negotiation of meaning and language acquisition. Quality classroom input must have two characteristics:

(1) It needs to be at an appropriate level;
(2) Learners should be engaged with the input (they interact with it).

Learners acquire language through comprehension but they don't simply absorb everything they hear or read. They very often can't attach

> Classroom input must have two characteristics:
> - It needs to be at an appropriate level;
> - L2 learners must interact with it.

meaning to the language input they are exposed to during comprehension. Their language systems process, organize, and store linguistic data while continuously interacting with language input. To make its way through the system that input (see following example in Italian) must be simplified input (insegnante = teacher; studente = student).

INSEGNANTE: Ciao, mi chiamo Alessandro? Come ti chiami? (My name is Alessandro. What is your name?

STUDENTE: [silenzio – pause]

INSEGNANTE: Come ti chiami? Ti chiami Robert? Paul? Come ti chiami? (What is your name? Are you Robert? Paul? What is your name?

STUDENTE: Oh, uh, Frank.

INSEGNANTE: Bene, Grazie. Tony [un altro] Ciao. Mi chiamo Alessandro. Come ti chiami? Thanks. Tony (somebody else) Hello. My name is Alessandro. What is your name?

STUDENTE: Uh, Grace.

INSEGNANTE: Bene. [alla classe] Ecco due studenti. Si chiama Frank. Si chiama Grace. E tu come ti chiami?
Right. (to the entire class). We have two students. He is Frank and she is Grace. And you, what is your name?

STUDENTE: Alex.

> ## Consider this …
>
> How would you use the target language with L2 learners who do not have any knowledge about the new language?
> What other means would you consider?

TEACHER: Ti chiami Alex? (Are You Alex?)

STUDENTE: [gesto con il capo] (nodding)

INSEGNANTE: (all class) Si chiama Alex. E tu come ti chiami? (to the entire class, he is Alex. And you, what is your name?)

There are four features in the preceding exchanges that should be considered to make input language easy to understand and process.

- Short sentences (e.g., simpler syntax is easy to process)
- Slower rate (e.g., extra stress in nouns makes input easy to process)
- Rephrasing (e.g., interactions offer opportunities for negotiation)
- Content is clear (e.g., easy language input is more processable)

The teacher is focused on getting everyone's name out so that learners can know each other.

> ## Consider this …
>
> Would L2 learners understand every word they hear or read? Is this crucial?

The content of the input is made clear as instructors use linguistics and nonlinguistics means to make input comprehensible (pictures, cartoons, gestures).

To recap so far:

- Input is central to the classroom, not something to be added on.
- Input must be simplified, comprehensible, and processable.
- Input must be message oriented.

Consider this

How do we make input more comprehensible and message oriented? Provide three examples:

1.
2.
3.

With the key characteristics of good input in mind let's now turn to the development of effective listening and reading comprehension tasks.

How Do You Develop Effective Listening Comprehension Tasks?

The Nature and Role of Listening

Listening is one of the language skills most frequently used. L2 learners receive a great amount of information through listening from instructors and other interlocutors. Listening can be defined an "active skill" as learners are actively involved in interpreting what they hear. L2 learners bring to a listening task their own background and linguistic knowledge to be able to process and understand all the information contained in what they hear. L2 learners are exposed to different listening tasks that often require different listening skills. They need intentional listening that requires the use of specific listening strategies for identifying sounds, understanding vocabulary, grammatical structures, and meaning.

Listening is a process of receiving what the speaker says (receptive orientation); constructing and representing meaning (constructive orientation); negotiating meaning with the speaker and responding (collaborative orientation); and creating meaning through involvement, imagination, and empathy (transformative orientation). It involves a sender (e.g., a person, radio announcement, and television program), a specific message, and a receiver (the listener).

Listening is a very complex process in second language acquisition as the listener needs to cope with the sender's choice of vocabulary, structure, and speed of delivery. Given the importance of listening it is essential for language instructors to help learners become effective listeners. That means that we should model listening strategies and providing listening practice in authentic situations that are the ones that L2 learners are likely to encounter when they use the language outside the classroom context.

The role of comprehensible input and conversational interaction has assumed greater importance in second language teaching. Considering that input is seen as a vital ingredient for acquisition, listening is seen as a skill that has acquired an important role in the language classroom. Language learning depends a great deal on listening as it provides the aural input that serves as the basis for language acquisition and enables learners to interact in spoken communication. Learners make use of listening strategies (bottom-up and top-down) that help them to understand language input.

Bottom-Up Strategies

L2 learners use bottom-up strategies that are text based. This means that the listener relies (to understand) on the language in the message, that is, the combination of sounds, words, and grammar that create meaning. Bottom-up strategies include listening for specific details, recognizing cognates, and recognizing word-order patterns. However, listening is not just a bottom-up process where learners hear sounds and need to decode those sounds from the smaller units to large texts but it is also a top-down process where learners reconstruct the original meaning of the speaker using incoming sounds as clues. In this reconstruction process, listeners use prior knowledge of the context and situation within which the listening takes place to make sense of what they hear.

Top-Down Strategies

Top-down strategies are listener-based where the listener uses his/her background knowledge of the topic and considers the specific situation, the type of text, and the language to interpret the message. Top-down strategies include listening for the main idea/concept, predicting, drawing inferences, and summarizing. Learners' comprehension improves and their confidence increases when they use top-down and bottom-up strategies simultaneously to construct meaning. Learners also tap into metacognitive strategies to plan, monitor, and evaluate their listening. They select the best listening strategy to use in a particular situation. They monitor their comprehension and the use of the chosen strategy. They evaluate whether they have comprehended the message. Monitoring comprehension helps learners detect inconsistencies and comprehension failures.

Listening as an Active and Interactive Skill

Listening is an active and productive skill. L2 learners are actively involved in constructing meanings from the message they hear. For example, learners hear a sentence and need to understand the relevant information to comprehend the meaning of the message. L2 learners must be exposed to listening comprehension tasks in which they are actively engaged in processing language to extract the meaning. In some cases, by processing every single item; in other cases by extracting the message using other clues. Therefore, listening comprehension is neither a top-down nor a bottom-up processing, but an interactive, interpretive process where listeners use both previous knowledge and linguistic knowledge in understanding messages.

The use of one process or the other will depend on a series of factors (e.g., language knowledge, topic familiarity, listening purpose). Listening for "gist" involves primarily top-down processing, whereas listening for specific information, as in a weather broadcast, involves primarily bottom-up processing to fully comprehend the passage.

> Listening comprehension is neither a top-down nor a bottom-up processing, but an interactive, interpretive process where listeners use both previous knowledge and linguistic knowledge in understanding messages.

Listeners must be active participants during listening comprehension activities. They make use of a series of mental processes and prior knowledge sources to understand and interpret what they hear. Listening is a very active skill given that learners are actively engaged in different processes while they are exposed to aural stimuli. We can distinguish between three main processes:

- Perceiving;
- Attending;
- Assigning meaning.

Perceiving refers to the physiological aspects of listening. The actual sounds entering into our ears, reaching our brain through the ear canals. Attending requires an active concentration by the listener, who would need to select what to pay attention to in the passage they hear. Assigning meaning involves personal, cultural, and linguistic matters interacting in complex ways.

Research from cognitive psychology has shown that the ability to develop listening skills can't be associated only to the ability to extract meaning from incoming speech. Developing listening skills is instead a process of matching speech with what listeners already know about the topic.

Language teachers must take all this various information about the characteristics of listening into consideration when developing effective listening comprehension tasks. These tasks must facilitate L2 learners' activation of prior knowledge and allow them to make the appropriate inferences essential to comprehending the message. Language instructors need to help students organize their thoughts, to activate appropriate background knowledge for understanding the listening text, to make predictions, and to be well prepared for listening. This significantly reduces the burden of language processing for the listener.

Developing Interactive Tasks

Other factors that must be taken into consideration when developing a listening task are the difficulty of the listening task and the type of classroom task we intend to develop.

Difficulty of a Listening Task

In the case of task difficulty, we need to take into consideration some of the following factors that might increase or decrease the level of difficulty of a listening comprehension task: speed and level of listening passage; listeners' role in the listening task; listeners' motivation; content and complexity (e.g., vocabulary, grammar) of the listening passage; nonlinguistics items in support of the listening task (e.g., pictures, visual aids). Listeners do not pay attention to everything they hear but they tend to select information they focus on and this depends on a number of factors including the actual purpose of the listening task.

We can differentiate between an interactional and a transactional purpose for listening comprehension: (1) interactional listening/two-way listening (e.g., talks, conversations) is highly contextualized and involves a strong interaction component with a speaker; (2) transactional/one-way listening (e.g., news, broadcasts) is more message oriented and is used primarily to communicate information requiring accurate message comprehension. Knowing the communicative purpose of a text will help the listener determine what to listen for and, therefore, particular processes will be activated. As with the advantages of knowing the context, knowing the purpose for listening also greatly reduces the burden of language processing and comprehension because listeners know that they need to listen for something very specific, instead of trying to understand every word in the passage.

Type of Classroom Task

In the case of type of classroom tasks that might facilitate the development of listening comprehension skills, classroom research suggests that listening tasks should be well structured to allow active participation and interaction from the listener. Task types can be classified in different ways and in the next section we will examine some of these listening comprehension tasks.

Traditional approaches to listening comprehension encourage passive listening. In traditional practice to listening comprehension, L2 learners listen to the teacher or an audio-recorded passage and they are usually asked to answer questions related to the text or to fill in the gap activity. The gap usually highlights the linguistic elements rather than the communicative elements in the passage.

In a more interactive approach to listening comprehension, L2 learners would play the role of active listeners. They listen to a passage to understand and they are required to understand the meaning conveyed. In this more communicative approach to listening comprehension tasks, language teachers should help L2 learners to develop a series of listening strategies (e.g., listening for gist, listening for purpose; see a list and examples of key strategies in the following text) and the ability to use them in different listening situations.

In adopting a principled and evidence-based approach to the teaching of listening comprehension, a series of factors need to be taken into consideration to foster the development of listening skills:

(1) The role of L2 learners
(2) L2 learners' strategies
(3) The type of listening tasks used

Key Strategies

Listening for gist: Is the passage about describing living in the city or living in the countryside? Is it a positive or negative view about the current political situation?

Listening for purpose: Is the speaker buying a ticket or making an enquiry? Does John agree or disagree with the death penalty?

Listening for main concepts: Does the speaker like or dislike President Obama? Did John like or dislike the book?

Listening for specifics: How much does the room cost? What time does John meet with Laura?

In everyday life people engage in a variety of situations during which they listen to a passage, a conversation, an announcement, a video, music, and TV programs. In developing specific classroom listening tasks we also need to consider two types of tasks:

– Collaborative or reciprocal listening tasks
– Non-collaborative or nonreciprocal listening tasks

Collaborative or reciprocal tasks involve both an exchange between interlocutors and negotiation of meaning on both parts (the speaker and the listener). Listeners play an important role in constructing the discourse. In noncollaborative tasks there is no negotiation of meaning and the listener is only an observer. L2 learners are generally engaged in listening tasks that are collaborative and noncollaborative (particularly in the language laboratory). The main challenge is to develop a listening task that will stimulate the development of listening skills while ensuring L2 learners make use of their own listening strategies (e.g., to listen for specific information, to obtain information for a specific purpose, to personalize). Language teachers also need to ensure that L2 learners must be engaged in listening tasks where they make use of bottom-up and top-down strategies.

Listeners use metacognitive, (e.g., to apply a specific technique to a listening task), cognitive strategies (mental activities used by L2 learners to comprehend and store information in short-term memory), and socio-affective strategies (e.g., to verify understanding) to facilitate their comprehension. Metacognitive strategies (e.g., assessing the situation, monitoring, self-evaluating, self-assessing) are used to regulate or direct listeners' language learning process. When listeners know how to analyze the requirements of a listening task, they activate the appropriate listening processes required, make appropriate predictions, monitor their comprehension, evaluate the success of their approach, and will be more successful in developing listening comprehension skills.

The following is a list of normal tendencies that successful language listeners might display when processing language:

– They tend to predict about what they might hear or what might happen;
– They tend to guess about what they might hear or what the speakers might have said;
– They tend to focus on key words and select key information;
– They tend to monitor their understanding of the meaning of what they hear;
– They tend to reflect on what they heard and attempt to formulate an opinion, and/or to interact with a speaker, or to personalize the content.

Michael Rost has outlined the basic constructive strategies that successful L2 listeners tend to adopt when they encounter some uncertainty:

• Predicting: using real-world expectations to generate predictions about what the speakers will say and what might happen;
• Guessing: making inferences about what the speakers might have said or might have meant, even when "bottom-up" information about the language may be incomplete;
• Selecting: focusing on key words, trying to select targeted information that is adequate to complete a given task;
• Clarifying: monitoring one's level of understanding and identifying questions that can be asked to supplement partial understanding or correct misunderstanding, and revising one's representation of meaning;
• Responding: react or attempt to formulate an opinion, interact with the speaker, personalize the content, focus on what was understood, or attempt to talk about the input or conversation in a comfortable way.

If we teach these strategies explicitly and persistently, and if we incorporate their use directly into our listening tasks, we will help L2 learners gain control over the listening process. When we develop a listening task, we should consider all these strategies and incorporate their use directly into our listening tasks.

Now if we look at listening in the language classroom the two main questions to ask are:

1. What kind of listening tasks should L2 learners be engaged with in the classroom?
2. Do they have the opportunity to use and develop their skills and strategies during the listening tasks?

To answer the preceding questions appropriately and to ensure that language instructors develop listening tasks that integrate listening skills, we need to consider the following steps:

(1) Language teachers should develop listening tasks that have a specific communicative purpose;

(2) Language teachers should choose topics that are familiar and interesting for language learners. They must be able to extract meaning from the text. To do that, they need to figure out the main purpose for their listening;

(3) Language teachers need to design a listening task that will activate learners' background knowledge about the specific topic so that they will be able to predict the content of the task and to use appropriate listening strategies to complete it;

(4) Language teachers need to contextualize the listening task. They need to provide clues to meaning. They need to provide the listener with an idea of the type of information to expect and what to do with it before the actual listening begins;

(5) Language teachers need to define the task's instructional goal and type of response expected. Each listening and comprehension task should have as its goal the improvement of one or more specific listening skills;

(6) Language teachers should spell out the goal(s) of a listening comprehension task (e.g., recognizing specific aspects of the message, such as sounds, words, morphological distinctions; determining the topic about a message; comprehending main ideas);

(7) Language teachers should take into consideration the level of difficulty of the listening comprehension passage by considering the following factors: how the information is presented, how familiar learners are with the topic, whether the listening task offers visual support (e.g., maps, diagrams, pictures);

(8) Language teachers should make use of prelistening tasks to prepare students for what they are going to hear or view. Prelistening tasks would activate learners' knowledge and interest. The prelistening tasks assess learners' background knowledge, and provide them with the background knowledge necessary for

coping with language comprehension (e.g., reviewing relevant vocabulary or grammatical structures before listening to a passage; reading something relevant to the listening task; predicting the content of the listening text, think-pair share, brainstorming). Prelistening tasks help students make decisions about what to listen for and, subsequently, to focus their attention on meaning while listening. Language teachers need to raise learners' consciousness/ knowledge of the relevant topic. They also need to establish a listening purpose so that learners know the specific information they need to listen for, and they can make predictions to anticipate what they might hear.

(9) Language teachers should encourage the development of L2 learners' listening strategies by exposing learners to different ways of processing information such as bottom-up tasks (e.g., word sentence recognition, listening for different morphological ending), top-down tasks (identifying the topic, understanding meaning of sentence), and interactive tasks (e.g., listening to a list and categorizing the words, following directions).

(10) Language teachers must expose L2 learners to a variety of tasks to develop listening strategies such as looking for key words, looking for nonverbal cues to meaning, associating information with one existing background knowledge (activating schemata), guessing meanings, listening for the general gist, or seeking clarification. Tasks, where learners need to extrapolate meaning, can be grouped according to the response learners must produce. The two main categories are listening tasks where learners perform physical tasks and listening tasks where learners transfer information.

A Task-Based Approach to Listening

As argued before, the notion of tasks is central to language learning and teaching. In listening tasks, the "postlistening" stage of listening occurs in the few minutes following the actual exposure to the text. Effective listening tasks often involve an explicit "prelistening" step, which consists of some activities that the learner does prior to listening to the main input to increase readiness. This step is designed to activate what the learner already knows, provide an "advance organizer" to help L2 learners predict ideas and "prestructure" information. The main aim of the prelistening phase is to get L2 learners to warm up and familiarize with the topic ahead of the tasks. They are anticipating and predicting the content of the listening passage so that they are prepared. Learners might initially work independently and, subsequently, in small groups or pairs. The prelistening step may include explicit preteaching of vocabulary, grammatical or rhetorical structures, pronunciations of phrases, or ideas that are part of the upcoming input (see following example of a listening comprehension task).

Effective listening tasks include the following phases:
- Prelistening
- While listening
- Postlistening

Listening Text

Born on February 5, 1985, Cristiano Ronaldo dos Santos Aveiro is a Portuguese soccer superstar. By 2003 – when he was just sixteen years old – Manchester United paid £12 million (more than US$14 million) to sign him, a record fee for a player of his age. In the 2004 FA Cup final, Ronaldo scored Manchester United's first three goals and helped them capture the championship. He set a franchise record for goals scored in 2008, before Real Madrid paid a record $131 million for his services the following year. Among his many accomplishments, he has won a record-tying five Ballon d'Or awards for player of the year, and led Portugal to an emotional victory in the 2016 European Championship. In July 2018, Ronaldo embarked on a new phase of his career by signing with Italian Serie A club Juventus.

Ronaldo's earnings made him the highest-paid soccer player for the fourth year in a row and the highest-paid professional athlete of 2017. According to Celebrity Net Worth, as of 2017 Ronaldo's net worth is an estimated $400 million. Cristiano Ronaldo is dating the Spanish model Georgina Rodriguez; the couple were first seen together publicly around November 2016. In June 2017, the couple welcomed twins, a boy and a girl, via a surrogate. In November 2017 Rodriguez added to their family with the birth of another girl.

Prelistening phase

(1) An orientation task, designed to enable students to activate what they already know and to predict information.

Football champion Cristiano Ronaldo. What do you know about him? Work with a partner. List what information you have about him.

(2) A vocabulary and grammar task, designed to help students in advance with problematic vocabulary and structures related to the passage.

- He set a franchise record capture in the Champions League
- Accomplishments
- Embarked
- Surrogate

While-Listening Phase

(1) A table completion task, designed to be done during two or three listens.

Listen for dates and key events in his life. As you listen, look at the timeline that follows. Listen for one event for each date on the timeline. Write a short phrase for each event.

1985 – 2003 – 2004 – 2008 – 2016 – June 2017 – November 2017 – 2018

(2) Read these sentences. Some of these are in the passage. Listen again. Which of these phrases are in the passage? Check them.
- From the time he was a child, it was clear that he was a natural-born athlete.
- He decided to focus primarily on football.
- By June 2004 he was the top-ranked footballer in the world.
- Net worth is an estimated $400 million.
- He is dating the Spanish model Georgina Rodriguez.
- He has won a record-tying six Ballon d'Or.

Now work with a partner. Can you change these sentences to match the passage? Listen again and check.

Postlistening Phase

(1) Work with a partner. Compare your timelines. Give extra information about each event.
(2) Do you have any questions about the passage? Are there any new vocabulary words? Ask your teacher now. Use these phrases:
- What does ".... " mean?
- I heard a phrase that sounded like ".....". I'm not familiar with that.
- I couldn't catch the part after "... ".

(3) Listen to the passage one last time. In your own words, what is the theme? What feeling do you get when you listen to the passage?

When the learner begins listening to the input, there needs to be some expectation for concrete action. "While-listening" tasks can include guided note taking, completion of a picture or schematic diagram or table, composing questions, and any tangible activity that the learner does while listening to demonstrate ongoing monitoring of meaning. This stage of the listening task is usually the most problematic for the teacher to prepare because it involves designing a task that involves only minimal reading or writing.

   To summarize, a listening task should have the following characteristics:

- In the prelistening phase, language teachers should set the context, create motivation, and activate L2 learners' prior knowledge through cooperative learning tasks (e.g., brainstorming, think-pair-share). Effective listening tasks involve learners to predict ideas and prestructure relevant information in the text. Prelistening tasks include vocabulary learning and/or identifying key ideas contained in the upcoming input;
- In the while-listening phase, L2 learners are required to listen for main ideas to establish the context and transfer information. Learners are exposed to

listening bottom-up tasks (e.g., word sentence recognition, listening for different morphological ending), top-down tasks (identifying the topic, understanding meaning of sentence), and interactive tasks (e.g., listening to a list and categorizing the words, following directions). Main listening tasks at this stage include guided note taking, completion of a picture or schematic diagram or table;

– The postlistening phase helps learners to examine the functional language and infer the meaning of vocabulary (e.g., guess the meaning of unknown vocabulary, analyze the success of communication in the script, brainstorm alternative ways of expression). In the final stage, language learners are given postlistening tasks that involve reading, writing, speaking, and interaction activities. Postlistening activities are both oral and written and allow teachers to bring together some of the key topics and areas of language learners have worked on in the previous stage.

The exemplary study that follows provides positive evidence for the use of task-based listening activities to facilitate the development of learners' listening self-efficacy. Listening comprehension tasks of this kind are preferable and more effective than traditional practice in teaching listening which is based on merely the Q/A paradigm.

Exemplary Study

Motallebzadeh, K. (2013). The Effects of Task-Based Listening Activities on Improvement of Listening Self-Efficacy among Iranian Intermediate EFL Learners. *International Journal of Linguistics*, 5, 24–34.

Participants:

* Fifty native-speaking Iranians
* Adults
* All learning English at intermediate level

Materials and procedure:

* Two groups were formed: experimental ($n = 26$); control ($n = 24$).
* Experimental = received task-based listening activities
* Control = received traditional practice (Q/A)
* Nineteen sessions of instruction (thirty minutes)
* Pretest and posttest design using self-efficiency questionnaire (twenty items)

Results:

- The results of independent t-test revealed that the participants' levels of listening self-efficacy in the experimental group was significantly higher than those in the control group (p = 0.05).
- The results showed that the experimental group, in which task-based activities were applied, benefited significantly from the treatment.
- The comparison between the mean values of the two groups demonstrated a significant change in the improvement of listening self-efficacy.

Conclusion:

- Using task-based listening activities, the development of learners' listening self-efficacy will be facilitated and this method is preferable to the traditional method of teaching listening that is based on merely asking and answering questions.

Recap

In developing listening tasks keep the following in mind:

- Choose input that will engage learners, arouse their curiosity, and make them want to remember what they are learning.
- Design clear tasks that focus on meaning. A task is designed for the purposes of increasing learning, exposing learners to meaningful input. A task should have a clear set of procedures, and it can be monitored and evaluated by the teacher.
- Maximize acquisition by creating prelistening tasks (e.g., prelistening surveys, pair questionnaires, or prediction activities using key vocabulary from the extract) that activate learners' knowledge and interest.
- While-listening tasks can include guided note taking, completion of a picture or schematic diagram or table, composing questions and any tangible activity that the learner does while listening to demonstrate ongoing monitoring of meaning.
- The postlistening phase of listening occurs in the few minutes following the actual attending to the text. This is probably the most important part of listening instruction because it allows the learner to build mental representations. Postlistening tasks can involve additional reading, writing, speaking, and interaction.
- Encourage the use of active listening strategies. A successful listener is someone who adopts active listening strategies. An active listening strategy is an attempt to gain some control over the listening process.

- Build steps into activities that enhance language awareness. One goal of listening instruction is to help learners "notice" more of the input and utilize more information from the input as they construct meaning.

How Do You Develop Effective Reading Comprehension Tasks?

The Nature and Role of Reading Comprehension

Reading is considered an interactive process between the reader and the text. The text presents letters, words, sentences, and paragraphs that encode meaning. The reader uses knowledge, skills, and strategies to determine what that meaning is.

Readers need to develop a variety of skills: the ability to recognize the elements of the writing system (e.g., words recognition, grammatical features); the knowledge of discourse and how different parts of the text connect with each other; the need to develop a knowledge about different types of texts; and the need to be able to use top-down and bottom-up strategies. Developing reading comprehension skills can be defined as the reader's ability to use and apply appropriate skills and strategies to successfully comprehend a written text. Research on word recognition has indicated that recognizing a word is a necessary component in comprehending a text. However, it is not sufficient to develop full comprehension. Readers must construct meaning from the words they can recognize. This means that language teachers should provide guided practice in reading to increase learners' comprehension and multiple exposures to vocabulary.

Bottom-Up and Top-Down Strategies

Developing learners' comprehension is the process of constructing meaning from a text. It involves word knowledge (vocabulary) as well as thinking and reasoning. This process involves making use of learners' prior knowledge. It involves drawing from internal strategies to process words and expressions in the input learners hear. Likewise, in the development of listening skills, reading skills are affected by two processing strategies: bottom-up and top-down. Bottom-up strategies are used by learners to gradually decode the linguistics information (e.g., orthographic knowledge, lexical and syntactic knowledge) in a written text: from the small to large units. Readers process letters and characters, and analyze and interpret the meaning of words and sentences. Top-down strategies involve processing beyond the analysis of linguistics information (e.g., knowledge of text structure) and prior knowledge (e.g., topics' familiarity, culture awareness).

The Schema Theory

The so-called Schema Theory suggests that as learners, our knowledge impacts on how we process and understand new incoming information. Research in reading has provided the following insights for developing reading skills:

- Learners benefit from prereading activities that are very effective to improve schema activation and use of reading strategies;
- Learners should be exposed to reading for a real-life specific purpose;
- Learners should read extensively;
- Learners should be encouraged to integrate information in the text with existing knowledge;
- Learners should be motivated and should engage in reading tasks with a specific purpose;
- Learners should be engaged in tasks stimulating different skills (e.g., perceptual processing, phonemic processing).

L2 learners tend not to transfer the strategies they use when reading in their native language to reading into another language. When reading a text from another language they exclusively rely on their linguistic knowledge (a bottom-up strategy). One of the language instructors' challenges is to help learners not to rely on this bottom-up strategy and to use top-down strategies as they do in their native language. Some of these strategies can help learners to read effectively in the language they are learning. Previewing of a text might help learners to develop a general understanding of the content of a passage.

Using readers' preexisting knowledge might help in making predictions about content, discourse structure, vocabulary, and main concepts in a text. Skimming and scanning might help learners to get the main ideas in the text and confirm or question predictions. Guessing from context might help learners to decode the meanings of unknown words rather than translating word by word. Paraphrasing might help learners to summarize the main ideas and concepts in a text using their own words.

Language teachers can help learners to use these reading strategies in several ways. They can take L2 learners through the processes of previewing, predicting, skimming and scanning, and paraphrasing. They should allow enough time in the classroom for group previewing and predicting activities in preparation for a reading comprehension task. Teachers should develop tasks that encourage learners to guess meaning from context. When language learners are able to use reading strategies, they will be able to effectively develop their ability to read into another language. Learners would find it difficult to process complex language and unfamiliar topics. It is desirable for teachers to select a text according to learners' topic familiarity.

An effective way to teach L2 learners reading comprehension abilities is for language instructors to help them develop reading strategies that they can use in different reading tasks. Reading is a key part of language instruction as it supports learning in multiple ways. When learners are exposed to a variety of materials to read, they have many opportunities to process vocabulary, grammar, and sentence structure in authentic contexts. Also, L2 learners develop a better picture of how these elements of the language work together to convey meaning. Reading for content information in the language classroom provides learners with both authentic reading material and an authentic purpose for reading. When reading to learn, students need to follow four basic steps:

1. Figure out the purpose for reading. Activate background knowledge of the topic to predict or anticipate content and identify appropriate reading strategies.
2. Attend to the parts of the text that are relevant to the identified purpose and ignore the rest. This selectivity enables students to focus on specific items in the input and reduces the amount of information they have to process and hold in short-term memory.
3. Select strategies that are appropriate to the reading task and use them flexibly and interactively. Students' comprehension improves and their confidence increases when they use top-down and bottom-up skills simultaneously to construct meaning.
4. Check comprehension while reading and when the reading task is completed. Monitoring comprehension helps students detect inconsistencies and comprehension failures, helping them learn to use alternate strategies.

Reading Comprehension Interactive Tasks

The pedagogical implication of the Schema Theory is the understanding that reading is an interactive process between readers and texts. Readers must associate elements in a text with their prereading knowledge. Reading activities in traditional textbooks consist mainly of two types:

- Translation tasks (read a passage and translate into French);
- Answer questions from a text (a typical task/exercise is: read the dialogue/text and answer the following questions).

Reading should be viewed as reading in another language rather than as an exercise in translation. The fact that language learners do not necessarily have the verbal virtuosity of a native reader means language teachers need to use some strategies to help them. The framework presented here takes into consideration the need to guide learners in their comprehension of a text. In adopting a principled evidence-based approach to the teaching of reading skills, a series of measures need to be taken into consideration. Language teachers should develop reading activities following a five-stage approach:

- Prereading stage;
- Reading stage;
- Text-interaction stage;
- Postreading stage;
- Personalization stage.

When designing a reading task, language instructors must keep in mind that we cannot expect learners to process all the information in a text. The purpose of the reading comprehension tasks is to bridge the gap between the reader and the information contained in the text. The tasks follow a five-stages approach with a prereading stage, a reading stage, a text-interaction stage, a postreading stage, and a personalization stage (see following example).

1. Prereading tasks must be included to improve the activation of learners' existing knowledge. To prepare L2 learners and activate the knowledge that is relevant to a particular reading text we want to present and use, many techniques are available:
   - Brainstorming as a whole class exercise or in pairs. This can take place before reading the text and should help to bridge the gap between the reader and a text;
   - Titles, subtitles, headings, divisions within the text, and illustrations can be exploited as a means to activate learners' background knowledge and or to predict content;
   - Scanning for specific information can be used in the case of a text that does not need extensive preparation. We could ask learners to scan the text for specific information, to skim to find the theme or main idea, and to elicit information activating appropriate prior knowledge.

Effective reading comprehension tasks include the following phases:
 – Prereading
 – Reading
 – In-text interaction
 – Postreading
 – Personalization

   In the prereading stage, learners are asked to read the title of the text and based on that to write down some of the issues they expect to find in the text. Before this prereading task, learners are asked to work in pairs and talk about some of the issues related to the main topic of the reading text. Both tasks are designed to activate readers' knowledge that will be needed to understand the information in the text. This is an attempt to bridge the gap between the readers and the text. Prereading tasks serve the purpose of mainly preparing learners for the reading task. However, during prereading, language teachers have the opportunity to assess learners' background knowledge of the topic and linguistic content of the text; to provide learners with the background knowledge necessary for the comprehension of the text; to activate their existing knowledge; and to clarify key issues that may be necessary to comprehend the passage.

2. During the reading stage learners are asked to scan the text for specific information. Initially, readers should process the text to understand the general

meaning. Learners are asked to quickly scan the text to establish whether they have guessed the content of the text during prereading activities.

3. In the text-interaction stage learners explore fully the content of a text. We should provide a guide to this process so as to avoid learners reading word for word. Language instructors must make sure that learners understand what the purpose of reading is. Learners must get the main ideas, obtain specific information, and gradually understand most of the message. Recognizing the purpose of reading will help students select appropriate reading strategies. This stage consists of a combination of two types of tasks:
   - Management strategies in which we suggest ways to divide a text and divide it into small parts;
   - Comprehension checks implemented during the guided interaction phase so that readers are monitored in an ongoing way.

   In the text-interaction tasks, L2 learners must check their comprehension as they read.

4. In the postreading stage learners are given a series of tasks in which they organize the information in the text. Postreading tasks are designed to check and verify comprehension. The purpose of these tasks is to encourage readers to learn from what they have read.

5. In the personalization stage learners are encouraged to exploit the communicative function of the reading text through the use of the text to accomplish a specific task (e.g., solve a problem, create a poster, apply main concepts to another context, relate key issues to a different context).

Developing reading comprehension skills involves the interaction of a variety of knowledge sources. An interactive model for the comprehension of written language has been proposed. This model envisages that L2 learners make a positive contribution to their learning. The proposed framework for developing reading comprehension tasks comprises different stages. Based on the principles highlighted in this chapter, instructors should be supplied with the following guidelines for the development of effective reading comprehension tasks:

– Reading comprehension tasks should be constructed around a purpose that has significance for learners. This will stimulate their motivation and interest;

– Reading comprehension tasks should be developed by language instructors for a specific purpose and language instructors should make sure that L2 learners understand what the purpose of reading is. A task can have more than one instructional purpose (e.g., practicing a specific grammatical structure, introducing new vocabulary, familiarizing learners with a particular topic); reading comprehension tasks should have a defined goal and develop tasks for learners to deliver appropriate responses;

- Use prereading tasks/activities to prepare students for reading and activate their background knowledge;
- Use text-interaction reading tasks to gradually bridge the gap between the text and the reader;
- Use postreading tasks to check and verify comprehension;
- Use personalization tasks to encourage learners to exploit the communicative function of the reading text.

Stage 1– Prereading Phase

Discuss with your partners the following questions around "racism."

- What do you think about the issue of "racism"?
- What are the reasons?
- What would you do to solve the problem?

Read the text file and write some ideas/concepts that you predict to find in the main text.

Racism and Discrimination

Stage 2 – Reading Phase

Read the text quickly to find out if you have correctly guessed the ideas.

1. Racism has many dimensions. It can be defined as the set of ideas, attitudes, and actions that seek to inferior ethnocultural minorities in social, economic, and political terms, thereby preventing them from participating fully in society.

   Racism is now mainly claimed by neo-Nazi and supremacist groups. This ideology presents a cultural group, defined by the color of the skin or by cultural or religious characteristics, as superior to others and that must therefore be the only one to fully enjoy the rights guaranteed by the state. This ideology no longer garners the support of modern democratic states as a result of the crimes and atrocities it has caused in the past. However, prejudices and discrimination against people from cultural communities still exist in contemporary societies.

2. Discrimination is a distinction, exclusion, or preference based on grounds prohibited by the Quebec Charter of Rights and Freedoms that has the effect of destroying or compromising the exercise of rights and freedoms. These grounds are: "race," color, sex, pregnancy, sexual orientation, marital status, age except to the extent permitted by law, religion, political beliefs, language, ethnic or national origin, social condition, and disability or the use of a means to overcome this handicap. Discrimination can manifest itself as much by exclusion as by harassment or unfavorable treatment.

Harassment is a particular form of discrimination. It may occur to a person or a group of people, including words, acts or repeated acts, vexatious or contemptuous. A single serious act causing a continuing harmful effect may also constitute harassment.

3. Direct discrimination occurs when the distinction, exclusion, or preference is clearly based on one of the grounds prohibited by the Quebec Charter. For example, an employer who refuses to hire a black man just because he is black makes direct discrimination. Indirect discrimination arises from the application of a seemingly neutral practice that is applicable to all, but that has detrimental effects on groups defined on the grounds of discrimination prohibited by the Charter. Thus, setting a high size for access to certain trades, and for no reason related to the nature of the work, indirectly discriminates against women and people from cultural communities, whose average size is smaller. There is no intention to discriminate here. Discrimination comes from arbitrary norms and practices often inherited without critical examination of older eras. The analysis of practices is therefore necessary to detect it.

4. Racism and discrimination tend to diminish the chances of those who suffer from it to have a job commensurate with their skills and the same opportunities for promotion. When they fail to overcome the professional barriers they face and integrate into the labor market in a sustainable way, their standard of living is affected.

They therefore have less access to public and private services such as housing, education, and recreation in particular. According to the World Health Organization, racism has a negative impact on mental health because it creates psychological distress. In addition, people who feel rejected by society because of the prejudice they face may have a weak sense of belonging to this society, which is theirs. Racism and discrimination also have a negative impact on the society that tolerates them. Institutions, businesses, and society in general are depriving themselves of the potential, talents, and resources of people who are excluded because of prejudice.

Stage 3 – Interaction with the Text (While-Reading Phase)

Read the text (sections: 1–4) and reflect on its content. For each section write a short paragraph summarizing the main meaning.

-
-
-
-

Based on what you read, indicate if these statements are true or false.

	True	False
1. Racism could have an impact on people's health	☐	☐
2. Direct or indirect racism is very similar	☐	☐
3. Ignorance is the main reason people are racist	☐	☐
4. Racism has a negative impact on the economy	☐	☐

Find the synonym for the following words in the text.

1. Difficulties
2. Reasons
3. Goals
4. Sense of belonging

Stage 4 – Postreading Phase and Personalization

Step 1: Work with your partner and identify the four possible solutions to the problem of "racism."

-
-
-
-

Step 2: Work with other groups in the class to prepare a poster against "racism."

Work in a group to prepare an interview/questionnaire on the main issues concerning racism.

Questions

The main findings from the exemplary study that follows indicate that using task-based reading comprehension activities present a significant advantage for learners in terms of improvement of reading comprehension skills compared to a more traditional approach to reading (read and answer written questions and/or read and translate a passage). The exemplary study that follows investigates and provides some evidence on the positive role of effective reading comprehension tasks.

Exemplary Study

Azizeh, C. (2016). The Effects of Task-Based Instruction on Reading Comprehension among Iranian Intermediate EFL Learners. *Applied Research English Language*, 4, 19–29.

Participants:

- One hundred thirty-five Iranian native speakers
- Adults
- All learning English at intermediate level

Materials and procedure:

- Four groups were formed: two experimental and two control
- Experimental = received task-based reading tasks
- Control = received traditional instruction on reading comprehension
- Instruction measured over a period of four months
- Pretest and posttest design. Two tests were used and they measured reading comprehension ability

Results:

- The results showed that task-based reading comprehension activities were beneficial to participants.
- Task-based comprehension tasks improved learners' interaction skills, and maximized their understanding and use of the target language.

Conclusion:

- Using task-based reading comprehension activities presents a significant advantage for learners in terms of improvement of reading comprehension skills.

Recap

In developing reading tasks, language teachers should keep the following in mind:

- Reading comprehension should be considered as reading in another language and not merely an exercise in translation.

- Reading comprehension tasks comprises a text surrounded by a number of tasks with the aim to close the gap between the text and the reader.
- Reading and comprehension tasks need to include a number of components (prereading phase, while-reading phase, and postreading phase) to ensure interaction between text and reader is promoted.

REFERENCES AND READINGS

- Bernhardt, E. (1991). *Reading Development in a Second Language.* Norwood, NJ: Ablex.
- Brown, S. (2011). *Listening Myths.* Ann Arbor: University of Michigan Press.
- Dave, W., Willis, J. (2007). *Doing Task-Based Teaching.* Oxford: Oxford University Press.
- Ellis, R. (2003). *Task-Based Language Learning and Teaching.* New York: Oxford University Press.
- Field, J. (2008). *Listening in the Language Classroom.* Cambridge: Cambridge University Press.
- Grabe, W. (2009). *Reading in a Second Language: Moving from Theory to Practice.* New York: Cambridge University Press.
- Richards, J. C. (2012). *Tips for Teaching Listening.* London: Pearson.
- Rost, M. (2002). *Teaching and Researching Listening: Applied Linguistics in Applied Linguistics in Action.* London: Longman.
- Rost, M., Wilson, J. (2013). *Active Listening.* London: Pearson.
- Wilson, J. J. (2008). *How to Teach Listening.* Pearson Longman.
- Zhao, H. H., Anderson, N. J. (2009). *Second Language Reading Research and Instruction: Crossing the Boundaries.* Ann Arbor: University of Michigan Press.

DISCUSSION, QUESTIONS, AND RESEARCH IDEAS

1. Keeping in mind the main principles (1–8) for an effective listening activity, develop a pre-while-post- listening task for your language class.

2. Using the five-step (and looking at the preceding example) interactive approach to reading comprehension, develop a reading comprehension task for your language classroom.

3. Look at the listening and reading comprehension tasks presented in this chapter and answer the following questions.

1. Input selection	Will the input increase learner's motivation? Is it interesting? Is it relevant? Is it packaged in a way that makes it accessible?
2. Task design	Does the task promote learning? Is the task worth doing? Does the task focus on meaning? Does the task have pre-while-post- phases? Are the procedures clear? Are there clear outcomes? Can the tasks be repeated?
3. Strategy use	Are the learners encouraged to use active listening strategies? Are there opportunities in the task for predicting, guessing, selecting, clarifying, monitoring, responding, interacting, and reflecting?
4. Language awareness	Does the task promote language awareness? Are there opportunities for the student to notice new vocabulary and structures?

5 | What Is the Nature and Role of Grammar, Vocabulary, and Corrective Feedback?

Overview

In this chapter, the nature and role of grammar, vocabulary, and corrective feedback in second language learning and teaching is examined. Language is too abstract and complex to teach and learn explicitly. Language should not be treated as a subject matter. These two main concepts have profound consequences for how we organize language-teaching materials as well as how we approach the classroom. One of the key issues in second language teaching concerns the role and practice of grammar instruction. Does grammar instruction make a difference? How do we teach grammar in the language classroom? Is there an effective pedagogical intervention to teach grammar that is better than others? These are some of the questions that scholars, language instructors, and practitioners have addressed in their attempt to find the most appropriate and effective way to teach grammar and will be discussed in this chapter. While many scholars tackle some of these questions to develop a better understanding of how people learn grammar, language instructors are in search of the most effective way to approach the teaching of grammar in the language classroom. Teaching and learning vocabulary are key issues for language teachers. The role of vocabulary is explored and an effective way to teach vocabulary is examined.

The nature, types, and role of interactional modifications and corrective feedback in language learning and teaching is also discussed in this chapter. The role of corrective feedback is one of the key issues in second language acquisition theory, research, and pedagogy. Interaction refers to conversational exchanges between L2 learners and other interlocutors (e.g., native speakers and nonnative speakers, learner-teacher interactions). Conversational interaction between native speakers (NS) and nonnative speakers (NNS) can facilitate language development. Corrective feedback refers to utterances from a language instructor or another speaker that indicate that the learner's output is not correct. This feedback is usually provided though different conversational techniques and negotiation strategies (e.g., clarification requests, confirmation checks, repetition, recast) during interaction and classroom tasks. In providing corrective feedback, language teachers and/or language learners should consider the following:

- Should errors be corrected?
- How should we correct errors?

Theories in second language acquisition argue that input is a necessary ingredient in language acquisition. Despite this view, there is considerable debate over the nature of language. In Chapter 1, we argued that language is not something to be learned the way a person learns anything else. In fact, there are strong arguments that language can't be learned like a subject matter such as literature. Language is an abstract, complex, and implicit system and, as we know, L2 learners do not internalize rules. Language is something internal, not external. Each and every one of us creates a mental representation we call language. This is true for first, second, and subsequent languages. We create an abstract and complex system even though we don't know this. This is also why it is implicit. We know we have language in our heads, but we don't really know what the contents are. In addition to this, as stated before, communication and language are not the same thing.

So, what are some of the implications of the nature of language for "language teaching"? This first implication is this:

- Language as mental representation is too abstract and complex to teach and learn explicitly. In short, language as mental representation is not the rules and paradigms that appear on textbook pages.

The first implication leads us to a second implication:

- Explicit rules and paradigm lists can't become the abstract and complex system because the two things are completely different. This implication stems from the fact that there is no internal mechanism that can convert explicit textbook rules into implicit mental representation.

What Is the Role of Grammar Instruction?

How do we teach grammar? Language learners often expect to get presentation and explanation of grammar rules from the teacher. Language teachers often explain grammar rules, and this is followed by mechanical output practice (drills).

Let's quickly review basic facts about language and language acquisition before we discuss grammar instruction.

- *Language is abstract and complex.* It is too abstract and complex to teach and learn explicitly. There is no mechanism that turns explicit "rules" into the abstract and complex mental representation we call "language."
- *Acquisition is slow and piecemeal.* L2 learners don't acquire one thing and then move on to another, as suggested by typical syllabi and textbooks. L2 learners' minds are constantly working on various aspects of language simultaneously. Only over time the internal system builds up and begins to resemble the second language.

- *Acquisition is stagelike and orderlike.* In the acquisition of any structure there are stages that all learners go through regardless of their L1. There is no evidence that stages can be skipped, or orders can be altered.

As the research on the preceding points emerged, scholars began to ask, "Can instruction influence acquisition? What role does instruction play in these observations?" This research has led us to three more basic facts.

- *Instruction does not affect the stagelike or ordered nature of acquisition.* That is, instruction does not allow learners to skip stages or alter ordered acquisition.
- *There are internal constraints on acquisition.* Something inside the learner's mind/brain processes and organizes language in ways that can't be manipulated by outside forces such as instruction and practice.
- *Input provides the data for acquisition.* Language that learners hear and see in communicative contexts forms the data on which the internal mechanisms operate.

> Instruction has a limited role and it is constrained. However, a grammar component has a facilitative role.

Overall, research investigating the role of grammar instruction in second language acquisition has indicated the need for a grammar component in second language instruction. The question is how this component should be provided.

There has been a dramatic shift from traditional grammar oriented to more recent communicative approaches to grammar instruction. In traditional grammar-oriented teaching approaches, one of the main assumptions was that a second language is learned through the deduction of the grammatical properties of L2 and this would allow learners to develop a conscious and explicit representation of that language in their internal system. Grammar instruction consisted mainly in studying forms and structures with memorization and translation of texts (see "Grammar Translation Approach" in Chapter 2). It was also suggested that grammar is learned through the process of repetition, imitation, and reinforcement (see "Audio-Lingual Method" in Chapter 2). Grammatical structures are presented in a linear manner with no attention to meaning. This approach emphasizes the use of memorization and pattern drills as grammar teaching tasks.

A specific traditional grammar-oriented approach is the so-called PPP (presentation- practice- production). This approach proposes a three-stage model. The first stage consists of the internalization of a new form or structure that is usually presented through a text. The second stage implies the practice of the new form of structure through its systematic use. In the final stage activities are organized involving personal use of the target form or structure. The PPP suggests the use of activities that allow the learner to move from systematic to appropriate use of the language in context. It is only when learners have mastered the form that they will be able to use it in context where the message becomes more important than the medium.

In more recent communicative approaches to grammar instruction (see "Communicative Language Teaching" and "Task-Based Language Teaching" approaches in Chapter 2), learners are asked to perform tasks with large quantities of meaning-focused input that contain target forms and vocabulary. The main purpose of these approaches is to develop learners' ability to interpret and use meaning in real-life communication but at the same time to focus on the learning of forms and structures. A component of grammar instruction is incorporated within an overall focus on communication.

> Traditional grammar instruction consists of two components:
> – Paradigms
> – Drill Practice

A traditional grammar-oriented approach is often characterized by paradigmatic explanations of specific linguistic forms or structures (see following example). The paradigmatic explanation is followed by pattern practice and substitution drills (see following example). In this type of mechanical practice, real-life situations are completely ignored, and practice is implemented in a completely decontextualized way.

"Today we are going to learn about past tense forms. Does anyone know what the past tense is, how is it formed and how we use it? (silence from the class) Well, the past tense in Italian is formed by ... (present the class with a paradigm of past tense). For example, in this sentence we add/change ... (quizzical look from students) .... What is the past tense of the verb 'to go'? If I need to say 'Yesterday I went to the Cinema with a friend,' how do you say this in Italian? (one student ventures an answer)."

Paradigm
Il passato prossimo (simple past) è formato da due elementi: l'ausiliare: il verbo essere o avere (al presente indicativo) + participio passato del verbo.

Formazione del participio passato
Il participio passato si forma togliendo al verbo la desinenza dell'infinito (are; ere; ire) e aggiungendo la desinenza del participio passato:

ARE ⇒ ATO (cambiare ⇒ cambiato)
ERE ⇒ UTO (vendere ⇒ venduto)
IRE ⇒ ITO (partire ⇒ partito)
Ora osserva la tabella:
PASSATO PROSSIMO DEI VERBI:
CAMBIARE – VENDERE – PARTIRE

Soggetto	Ausiliare	Participio passato	Ausiliare	Participio passato	Ausiliare	Participio passato
io	Ho	cambiato	Ho	Venduto	sono	partito – a
tu	Hai	cambiato	Hai	Venduto	sei	partito – a
lui – lei	Ha	cambiato	Ha	Venduto	è	partito – a
noi	Abbiamo	cambiato	Abbiamo	Venduto	siamo	partiti – e
voi	Avete	cambiato	Avete	Venduto	siete	partiti – e
loro	Hanno	cambiato	Hanno	Venduto	sono	partiti – e

L'ausiliare avere si usa con i verbi transitivi, ovvero con quei verbi che rispondonoalla domanda: chi? che cosa?

Qualche esempio:

Ho mangiato (cosa?) una mela.

Abbiamo incontrato (chi?) Lucia.

L'ausiliare essere si usa con i verbi intransitivi, ovvero con i verbi che non rispondono alla domanda: chi? che cosa?

Per esempio: sono uscito presto stamattina.

L'ausiliare essere si usa con:

⇒i verbi di movimento: partire; uscire; tornare etc.

⇒i verbi riflessivi: alzarsi; svegliarsi; lavarsi etc. (mi sono alzato; ti sei svegliato)

Consider this ...

Why do you think paradigms and drills practice are so entrenched in the mind of many language teachers?

Mechanical Drill

Complete the sentence with the *passato prossimo*. (Complete the sentence in the past using the verbs provided in brackets.)

1. Ieri, Paolo _____ (andare) al mare.
2. Questa mattino, Stefano _____ (parlare) al telefono con sua moglie Elena.

To complete this mechanical drill, it is not necessary to understand any Italian. The learner must know how to conjugate the verb in the correct form and can ignore all the other language. More meaningful drills practice usually follows from the mechanical practice (see following example).

Meaningful Drill

Answer the following questions with a complete sentence using *passato prossimo*.

A che ora sei andato a scuola? (What time did you go to school?)

Learners would answer the above open-ended question with the correct answer demonstrating the ability to correctly use the passé compose.

Communicative Drill

Communicative drills instead ask learners to communicate information to each other, and there is more than one answer, usually limited to yes/no, and the correct form of the verb needs to be produced (see following example).

Talk in groups about what you did yesterday.

Sono andato al cinema (Model) (I went to the cinema)

STUDENT 1:   Ieri, sei andato al cinema? (Yesterday, did you go to the cinema?)
STUDENT 2:   Si sono andato/No, non sono andato. (Yes, I did/ No, I did not)

Communicative drills focus on a specific grammatical form and the answer is personalized. However, there is no burden of communication for the students. The learner does not need to understand what is said, as there is no step that asks them to demonstrate comprehension. Therefore, it is possible to complete the activity without comprehension.

Drills are problematic for two main reasons:

- They force L2 learners to produce grammatical forms before they can comprehend the forms, which leads to incorrect generalizations and overuse of the form when not necessary. Learners need the opportunity to comprehend language before being able to use it accurately.
- They don't allow learners to make form-meaning connections in comprehension and production. The idea that acquiring grammar can be simply achieved by learning about the grammatical rules of a target language and practice those rules through production tasks (very often mechanical and traditional) has been challenged by many scholars in the field of second language acquisition and language teaching. In recent years, findings from empirical research in instructed second language acquisition and theory have demonstrated that a component of focus on grammar "focus on form") might facilitate acquisition if it is provided in combination with a focus on meaning. The term "focus on form" is characterized by any pedagogical interventions that draw learners' attention to the grammatical properties of the target language by providing a focus on meaning and a focus on form.

What Are the Options to Effectively Teach Grammar?

Input-Based Options to Grammar Instruction

Input plays a key role in second language acquisition. Just to remind ourselves that input is the language we hear or read and has a communicative intent. And that input is the single most important concept in second language acquisition. Considering the limited role for instruction, and the importance of incorporating grammar in a more communicative framework of language teaching, teachers should look at devising grammar tasks that, on one hand, enhance the grammatical features in the input and, on the other hand, provide L2 learners with opportunities to focus on meaning. The question is to determine what type of grammar is more successful in terms of helping learners internalize the grammatical features of a target language. In the exemplary study that follows, a type of instruction called "processing instruction" is compared to output-based pedagogical interventions to grammar instruction.

Exemplary Study

Benati, A. (2005). The Effects of Processing Instruction, Traditional Instruction and Meaning-Output Instruction on the Acquisition of the English Past Simple Tense. *Language Teaching Research*, 9, 87–113.

Main aims of the study:

- Compare the effects of three pedagogical interventions to grammar instruction (processing instruction, traditional instruction, and meaning output instruction) on the acquisition of English past tense forms.
- Measure the effects of processing instruction in altering a processing strategy called the "Lexical Preference Principle" and ensuring language learners process this linguistic feature correctly.

Participants:

- First semester school learners in two different secondary schools in China and Greece.
- Forty-seven Chinese students studying English in a secondary school in China (all at the age of 12–13).
- Thirty Greek students studying English in a secondary school in Greece (all at the age of 12–13).

Materials and procedure:

- The population of this study was split into three groups using a random procedure from the beginning of the experiment.
- The participants selected in both schools were studying English and did not have any previous knowledge of the target feature.
- Pre- and posttest procedure was used, and instruction lasted for four hours.
- Interpretation and production sentence-level tasks were used.

Results and significance:

- Processing instruction is better than traditional instruction and meaning output-based instruction at helping learners to interpret sentences containing the target feature.
- Processing instruction is better than traditional instruction and meaning output-based instruction at helping learners to produce sentences containing the target feature.

Structured Input Tasks

In traditional grammar-oriented instructional approaches learners are provided with explicit information about a particular target form or structure, and this is followed by mechanical practice (this traditional type of grammar instruction is also called "focus on forms" as linguistic forms are taught explicitly without communication and meaningful input). Unlike traditional instruction, where the focus of instruction is in the manipulation of learners' output, processing instruction aims at changing the way input is perceived and processed by learners (input manipulations).

> Structured input tasks facilitate language processing and interpretation by making appropriate form-meaning connections

Processing instruction is an input-based approach to grammar instruction predicated on the Input Processing Theory (see Chapter 1). Input processing refers to the fact that language learners make use of processing strategies when exposed to language input. When L2 learners process input, they have limited resources to ensure that they make correct form-meaning connections. When they hear a sentence such as *passerò il fine settimana a Assisi* (I will spend my weekend in Assisi), understand that "*passerò*" means that the action is in the future, a form-meaning connection is made. L2 learners cannot just notice the form, as they need to comprehend the meaning that the particular form encodes. Learners use two main processing strategies when they are exposed to language input.

The first one is called the Primacy of Meaning Principle. According to this strategy, learners will first process input for meaning before they process the linguistic form. The result of this will be that they will not make natural connections between forms in the input and their meanings. The second one is called the First Noun Principle and argues that learners will tend to process the first noun or pronoun they encounter in a sentence as the subject or agent. The result of this will be that they will misinterpret sentences in which the first element in a sentence is not the subject or agent.

Structured input tasks aim at altering the processing strategies/principles learners take to the task of comprehension and to encourage them to make better form-meaning connections. It is an input-based option to grammar instruction that guides learners to focus on small parts/features of the targeted language when they process the input. In structured input tasks learners are pushed to process the form or structure to complete the task. In structured input tasks the input is manipulated in particular ways to make learners become dependent on form and structure to get meaning (see the following guidelines for developing structured input):

(1) Present one thing at a time.
(2) Keep meaning in focus.
(3) Move from sentences to connected discourse.
(4) Use both oral and written input.
(5) Have the learner do something with the input.
(6) Keep the learner's processing strategies in mind.

1. Rules should be broken down into smaller parts and taught one at a time during the lesson. Learners are presented with the linguistic feature before being exposed to structured input activities. We should avoid providing learners with lots of information and grammatical rules, as learners possess a limited capacity for processing information. Presenting learners with a smaller and more focused amount of information will clearly enhance the opportunity for learners to pay more focused attention.

2. Keeping meaning in focus is crucial when we develop structured input tasks. Tasks in structured input must be completed with focused attention to the referential meaning of the input to which learners are exposed. A good structured input task is the one where students must understand the meaning of the sentence to complete the task. To complete the task and express their opinions, learners must understand the meaning of each utterance.

3. L2 learners are first exposed to sentences, and at a later stage they should be provided with connected discourse. This should happen only when learners have already had opportunities to process the new form or structure.

4. Structured input tasks that combine oral and written input should be used because there are different types of learners. This is to account for individual differences. Hearing the forms allows only for sound-meaning connections, whereas written form-meaning connections are made through reading.

5. Structured input tasks should be designed to make learners do something with the input they receive (i.e., agreeing or disagreeing; false or true; likely or unlikely). During structured input tasks learners should be encouraged to make form-meaning connections. Learners must engage in processing the input (having a specific reason for processing input) and must respond to the input sentence in some way.

6. Learners' attention should be guided so as not to rely on natural processing strategies. Activities in which the input is structured to alter learner's reliance on one particular processing principle should be created. This is the main goal for structured input tasks: correcting inefficient processing strategies and instilling in learners more efficient ones.

So structured input is necessary, for example, in the case of verbal inflection; the Italian verbal inflection -*ato* encodes past as in *parlato* (talked). The same semantic notion is also expressed in Italian by words such as *ieri* (yesterday) or *l'anno passato* (last year). Given that L2 learners are driven to process a content word before anything else in a sentence, they would attend to lexical temporal references of "pastness" before verbal inflections of paste tense in Italian. Another example where structured input tasks would facilitate acquisition is in the case of a sentence such as *Alessandro viene baciato da* Bernadette (Alessandro is kissed by Bernadette). L2 learners would misinterpret the preceding sentence as if it were "Alessandro who kissed Bernadette." The meaning of the sentence is that "Bernadette kissed Alessandro." In figuring out who did what to whom, L2 learners rely on word order. Therefore, they assign the role of subject to the first element they encounter in the sentence (Alessandro). This leads to a misinterpretation of the sentence and subsequent delay in acquisition.

Consider this ...

Can you think of a grammatical item and based on the preceding guidelines prepare a structured-input task?

Structured-input tasks are of two types: referential and affective. Referential tasks are those for which there is a right or wrong answer and for which the learner must rely on the targeted grammatical form to get meaning. Some examples of structured-input tasks concerning Italian gender agreement and English causative are provided in the following text. Learners had to determine which of two people (male or female) was being described. Nouns and any other reference to gender were removed in the sentences to which learners were exposed (sentences like *È brutta* instead of *Jenny È brutta*), so that only the adjective encoded gender. (The subject pronoun is not obligatory in Italian.) Thus, learners were obliged to attend to the grammatical markers to establish to whom the sentence was referring. Ascolta le seguenti frasi e indica chi viene descritto. (Listen to the following sentence and choose the subject described.)

È buono   ☐   ☐
È bella   ☐   ☐
È piccolo
             ☐   ☐

È italiana.
☐   ☐
Picture of Reberto Benigni   Picture of Sofia Loren

In the referential structured input example that follows, the input is structured in a way that L2 learners need to rely on the causative structure to correctly understand meaning in the input. All the sentences are meaningful, and learners are asked to interpret input correctly.

Listen to the sentences and answer the questions. Pay careful attention to the structure of each sentence to understand **who** is performing the action.

Who mended the dress?   (a) Jane   (b) someone else
Who delivered the flowers?   (a) Penny   (b) someone else
Who painted the fence?   (a) Mary   (b) someone else

Instructor's Script

(1) Jane had her dress mended last Monday
(2) Emma had flowers sent to her boyfriend
(3) Mary had the fence painted pink

In the affective structure input activity that follows, L2 learners are asked to interpret the sentences containing English causative forms and then undertake several tasks afterward.

Step 1 Indicate which of the following things happened to you in real life. Be prepared to share with the class.

	Yes	No
1. I had my vehicle repaired last month.	☐	☐
2. I had my hair cut at least once last year.	☐	☐
3. I had my photo taken by a professional.	☐	☐
4. I had my bills paid by a relative.	☐	☐
5. I had my mobile phone stolen once.	☐	☐

Step 2 As the instructor reads the statements, raise your hand if it is true for you. Someone should keep a record on the board.

Step 3 Let's find out now which are the three most popular and the three least popular things to do among our class.

The main advantage for the use of structured input is that it is a pedagogical intervention that through the manipulation and restructuring of the input might help learners to acquire grammatical and syntactic features of a target language (make correct and appropriate form-meaning connections). It is an effective pedagogical intervention to alter a variety of L2 learners' processing strategies in different languages and with native speakers of a variety of L1s.

The following is a list of linguistic features that can be affected by processing principles and require structured input grammar tasks to ensure L2 learners process forms and appropriately connect them to meaning.

Example of Grammatical Features/Forms Affected by Principle the Primacy of Meaning Principle and Its Sub-Principles	Example of Grammatical Features Affected by the First Noun Principle
Tense markers when adverbials time are present	Word order
Subject-verb agreement when explicit subjects are present	Passive constructions
Aspectual markers when adverbials of aspect are present	Case marker
Mood when expression of uncertainty or emotion are present	Object pronouns
Subjunctive	Causative form
Adjective agreement	
Case markers	

Input Enhancement

Scholars in second language acquisition have agreed that learners must be exposed to input, and that input must be comprehensible and meaning bearing to facilitate the L2 acquisition. Learners require attention to process successfully forms in the input. What is meant by this is that L2 learners must first notice a form in the input for that form to be processed. Given the importance of "noticing" (see Chapter 1) a form in the input the question is: How can we best facilitate the noticing of a certain form in the input?

> Input enhancement is a pedagogical intervention to grammar instruction to enhance the target form in the input and to help L2 learners to notice that form

Input enhancement is a form of pedagogical intervention that enhances the input to allow learners to notice some specific forms in the input. This should have an effect in learners' linguistic competence. Various ways of enhancing the input have been proposed that differ in terms of explicitness and elaboration. A practical example would be to underline or to capitalize a specific grammatical item in a text to help learners notice that particular grammatical feature (textual enhancement). A different instructional intervention would be to modify a text so that a particular target item would appear repeatedly so that the text will contain many more exemplars of the same feature (input flood).

Input enhancement is a pedagogical intervention to grammar instruction through which input is made more noticeable to the learner. Input enhancement might help teachers to expose learners to comprehensible input and positive evidence while drawing learners' attention to some linguistic properties of the target language. To help learners notice a particular feature, teachers provide learners with typographical cues such as bolding and italics to draw their attention to grammatical forms in the text.

Textual enhancement is used to make particular features (in the examples that follow feminine gender agreement form -*a*- in Italian) of written input more salient with the scope to help learners notice these forms and eventually make form-meaning connections. The target form is enhanced by visually altering (see the following example in Italian enhancing gender agreement forms) its appearance in the text (italicized, bolded, underlined, see following examples). Oral input enhancement can also be provided by using special stress, intonation, and gestures in spoken input.

Step 1. Leggi il brano. (Read the text.)

La mia camera nuov**a** è molto spazios**a**. Nella mia camera c"è un tavolo grigi**o**, un armadio alt**o** e bianc**o** e un letto ampi**o** e comod**o**. La mamma ha messo una tenda legger**a** e un tappeto viol**a**. C"è anche una libreria pien**a** di libri.

Step 2. Disegna la camera descritta. (Draw the room described.)

Step 1. Leggi il seguente brano. (Read the following text.)

Oggi sul giornale ho letto una brutt**a** notizia! La vecchi**a** libreria dove compravo i libri quando ero piccol**o**, ha chiuso per sempre. Il signor Antonio, il suo proprietario, mi conosceva bene e mi consigliava sempre cosa leggere.

Al posto della piccol**a** libreria apriranno una famos**a** libreria che è conosciuta in tutta Italia. Sono molto arrabbiat**o** per questa notizia!

Step 2. Riordina gli eventi dal più vecchio al più recente. (Reorder events from the oldest to the most recent.)

– Aprono una libreria famos**a**
– Sono molto arrabbiat**o**
– Antonio mi consigliava
– Ho letto una brutt**a** notizia
– La vecchi**a** libreria ha chiuso per sempre

Designing input enhancement tasks will involve following these guidelines:

(1) Choose a grammatical feature that L2 learners need to pay attention to. There are "forms" that language learners would find difficult to learn because the lack of frequency, saliency, or redundancy, for example (see Chapter 1 for a definition of these terms);
(2) Highlight the feature in the text using a textual enhancement technique (e.g., bolding, underlining). This is a technique to increase saliency of this form in the input so as to increase opportunities for noticing;
(3) Keep learner's attention on meaning. Again, the main objective is to enhance the opportunities to make form-meaning connections;
(4) Do not provide any metalinguistic explanation.

The advantages of this textual enhancement activity are as follows: learners can be exposed to more instances of the target form; therefore there are more chances that they will notice the form; learners will be exposed to meaning-bearing input from this type of tasks; and it is a form of input enhancement that can be easily integrated and is easy to use. Success in using textual enhancement depends on the following: proficiency level of language learners; the developmental stage and the degree of readiness of the learner; the type of form chosen; and the intensity of the treatment.

Input Flood
Input flood is a more implicit pedagogical intervention to grammar instruction. The input learners receive is saturated with the form that we hope learners will notice and possibly acquire. The form is not highlighted in any way. When designing input flood activities, the following guidelines should be followed:

(1) Grammatical tasks using input flood should either be used in written or oral input;

(2) The input learners receive must be modified so that it contains many instances of the same form/structure. This is to provide language learners with ample opportunities to encounter a certain linguistic feature (increase frequency in the input). Learners are likely to notice the form, and its meaning unconsciously and without metalinguistic explanations or error corrections;

(3) Input flood must be meaningful and learners must be doing something with the input (i.e., reconstruct a story, draw a picture, answer content questions).

Input flood is an implicit pedagogical intervention to grammar instruction where L2 learners receive input saturated with the target form.

The main purpose of designing input flood activities is to help learners be exposed to a greater amount of input (through this technique) containing the target form (past tense in Italian is flooded in the example that follows) that will allow (hopefully) L2 learners to notice and subsequently acquire this form.

Sabato scorso, Gaia è saltata giù dal letto alle 8 del mattino. Si è versata tre forti tazze di caffè per svegliarsi completamente. Ha guardato la TV ed è uscita. Ha lavorato a Starbucks tutto il giorno. Dopo ha preso l'autobus per tornare a casa. Per il traffico ha aspettato più di un'ora per l'autobus. Alla fine è arrivata a casa e ha bevuto un te ed è andata a dormire.

(Text continues)

Follow-up: dopo aver ascoltato il testo, cerca di ricordarti il giorno di Gaia … in coppia cerca di ricordarne il maggior numero di cose che ha fatto. Vince chi si ricorda il maggior numero di cose. Hai tre minuti.

After having listened to the text, try to remember the day of Gaia. In pairs, try to remember the greatest number of things she has done.

The winner is the one who remembers the greatest number of things. You have three minutes.

Overall advantages for input flood are that input flood material can be accommodated easily to any subject in which learners are interested and the instructor can simply manipulate any materials so that this input contains many uses of a particular target form. Input flood might be an effective "focus on form" subject to factors such as the length of the treatment and the nature of the linguistic feature. The main advantage of input flood is that it provides comprehensible meaning-bearing input. It is also effective, as it does not disrupt the flow of communication. However, as this technique is so implicit, it is difficult for instructors to know whether learners are learning anything through the flood.

Structured-Based Focused Options

Making certain features salient in the input might help drawing learners' attention to those specific features and facilitate acquisition. Enhancing the input through different techniques might be sufficient in helping learners paying attention to the formal properties of a targeted language without the need of metalinguistic discussion. Consciousness-raising tasks refer to external attempts to drawn learners' attention to formal properties of a target language.

Consciousness-Raising Tasks

The goal of consciousness raising is to make learners conscious of the rules that govern the use of particular language forms while providing the opportunity to engage in meaningful interaction.

During consciousness-raising tasks L2 learners develop explicit knowledge about how the target language works and are pushed to negotiate meaning. Explicit knowledge should help learners notice that form in subsequent communicative input, while negotiation of meaning (interaction) can expose learners to more comprehensible input. During consciousness-raising activities, learners are encouraged to discover the rules in consciousness raising. They are provided with some data and then asked to arrive (through some practice/tasks) at an explicit understanding of some linguistic property of the target language. Raising consciousness about a particular form enables learners to notice it in communicative input.

> Consciousness-raising tasks make learners conscious of a target form.

There is a clear distinction between traditional grammar instruction and consciousness raising. Traditional practice is production-based whereas the main aim of a consciousness-raising task is to construct a conscious representation of the target feature. In consciousness-raising tasks greater attention is paid to the form-meaning relationship while there is an attempt to situate grammatical structure and elements in questions within a broader discourse context. With this pedagogical intervention there is an attempt to equip the learner with an understanding of a specific grammatical feature.

In the case of a consciousness-raising task, L2 learners are provided with some language data and are required to provide an explicit representation of the target linguistic feature.

Consciousness-raising tasks (see following example) should be designed with the following guidelines in mind:

(1) The task focuses on a source of difficulty for second language learners;
(2) The data provided is adequate to make learners discover the rule;
(3) The task requires minimal production on the part of the learner; and
(4) There is an opportunity for applying the rule to construct a personal statement to promote its storage as explicit knowledge.

Step 1
Here is some information about where three people live or have lived.

Name	Dove abita/ha abitato	Da quanto tempo
Alessandro	Canada	5 anni
Bernadette	Dubai	6 mesi
Stefano	Milano	10 giorni

Step 2
Study these sentences about these people. When is "per" used and when is "da" used?

(a) Alessandro abita in Canada da 5 anni.
(b) Bernadette ha abitato a Dubai per sei mesi.
(c) Stefano abita a Milano da 10 giorni.

Step 3
Which of the following sentences are ungrammatical? Why?

(a) Bernadette abita a Dubai da 6 mesi.
(b) Alessandro ha abitato in Canada per 5 anni.
(c) Stefani ha abitato a Milano per 10 giorni.

Step 4
Try and make up a rule to explain when "per" and "da" are used.
   The advantages of consciousness-raising tasks are as follows:

(1) Learners can be exposed to grammatical forms or structures and they are given opportunities to work out the grammatical properties;
(2) Attention is given to the form-meaning relationships in a broader discourse context; and
(3) Learners are exposed to meaning-bearing input.

Consider this ...

Can you develop a consciousness-raising task?

Output-Based Options to Grammar Instruction
In this section, output-based options to grammar instruction will be considered. The role of output in second language acquisition has been considered from two main perspectives: skill-building hypothesis and comprehensible output hypothesis.

From the skill-building hypothesis perspective, L2 learners should first learn rules or items consciously and then gradually automatize them through practice. From a comprehensible output perspective, comprehensible input is not sufficient for developing nativelike grammatical competence. Learners need opportunities for *pushed output* (speech or writing that demands learners to produce language correctly and appropriately in a meaningful context).

Output might contribute to language acquisition in various ways:

(1) Learners can test out their hypotheses about how they express their meaning in a second language. Learners may use language production as a way of trying out new language forms and structures as they stretch their interlanguage (new language they are acquiring). They may use their output to test what works and what does not;

(2) Learners might notice a gap in their linguistic ability. Producing the target language may prompt second language learners to recognize consciously some of their linguistic problems;

(3) Learners can reflect consciously on the target language. These reflections produced in the context of making meaning may serve the function of deepening learners' awareness of forms and rules and the relationship of those forms and rules to the meaning they're trying to express;

(4) Through output meaningful production, L2 learners might negotiate meaning and provide language input for somebody else;

(5) Learners can pay attention to the means by which meaning is expressed. Output helps the development of discourse skills. Learners can move from sentence to discourse production.

Dictogloss

Dictogloss is a type of collaborative output task that aims at helping learners to use their grammar resources to reconstruct a text and become aware of their own shortcomings and needs. It consists of a listening phase and a reconstruction phase where learners are asked to reconstruct a text rather than write down the exact words they hear during the listening phase. As the text is read at a natural speed, learners are asked to focus on the key words to understand the meaning of the texts and use the information they have processed to reconstruct the passage.

> Dictogloss is a collaborative output task aiming at developing L2 learners' ability to understand and reconstruct a language text.

There are four stages to follow to develop dictogloss tasks:

(1) Preparation stage: when L2 learners are informed about the topic of the text and through a series of warm-up discussions they are given the necessary vocabulary to cope with the task. It is at this stage that they are also organized into groups;

(2) Dictation stage: this is the stage when L2 learners hear the text for the first time at natural speed. The first time they do not take any notes. The second time, learners are asked to note down key words to help them remember the content and reconstruct the text;

(3) Reconstruction stage: when L2 learners work together in small groups and they need to reconstruct the text with correct grammar and content; and

(4) Analysis and Correction stage: when L2 learners analyze, compare, and correct their texts. This is achieved with the help of the teacher and the other groups.

A dictogloss is a very effective output task for many reasons:

- Learners are encouraged to focus their attention on form and meaning and all four language skills are practiced;
- Learners develop a need for communication and for group work; learners can monitor and adjust their interlanguage; and
- Learners have ample opportunity for discussion and negotiation.

In the following example, learners are encouraged to monitor and reflect on grammatical properties of the new language.

In dictogloss tasks, the language teacher introduces the main idea of the story and distributes copies of a passage/or reads the passage to the participants (Stage 1). Then, they are asked to form pairs and to understand the meaning of the story (Stage 2). The teacher collects the copies from the students and asks them to reconstruct the passage in pairs as close to the original passage as possible. The teacher stresses the usage of passive voice when appropriate (Stage 3). The teacher gives back the original passage to the students and asks them to compare their constructed passage to the original passage and make notes on places that are different from the original passage (Stage 4).

Stage 1
Listen to the text and take note of as many words as possible.

Stage 2
Compare your notes with your partner and try to put the text together.

Stage 3
Compare the text version with another pair and look at the similarities and differences.

Stage 4
Similar, different?

Structured Output Tasks

Input is not enough for developing the ability to use language in communicative context. L2 learners need opportunities to express a particular meaning by retrieving a particular form or structure (the ability to string structures and forms together) from their internal language system. The fact that learners incorporate structures and forms in the language system does not mean they can have automatic access to them for speech production.

Mechanical exercises (see following example) do not make use of the same brain processes involved in accessing language. They bypass deeper levels of processing where form-meaning connections are involved.

Use the following verbs to describe what you have done this weekend.

Model: work → *I have worked at the bar this week*

1. Study
2. Write
3. Speak

Can classroom output practice focusing on form also be practice that focuses on information exchange? Structured output tasks are an effective alternative to mechanical output practice. Structured output activities have two main characteristics:

– They involve the exchange of previously unknown information; and
– They require learners to access a particular form or structure to process meaning.

To develop structured output tasks the following guidelines should be followed:

(1) Present one thing at a time (one form/one function).
(2) Keep meaning in focus (obtaining information).
(3) Move from sentences to connected discourse (string sentences together).
(4) Use both oral and written output (prepare questions and interview somebody).
(5) Others must respond to the content of the output (the output created contains a message and someone must respond to the content of the message, e.g., comparing, taking notes, filling out a grid or chart, signing something, indicating agreement, responding).
(6) The learner must have some knowledge of the form or structure (should follow structured input tasks).

In the following example the focus is on one form and one meaning and learners must respond to the content of the output.

> Structured output tasks involve the exchange of previously unknown information. Learners access a form/structure to process meaning.

Step 1. Indicare se si eseguono ciascuna delle seguenti attività spesso o raramente.

Activities	Spesso	Raramente
Giocare a calcio		
Andare in piscina		
Guardare la TV		
Leggere un libro/giornale		
Ascoltare la musica		

Step 2. Utilizzando le informazioni del passaggio 1, crea una serie di domande da porre al tuo compagno durante un'intervista.

Step 3. Intervista il tuo compagno di classe.

Step 4. Prepara una serie di affermazioni in cui confronti ciò che stai facendo e ciò che il tuo compagno di classe sta facendo usando i pensieri del punto 1.2.3. Presenterai i tuoi risultati alla classe e, dopo aver ricevuto feedback dagli altri compagni di classe, tracciare le abitudini di alcuni studenti.

The other example of structured output tasks uses the English causative and the he "form" to practice.

Step 1. Indicate which of the following activities you did **yourself** and which **you asked someone else** to do for you last week.

Example: "I tidied my room last week, but I had my desk dusted by my brother, because I'm allergic to dust."

Chores	Done by Myself	Have It Done by Someone Else
Clean the windows		
Mop the floor		
Do the dishes		
Cook dinner		
Iron the clothes		
Repair something		
Do the laundry		

Step 2. Using the information from step 1, create a series of questions (maximum 5) to ask your classmate during an interview.

Example: "Did you tidy your room yourself or did you have it tidied by someone else last week?"

Step 3. Interview your classmate. Be sure to write down your classmate's responses because you will need them later.

Step 4. Prepare a set of statements (maximum five) in which you compare the chores you ask someone else to do for you with the chores your classmate asks someone else to do for him/her using the ideas from steps 1, 2, and 3. You will present your results to the class, and after you have received feedback from other classmates you will draw some conclusion about which chores are the least popular among the students of your class.

As we have previously said, traditional grammar instruction is not an appropriate way to approach the teaching of grammatical forms and the structure of a second language. Paradigmatic explanation of a grammatical rule followed by mechanical and meaningful drill practice is not an effective way to focus on form in the language classroom.

However, there are types of "focus on form" pedagogical interventions to grammar instruction, as described in this chapter, that can in certain cases and conditions enhance and speed up the way languages are learned and are an effective way to incorporate grammar teaching and grammar tasks in communicative language teaching.

Consider this ...

Why is it important for L2 learners to attend to meaning in output tasks?

Can you underscore the difference between structured input and structured output?

If we are going to focus on form (grammatical form, grammatical structure) in any way in the classroom, it ought to be input based and meaning oriented. This idea falls out of what we know about the nature of acquisition; that is, how it is tied to input within communicative settings and not explanation + practice. What implications are there for instruction?

Focus on Form Is Not a Singular Thing. There Is No One Way to Do It. Language Teachers Have Options.

What this implication means is that focus on form or input enhancement comes in a variety of different pedagogical interventions. In addition to those presented here, there are others. Teachers are free to explore how to focus on form in the communicative classroom. As we have said before, there is no one way to provide effective focus on form instruction. As this book has tried to show, there should be principles that guide teachers in decision making to fashion their own curricula. Likewise, understanding what the parameters are for a focus on form allows teachers to make decisions about what to do and when to do it. This reflection leads us to a follow-up implication.

Because Focus on Form Exists Does Not Mean Teachers Have to Focus on Form.

The research on focus on form is wobbly; that is, the results of the research are not always clear. One of the problems with the research is the way scholars measure outcomes of the intervention. Just how do we know acquisition has happened after an intervention? Some scholars have argued that there is a huge bias toward explicit testing and tapping of explicit knowledge in the research on focus on form. What is more, given what we know about the slow and piecemeal nature of acquisition, it is hardly probable that focus on form causes instantaneous acquisition of a particular property of language. In fact, it is probably impossible. That is, if we conduct one experiment, what do we really show in that one experiment? But researchers and teachers cling to the idea that we can make a difference in acquisition in some way by focusing on grammar. After all, isn't that what instruction is supposed to do? I would argue that we are doing precisely that – making a difference – by offering a communicatively oriented approach to focus on form. Because of how language grows in the mind and communication develops over time, a communicative and truly proficiency-oriented classroom is already doing what it is supposed to do: helping the learner. In the case of focus on form teachers should move from input options to output options, from structured input to structured output tasks. This is in line with how acquisition happens (see Chapter 1 and the figure that follows).

Input →Intake →Language System →Output →

    ↑   ↑

Textual Enhancement   Structured Output

Input Flood   Dictogloss

Structured Input

What Is the Role of Vocabulary?

Joe Barcroft has suggested that, based on existing research in second language acquisition, the following principles would promote effective vocabulary acquisition:

(1) Ensure we develop vocabulary tasks to target what vocabulary learners are going to be exposed to;

(2) Present new words frequently and repeatedly in the input. There's a great deal of research suggesting that frequency and repeated exposure is useful for learners and learning;

(3) Promote incidental vocabulary learning. Incidental vocabulary learning is when L2 learners pick up new words when they are still exposed to them in the input and, again, preferably multiple times, frequently, and repeatedly;

(4) Use comprehensible and message-oriented input when presenting new words; and

(5) Present new words in an enhanced manner. Most research on input enhancement has – to date at least – focused on enhancement for the acquisition of grammatical forms in second language, but there is some growing body of research on different types of enhancements that you can use to facilitate the acquisition of a target vocabulary.

Language teachers would need to plan for vocabulary learning. In traditional instruction vocabulary is often learned by heart, and there is time assigned by the teachers to language learners for learning specific words. In a more communicative approach to language teaching, all words and lexical items are presented in the input in a frequent and repeated manner.

To make vocabulary easy to understand and process, teachers might consider presenting vocabulary using pictures to clarify meaning, providing definitions of words or giving learners a list of words to familiarize with ahead of time.

Teachers should ensure that vocabulary is used within a meaningful context where the input is simplified and easy to comprehend. Words can be enhanced in the input to facilitate comprehension and processing. A good example of vocabulary teaching in information exchange tasks is the one we presented in Chapter 3 and we now present in the following section.

Vocabulary

Once the interactive information exchange task has been set, the question is: What kind of vocabulary do learners need to complete the task? Therefore, we develop a series of subtasks so that we provide the necessary lexical tools for learners to complete the task. We expect learners to become familiar with words such as *reading books, watching movies, hobbies, sports, writing poetry/ prose, learning to play the piano/violin*, and so forth. Additionally, they will need to know some temporal expressions such as: *in the morning, afternoon, evening,* and so forth. They will probably need to know how to say the days of the week (*Monday, Tuesday*) because activities may vary depending on the day. Several lesson subgoals may include work with these lexical items (see Activity A that follows).

Activity A

Step 1. Write three things that one of your classmates does in his or her free time but you do not think your instructor does. Make a list of three things that your classmate does in his or her free time and your instructor does as well.

Step 2. A volunteer reads his or her statements to the class and someone should write then on the board in two columns. Once the volunteer has finished, classmates should continue reading new statements aloud to make the lists on the board as complete as possible.

Subgoal tasks for the days of the week and expression of time can also be planned, as in the following example (see Activities B and C that follow).

Activity B

Step 1. Write a few sentences about activities you do in your free time each day of the week. Leave a blank after each one.

EXAMPLE: I go to the gym every Monday. _____

Step 2. Now go about the room telling different classmates about your classes and ask them if they do the same. If so, get that person's signature in the blank. If not, move on to someone else. You must try to obtain five different signatures for the five different days of the week. Be prepared to answer questions that your instructor will ask when you are finished obtaining signatures.

Activity C

Step 1. Using time expressions that you have learned in this lesson, indicate when you do the following activities on a particular day of the week. The last items indicate that you should come up with two activities not on the list.

EXAMPLE: On Sunday afternoon, I watch TV.

watch TV
go out with friends
walk in nature and take photographs
read a book
exercise
?_____
?_____

Step 2. Break into groups of three and present your sentences to the two other classmates. They should indicate whether they do the same things. When you have finished, they should add any activities that they do, and you did not mention.

EXAMPLE: (you say) I watch TV on Saturdays, but usually in the morning.
            (Other person) Me, too.
            or
            (Other person) I don't. I only watch TV at night.

In each of the activities we see that the tasks require students to use language in a manner similar to that required for the final lesson task. In Activity B they use the days of the week to make statements about themselves and to get information from someone else. In Activity C they must choose time expressions to make sentences about themselves. These tasks indicate that learners have achieved a certain lesson subgoal: the ability to use certain words from the vocabulary to exchange information related to daily routines.

Recap

- Structured input tasks help language learners to process input correctly and efficiently and therefore increases the learner's intake.
- Input enhancement provides language learners with access to comprehensible input, furnishes positive evidence, and helps them to pay attention and to notice grammatical forms in the input.
- Consciousness-raising tasks help learners pay attention to grammatical forms in the input while providing the necessary input language learners need to acquire a L2.
- Collaborative output tasks are useful tasks as they provide language learners with an opportunity to produce output, promote negotiation of form, and at the same time develop learners' linguistic skills.
- Here are some of the principles language teachers should consider when developing grammar tasks and providing grammar instruction in the language classroom:
  - Grammar tasks should be developed to ensure that language learners process input correctly and efficiently;
  - Grammar tasks should be designed for language learners to notice and process forms in the input and eventually make correct form-mapping connections;
  - Grammar tasks should include both a focus on form and a focus on meaning;
  - Grammar tasks should move from input to output practice. Structured output tasks should be used to promote language production and the development of grammatical skills.
- Vocabulary instruction should keep in mind the following: present new word repeatedly and frequently in the input; use comprehensible and meaningful input when processing new words; and make available words in an enhanced manner.
- Vocabulary tasks should be input oriented (activities or quizzes).

What Is the Nature of Corrective Feedback?

Should Errors Be Corrected?

Interactional input refers to input received during interaction where there is some kind of communicative exchange involving the learner and at least another person (e.g., conversation, classroom interactions). Through these interactions, learners have the advantage of being able to negotiate meaning and make some conversational adjustments. This means that conversation and interaction make linguistics features salient to the learner who may be able to notice specific linguistic features they would not notice otherwise. The ability for language learners to notice might influence their acquisition of a new language. How learners are led to notice things can happen in several ways.

> Interactional input refers to input received during interaction where there is some kind of communicative exchange involving the learner and at least another person.

Learners can be exposed to modified input. Input modifications happen when the other speaker adjusts his or her speech due to perceived difficulties in learner comprehension. Learners can then receive some corrective feedback. The other speaker indicates in some way that the learner has produced something nonnativelike. Conversational interaction and negotiation can also facilitate acquisition.

A typical interactional feedback exchange is the following:

TEACHER/NS: Where did you go last summer?
STUDENT/NNS: I was in vacation in Italy.
TEACHER/NS: Oh, where were you on vacation in Italy?
STUDENT/NNS: I was in Tuscany.
TEACHER/NS: Oh, you where were on vacation in Tuscany?
STUDENT/NNS: Yes, on vacation in Tuscany.

Learners sometimes request clarifications or repetitions if they do not understand the input they receive. In the attempt to facilitate acquisition, one person can request the other to modify his/her utterances or the person modifies his/her own utterances to be understood. Various kinds of interactional feedback have been associated to language acquisition. Among these types of corrective feedback techniques used for modifying interaction the most common are:

- *Clarification requests* can be defined as an expression used to clarify learners' utterances (e.g., cosa hai detto? What did you say?);
- *Confirmation checks* are used by learners and teachers when it is not clear what has been said (e.g., ho capito bene … .? Did I understand correctly?);
- *Comprehension checks* are used when one speaker is not convinced that the other speaker has understood what has been said (e.g., hai capito cosa voglio dire? Do you know what I mean?);
- *Recast* is the reformulation of a speaker's erroneous utterance.

Consider this ...

Do you know what recast is? Can you provide an example?

From a universal grammar perspective, the application of corrective feedback has little impact on second language acquisition because it merely affects performance and leaves the underlying competence untouched. Stephen Krashen has argued for no effects of corrective feedback as he believes that knowledge consciously learned through explicit instruction cannot have a significant impact on second language acquisition.

From an interaction perspective, however, Michael Long has argued that corrective feedback is effective as it provides direct and indirect information about the grammaticality of the utterances as well as additional positive evidence that may otherwise be absent in the input.

In particular, negotiation for meaning triggers interactional adjustments and facilitates second language acquisition as it connects input, internal learner capacities, particularly selective attention, and output in productive ways. James Lee has defined negotiation of meaning as interactions during which speakers come to terms, reach agreements, solve a problem, or settle an issue by conferring or discussing.

Nine main corrective feedback techniques have been researched and proposed to support the view that errors should be corrected: recast, explicit corrective feedback, metalinguistic information, elicitation, clarification requests, repetition, prompt, translation, and nonverbal feedback.

Corrective feedback techniques:

- Recast
- Explicit corrective feedback
- Metalinguistic information
- Elicitation
- Clarification requests
- Repetition
- Prompt
- Translation
- Nonverbal feedback

These types of interactional feedback have positive effects on the acquisition of a language. However, comprehensible input and interaction might not be sufficient to develop nativelike grammatical competence, and L2 learners also need comprehensible output. Language teachers should always expose learners to comprehensible input and give them the opportunities to communicate and interact with each other during instruction. Learners should be involved in learning tasks where they have opportunities to communicate and negotiate meaning.

Research conducted on the effects of interactional feedback provide support for the overall role of corrective feedback:

- Corrective feedback techniques should be used to elicit student-generated repairs (self-repairs);
- Single linguistic feature (one at a time) should be targeted;
- One size does not fit all;
- Self-correction should be encouraged.

What Is the Role of Corrective Feedback?

Corrective feedback can occur in two different ways: reformulations and elicitation techniques. Reformulations are those corrective feedback techniques such as recast. Elicitations refer to other corrective feedback techniques that do not provide L2 learners with the correct form. Repair techniques such as clarification requests do not provide language learners with targetlike forms. Learners are encouraged to repair their own errors by providing them with a prompt and thus a chance to reformulate their utterance. Rod Ellis has renamed these two interactional feedback approaches as: input providing and output prompting approaches.

There are also two main types of learners' uptake (learners' reaction following language teachers' feedback): uptake that produces a new sentence still needing repair and uptake that produces a repair of the error on which the language instructor's feedback is focused.

> Two types of uptake:
>
> - Uptake that produces a new sentence still needing repair; and
> - Uptake that produces a repair of the error on which the language instructor's feedback is focused.

How Should We Correct Errors?
Recast
Recast was originally used in L1 research to investigate responses by adults to children's utterances. In second language acquisition recast can be defined as teacher's reformulation of all or part of a student's utterance, minus the error. Two main

classifications of recast have been proposed: (a) simple recast deals with minimal changes to the language learner's utterance and (b) complex recast is concerned with providing the language learner with substantial additions. Recast is used by teachers to make sure that the speaker becomes aware that something is wrong in their speech production. The following is one example of how recast can be used:

NNS: It bugs me when a bee stving me.
NS: Oh, when a bee stings me.
NNS: Stings me.
NS: Do you get stung often?

In the preceding example, the nonnative speaker produces a sentence that contains an error. The native speaker (language teacher) provides recast by reformulating learner's incorrect form into a correct form. The successful correction made by the nonnative speaker is called uptake. The native speaker continues the interaction in the attempt not to break the flow of communication. The degree of explicitness in using this technique would vary also depending on the use of intonational signals. In the example that follows the added stress makes the recast more explicit:

NNS: It bugs me when a bee sting me.
NS: Oh, when a bee STINGS me.
NNS: Stings me.
NS: Do you get stung often?

Recasts are an interactional and implicit corrective feedback technique that can be implemented in different ways. The NS reformulated the NNS utterance with the intention to correct one or multiple errors. There is no general agreement among language researchers and practitioners regarding the effectiveness of recasts.

Explicit Corrective Feedback

Explicit corrective feedback is characterized by an overt and clear indication of the existence of an error and the provision of the targetlike reformulation and can take two forms: explicit correction and metalinguistic feedback. In explicit correction, the teacher provides both positive and negative evidence by clearly saying that what the L2 learner has produced is erroneous (You don't say *goed* ... you say *went*.)

Metalinguistic Feedback

In metalinguistic feedback, the focus of conversation with the language learner is diverted toward rules or features of the target language. Metalinguistic feedback is divided into three subcategories: metalinguistic comments, metalinguistic information, and metalinguistic questions. The least informative one is metalinguistic comments that only indicate the occurrences of an error. Metalinguistic information not only indicates the occurrences or location of the error but also offers some metalanguage that alludes to the nature of the error. Metalinguistic questions point to the nature of the error but attempt to elicit the information from the learner. Metalinguistic feedback provides NNS with a metalinguistic cue in the input and/or metalinguistic feedback about the correctness of an utterance (see following examples).

> NNS: I see him in the office yesterday.
> NS: You need a past tense (metalinguistic cue)
> NNS: He catch a fish.
> NS: Caught is the past tense. (metalinguistic feedback and correction)

Elicitation

Elicitation is a correction technique that prompts the L2 learner to self-correct and may be accomplished in one of the following three ways during face-to-face interaction, each of which vary in their degree of implicitness or explicitness. One of these strategies is request for reformulations of an ill-formed utterance. The second one is using open questions. The last strategy, which is the least communicatively intrusive and hence the most implicit, is the use of strategic pauses to allow a learner to complete an utterance. With direct elicitation the NS attempts to elicit relevant information from the NNS. There is no correction but an opportunity for self-repair/correction (see following example).

> NNS: And when the young girl arrive, ah, beside the old woman.
> NS: When the young girl ...?

Clarification Requests

Feedback that carries questions indicating that the utterance has been ill-formed or misunderstood and that a reformulation or a repetition is required are identified as clarification requests. Clarification requests, unlike explicit error correction, recasts, and translations, can be more consistently relied upon to generate modified output from learners because it might not supply the learners with any information concerning the type or location of the error. Clarification requests occur when there is a breakdown of communication between two speakers. One speaker asks the other speaker to clarify his/her utterance. It does not provide the speaker with the correct form; however, it gives the other speaker the opportunity for self-repair. Phrases such as "sorry?" or "what did you say?" or "say it again, please" provide the learner with an opportunity to clarify and/or make his utterance more accurate. The following is an example of clarification requests.

NNS: I can find no [ruddish].
NS: *I'm sorry. You couldn't find what?*

Prompt

In the related literature two other terms are used interchangeably to refer to this kind of feedback; that is, negotiation of form and form-focused negotiation. Prompts consist of four prompting moves: elicitation, metalinguistic clue, clarification request, and repetition. All these moves offer learners a chance to self-repair by withholding the correct form.

Repetition

Another approach to provide corrective feedback is repetition that is less communicatively intrusive in comparison to explicit error correction or metalinguistic feedback and hence falls at the implicit extreme on the continuum of corrective feedback. This feedback is simply the teacher's or interlocutors' repetition of the ill-formed part of the student's utterance, usually with a change in intonation.

Translation

Translation was initially considered as a subcategory of recasts, but what distinguishes it from recast is that the former is generated in response to a learner's ill-formed utterance in the target language while the latter is generated in response to a learner's well-formed utterance in a language other than the target language. What translation and recast have in common is that they both lack overt indicators that an error has been produced. This shared feature places both toward the implicit end of the corrective feedback spectrum, though the degree to which translations are communicatively obtrusive can also vary. Translations also have another feature in common with recast as well as explicit error correction, that is, they all contain the targetlike reformulation of the learner's error and thus provide the learner with positive evidence.

Nonverbal Feedback

Nonverbal feedback is also another form of corrective feedback. Body movements and signals such as gestures, facial expressions, rolling your eyes, crossing your arms, head, hand, and finger movements are all different forms of feedback. Nonverbal feedback is feedback that the teacher provides to students with their actions (e.g., smiling, patting a student's shoulder).

Consider this ...

What are the advantages to using communicative tasks? How can they facilitate corrective feedback?

Exemplary Study

In the exemplary study described in the text that follows six different corrective feedback types and two main types of learners' uptake (learners' reaction following language instructor's feedback) are identified: uptake that produces a new sentence still needing repair and uptake that produces a repair of the error on which the language instructor's feedback is focused.

The results from this study showed that recasts and explicit correction did not result in learner-generated repair. However, when learners were more engaged in the language process using other techniques (e.g., elicitations, clarification requests), they were able to self-repair.

Lyster, R., Ranta, L. (1997). Corrective Feedback and Learner Uptake: Negotiation of Form in Communicative Classrooms. *Studies in Second Language Acquisition*, 19, 37–66.

Main aims of the study:

- The purpose of this study was twofold: (1) to develop an analytic model comprising the various moves in an error treatment sequence and (2) to apply the model to a database of interaction in four primary L2 classrooms with a view to documenting the frequency and distribution of corrective feedback in relation to learner uptake.

Participants:

- Six French immersion classrooms in the Montreal area.
- Transcripts for about eighteen hours of classroom interaction over fourteen subject-matter lessons and thirteen French language arts lessons.

Materials and procedure:

- This observational study has yielded 100 hours of audio recordings of a variety of lessons in four Grade 4 classrooms (including one "split" Grade 4 and 5 class) and two Grade 6 classrooms across two different school boards.
- COLT (Communicative Orientation Language Teaching) and audio recordings were used to observe and capture interactions.

Results:

- The findings indicate an overwhelming tendency for teachers to use recasts despite the latter's ineffectiveness at eliciting student-generated repair.

- Four other feedback types – elicitation, metalinguistic feedback, clarification requests, and repetition – lead to student-generated repair more successfully and are thus able to initiate what the authors characterize as the negotiation of form.
- The results from this study showed that recasts and explicit correction did not result in learner-generated repair. However, when learners were more engaged in the language process using other techniques (e.g., elicitations, clarification requests), they were able to self-repair.

Conclusion:

- The data indicates that the feedback-uptake sequence engages students more actively when there is negotiation of form, that is, when the correct form is not provided to the students – as it is in recasts and explicit correction – and when signals are provided to the learner that assist in the reformulation of the erroneous utterance. Negotiation of form involves corrective feedback that employs either elicitation, metalinguistic feedback, clarification requests, or teacher repetition of error, followed by uptake in the form of peer- or self-repair, or student utterances still in need of repair that allow for additional feedback.
- L2 learners need opportunities for interaction and feedback in the classroom. From our previous discussion, the way to provide opportunities for communicative interaction is through the use of communicative tasks where L2 learners can interact, negotiate meaning, and produce language for a specific purpose.
- Interactional feedback has a positive effect on second language acquisition and teachers should consider the following: the type and nature of the target structure, target single rather than multiple errors, increase opportunities for negotiation, and provide feedback that promotes opportunities for modified output.

The following is a short recap of some of the main points raised in this chapter.

Recap

- Two questions addressed: Should we correct errors? How should we correct errors?
- Corrective feedback might play a facilitative role in second language acquisition.
- Corrective feedback techniques (although one size does not fit all) should elicit student-generated repairs.

- There are nine types of corrective feedback available to the teachers.
- Research has indicated the following
  - Corrective feedback techniques should be used to elicit student-generated repairs
  - Single linguistic feature (one at a time) should be targeted
  - One size does not fit all
  - Self-correction should be encouraged
  - Corrective feedback should be provided with some form of uptake

REFERENCES AND READINGS

- Barcroft, J. (2018). *Vocabulary in Language Teaching.* New York: Routledge.
- Benati, A., Lee, J. (2008). *Grammar Acquisition and Processing Instruction.* Clevedon: Multilingual Matters.
- Benati, A. (2005). The Effects of Processing Instruction, Traditional Instruction and Meaning-Output Instruction on the Acquisition of the English Past Simple Tense. *Language Teaching Research*, 9, 87–113.
- Benati, A., Schwieter, J. (2019). Pedagogical interventions to L2 grammar instruction. In J. Schwieter and A. Benati, (ed.) *The Cambridge Handbook of Language Learning* (475–495). Cambridge: Cambridge University Press.
- Doughty C., Williams, J. (eds.) (1998). *Focus on Form in Classroom Second Language Acquisition.* New York: Cambridge University Press.
- Lee, J., VanPatten, B. (2003). *Making Communicative Language Teaching Happen.* New York: McGraw-Hill.
- Long, M. (2007). *Problems in SLA.* New York: Lawrence Erlbaum Associates.
- Lyster, R., Ranta, L. (1997). Corrective Feedback and Learner Uptake: Negotiation of Form in Communicative Classrooms. *Studies in Second Language Acquisition*, 19, 37–66.
- Nassaji, H. (2015). *The Interactional Feedback Dimension in Instructed Second Language Learning.* London: Bloomsbury.
- Nassaji, H., Fotos, S. (2011). *Teaching Grammar in Second Language Classrooms.* New York: Routledge.
- Qin, J. (2008). The Effect of Processing Instruction and Dictogloss Tasks on Acquisition of the English Passive Voice. *Language Teaching Research*, 12, 61–82.
- Sheen, Y. (2011). *Corrective Feedback, Individual Differences and Second Language Learning.* New York: Springer.
- Nation, I. S. P. (2001). *Learning Vocabulary in Another Language.* Cambridge: Cambridge University Press.
- Wong, W. (2005). *Input Enhancement: From Theory and Research to the Classroom.* New York: McGraw-Hill.
- Wong, W., Simard, D. (2018). *Focusing on Form in Language Instruction.* New York: Routledge.

DISCUSSION AND QUESTIONS

1. Which of the input enhancement techniques or focus on form interventions do you see being able to use in the classroom? Why did you select this particular technique or techniques?

2. Let's imagine you are going to start a new unit called "What we did last night and what that says about us." Your first activity in class is to tell students the following: "OK, Class. I'm going to tell you five things I did last night [writes what last night means in the first language on the board]. Last night. Ready? I watched the news. I prepared dinner. I walked my dog. I drank a cocktail. I called my sister on the phone. OK. Let's see what you remember. Who did I call on the phone? What did I drink? What did I watch on TV? Excellent ! Good memory! OK. Look up here on the screen. [the same five activities are on the screen] OK. With someone next to you, I'm giving you two minutes to put these activities in the order in which I did them. Go ahead. One through five...." Also imagine this is the first time students are exposed to the past tense in the language you teach. How much do you have to explain about the past tense before you launch into this? Anything? All of it? Just a little bit? Think carefully about how this unit starts!

3. Identify a particular linguistic feature in a target language. Prepare two grammar tasks:
   - One input enhancement task
   - One structured input task

4. Read the following article and provide the requested info: Benati, A., Batziou M. (2019) The effects of structured-input and structured-output tasks on the acquisition of English causative. *IRAL*, 57 (3), 265–288. 10.1515/iral-2016-0038

Background
Motivation and Q/H
Methodology
Results
Significance of findings
Implications
Limitations and Further research

5. Based on what you read in this chapter and your knowledge about the subject, decide whether you agree or disagree with the following statements:
   Language instructors should make feedback salient and adopt techniques that require L2 learners to reflect on language structures or vocabulary.
   TRUE   FALSE

6. Language teachers should be eclectic in choosing an error correction technique depending on different factors (e.g., structures, levels of proficiency).
   TRUE   FALSE

7. Good language teachers understand that one size does not fit all. They might want to consider starting with less direct and implicit feedback and move progressively to more direct and explicit ones.
   TRUE   FALSE

8. Choosing to use a different type of corrective feedback that seems to produce student-generated repairs increases chances of reaching more learners.
   TRUE   FALSE

9. Why is it important to consider the nature of the instructional context when providing feedback?

10. In your opinion, what are the most effective characteristics of effective feedback? List them:

    1.

    2.

    3.

6 How Do We Carry Out Second Language Research?

Overview

In this chapter, the main characteristics of second language research will be outlined. Research design adopted to address questions in language learning and language teaching will be briefly presented. A minimal definition of second language research is the one that involves several interlinked stages. (1) There is an attempt to investigate a particular language behavior that is not clearly understood. (2) An initial hypothesis/question is formulated to investigate that behavior. (3) An observation of that behavior is carried out. (4) Some possible explanations about that behavior are suggested. (5) Data analysis shows that one possible explanation is considered the right one. Second language research has theoretical, methodological, and pedagogical purposes. Researchers are interested in testing and verifying a theory to develop a better understanding of how learners comprehend, process, and produce a second language. Researchers tend to address theoretical questions aimed at describing how learners develop an internal system and eventually can tap into that system for speech production. However, scholars often investigate the effectiveness of a particular theory, account, or hypothesis to offer practical implications for second language teaching and language teachers. Despite the fact that not all research is tied to instructional potential, research findings from classroom-based research, for instance, could lead to a revision of how best we teach languages.

What Are the Main Characteristics?

Research is cyclical and involves interrelated phases (see Figure 6.1). Initially, the researcher develops an interest. Reviewing the existing literature about a specific topic leads to the formulation of questions. Then the researcher establishes what kind of data would provide the appropriate evidence to address those questions. At this point, a research design must be chosen.

Once data are collected and analyzed, the findings are interpreted and related to the research questions raised at the beginning

Research as a cyclical process involving interrelated phases.

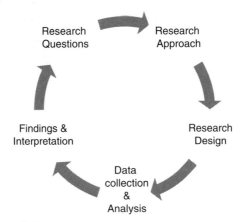

Figure 6.1. Research as a cyclical process

of the process. The answers obtained, however, do not close the research cycle as other questions might arise and further research avenues explored.

Research designs are usually chosen based on how best they address the purpose and the questions of a particular study. There are two types of research approaches: qualitative and quantitative.

A qualitative approach (see Figure 6.2) is usually an observation of human behaviors in the natural context. It involves the study of the characteristics of a group in the real world with no manipulation. The analysis of the data leads the researcher to the discovering of several phenomena such as patterns of learning behavior. The data can generate hypotheses that need further research to be tested. Common qualitative data collection instruments are observations, interviews, questionnaires, and diaries.

Example: You can conduct a study to develop an understanding of the type and amount of language that is learned by one subject to communicate with native speakers and to understand how conversational interaction contributes to learning a specific language. Journal entries and a diary can be used to collect your data.

> A qualitative approach is usually an observation of human behaviors in the natural context.

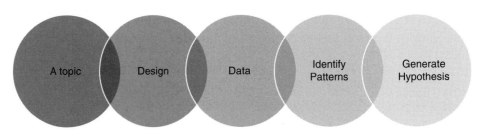

Figure 6.2. Qualitative research

A quantitative approach is normally used in experiments conducted to investigate the possible relationship between two variables (a teaching method and the measurement of the method, for example). It involves the formulation of questions/hypotheses before the experiment begins. The analysis of the data should provide an answer to the questions/hypotheses raised in the experiment. Tests, questionnaires, and observation schemes are used to collect data.

Example: You can carry out a study investigating the effects of two types of error corrections techniques (corrective feedback). Your population will be assigned to groups receiving a different treatment condition over a period (instructional period). A pretest/posttest procedure would be adopted measuring the effects of treatments. A quantitative research approach begins. A methodology is developed, and the data generated by the study are analyzed. The results obtained allow the researcher to deduct whether the hypothesis/hypotheses is/are true or false (see Figure 6.3).

> A quantitative approach is normally used in experiments conducted to investigate the possible relationship between two variables.

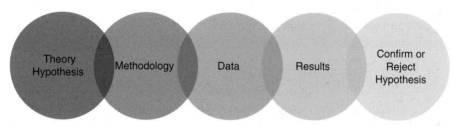

Figure 6.3. Quantitative approach

What Are the Main Research Designs?

Action Research Design

Action Research is a very effective research approach to undertake a small-scale investigation by a teacher in the language classroom. Through Action Research, language teachers can engage in research related to specific language problems to improve teaching materials, language teaching methodologies, and curriculum development. They can also undertake research for their own professional development, very often as part of school requirements. Action Research is often motivated by teachers reflecting on their own current teaching and developing ideas and intuitions about a specific problem or topic.

An action researcher may undertake a project individually in the classroom or cooperate with colleagues in investigating a question or a problem. Action Research can be defined as a process designed to address more effective ways in teaching languages and facilitating learning through identifying a specific

Action Research is one form of classroom-centered research that is seen as being small scale and situational trying to understand and perhaps solve some concrete problem in an individual teacher's classroom.

problem, targeting the causes of the problem through systematic data collection procedures (e.g., surveys, observation, interviews), and applying an effective solution to the problem as a result of the data being collected and interpreted.

If teachers are kept up-to-date with theory and research findings in language learning, not only would they improve their pedagogical practices, but they would also find the stimulus to conduct their own research to micro-evaluate teaching materials, or address particular teaching and learning problems arising in their own classroom.

The fundamental steps in Action Research are:

- Identifying a "problem" (Stage 1)
- Describing the "problem" (Stage 2)
- Planning the research (Stage 3)
- Intervening (Stage 4)
- Evaluating the results (Stage 5)
- Writing a report and disseminating results (Stage 6)
- Following up (Stage 7)

At the beginning the teacher identifies an issue or a "problem" concerning an aspect of language teaching or language learning in a classroom context (Stage 1). The "problem" is often something that is noticeable and persistent. The teacher decides to evaluate the extent of the "problem" through reflection, observation, and discussion with the students and other colleagues (baseline data).

Let's assume that the problem the teacher has identified is that students in the classroom always find it difficult to learn a specific grammatical feature of the language they are currently learning. The teacher finds and reads relevant texts that provide him/her with a better understanding of the specific problem. He/she hopes that research could somehow help him/her find some solutions to the problem. The following step is to describe the "problem" and to find out whether it is a common issue (Stage 2). The teacher spends time observing the class and taking notes on their students' behavior. After observation, the teacher forms a question or hypothesis as to the cause of the problem. He/she reaches this stage by reading and reflecting on literature (articles, surveys, reports) that has described similar problems. The cause of the "problem" might be that students need better practice and need to be exposed to more effective materials to master the grammatical feature.

At this stage (Stage 3) the teacher decides to engage in some form of systematic investigation to solve the problem. He creates an Action Research plan (Stage 4) that includes the following:

- A specific purpose
- Actionable research questions
- Ideas for data collection and analysis
- Timeline
- An evaluation plan

Three main components are the main characteristic of the Experimental Design:

Population
The Treatment
Measurements of the Treatment

To this end, s/he produces some "new material" to teach the students the target grammatical form. The teacher implements the new pedagogical approach in the classroom in the attempt to solve the problem. After a few weeks, the teacher observes a higher level of performance among students; previously, most of the students were making mistakes and not responding well to the material used. Several of the students now have improved in accuracy and fluency in using the particular target form. S/he sees a dramatic turnaround in students' ability to use the form correctly and appropriately and the teacher concludes that this is in part due to the data gathered through action research. The teacher is now ready to share the findings with others (Stage 6). The teacher has noticed that students understand better and perform much better than before. S/he then decides to disseminate and to share his/her findings with other teachers. Teachers can share the findings of their action research projects in local teacher's meetings as a presentation, in informal meetings with other colleagues, or by publishing their results for a larger body of readers. Action research reports get read and appear to have greater immediate impact on the lives and practices of other classroom teachers than the findings of second language researchers. The teacher looks now for other methods to solve his original classroom problem (Stage 7). The teacher makes some recommendations and suggests that the new approach used (the one used in the data collection) is a very effective way to learn and teach the grammatical feature. The follow-up of the action research is to show other teachers that the dynamics/problems present in a particular context might also be present in their contexts. This will hopefully spur other teachers on to starting action research projects of their own.

Exemplary Study

Sampson, Richard. 2012. The Language-Learning Self, Self-Enhancement Activities, and Self-Perceptual Change. *Language Teaching Research*, 16, 317–335.

Participants:

- Thirty-four Japanese native speakers
- Adults
- All learning English with mixed ability

Materials and procedure:

- Introspective methods were used in this study, particularly with the main purpose of collecting learners' views about learning experiences and their self-images.
- Free writing activity was used to collect information from students on their ideal life in the future after studying English.
- Students were asked to provide feedback on learning and practices. They were asked to complete a session entry in their learning journal. They were asked to reflect, at the end of each session, on the tasks and learning experience during the class.
- Students were asked to make a conversation skit reflecting on the semester's main tasks.
- A learning experience questionnaire was administered to all students at the end of the process. The questionnaire was both quantitative and qualitative measure in nature (numerical scale with additional open-ended components).

Results:

- The results from the free-writing task clearly indicated that only few students had a developed vision about their future self.
- The analysis of the learning journal entries, the reflective skit, and the final questionnaire provided the following findings:
  - Activities focusing on steps toward the development of the ideal self were considered highly motivating;
  - Activities focusing on the ideal future self or those that focused on the "failed" future self were also considered motivating activities by students; and
  - Activities that include a social component helped motivate students in several ways: broadening their thinking; improving a greater sense of possibility; and providing support for thinking about one's future self.

Conclusion:

- The results of this study confirmed that consultation with students about their self-images helps in creating motivating lessons enhancing learners' self-images.

Consider this ...

Consider a language classroom and think of a problem you have encountered (learning or teaching issues). Use the Action Research fundamental steps to prepare a plan.

Experimental Research Design

An alternative design to Action Research is the Experimental Research Design. It is the most common research design currently used in second language research. One of the essential characteristics of this design is that the researcher must systematically control and manipulate many variables to establish a significant relationship between them and avoid that extraneous variables might be influencing the outcomes of a study.

The Experimental Research Design consists of at least three components:

1. Questions and or hypotheses;
2. Data collection procedures;
3. Data analysis procedures to analyze and interpret the data collected.
   (1) Questions and/or hypotheses are generated as a result of critically analyzing existing theoretical views and current empirical research on a specific area of enquiry in second language learning.
   (2) To attempt to address research questions or hypotheses formulated on a specific area of enquiry, several data collection procedures can be used according to the nature of the experimental study. A standard procedure used is the pre- and posttest procedure.
   (3) To analyze and interpret the data collected, several data analysis procedures can be used. The analysis and interpretation of the data collected will provide an answer to the questions and/or hypotheses raised.

Experimental research is carried out to explore the strength of a relationship between independent and dependent variables. Scholars and practitioners are often interested in investigating the effects of factors such as a particular "teaching approach" or "technique" on language learners' performance. Learners' performance is usually measured through a test. The "teaching approach" is given the label of *independent variable*, and it is expected that this variable would influence the other variable (the test), called the *dependent variable*.

Experimental research is carefully planned and constructed so that the variables involved in the study are controlled and manipulated. Three main components can be identified in experimental research framework:

1. Participants ("units of assignment");
2. Instructional treatment ("treatment" or independent variable); and
3. Measurement of the instructional treatment ("outcome measure" or dependent variable).
   (1) The main objective of experimental research is to measure the relative effects of different instructional treatments given to participants arranged in groups. Comparison is the essence of experimental research. Groups can be formed by the researcher specifically for an experiment or preexisting

groups can be used. In forming groups for a study, researchers need to consider a subject's variability. Randomization or matching procedures are normally used to make sure that individual variables are distributed homogenously across groups. Randomization involves the random distribution of individual to groups. Matching involves the distribution of individual to groups by matching certain characteristics (e.g., age, gender, background). Researchers must make any efforts and take actions to control, to reduce, or possibly to eliminate other factors, except the ones under investigation, that might have an effect on the results of the study. For instance, the research might ensure that the groups are taught at the same time of the day to eliminate the "fatigue" factor.

2) The instructional treatment is the independent variable in an experimental research design, and it is specifically constructed for the experiment. An instructional treatment refers to a technique, method, or material presented under controlled circumstances. It is the variable that the researcher suspects may influence the dependent variable. A new grammar method might be very effective in improving learners' accuracy in producing a sentence or discourse containing a particular grammatical feature. The researcher chooses independent variables to measure their effects in relation to the dependent variables.

3) The measurement of the instructional treatment is the way in which the effects of the treatment are evaluated and observed. Different types of tests are the logical way to evaluate the effectiveness of a treatment. Scores from a data-gathering instrument usually provide information about the effectiveness of the independent variable. The dependent variable is the major and central variable that will be measured in an experimental study. There can be more than one in a study. Participants are usually tested prior to receiving their treatment (pretest) and after the instructional treatment (posttest) to measure the possible effects of the treatment factor. Experimental research makes use of pretest/posttest designs.

Within the experimental research framework, the independent factor is therefore a stimulus (e.g., a new method, a new technique) and the dependent factor is a response to that stimulus (e.g., student's performance on a test). Experiments in classroom settings are usually of two types: quasi-experimental (without random assignment) or truly experimental (with random assignment).

Example: A researcher wants to investigate the effectiveness of a "new treatment" in the teaching of Japanese passive constructions. A treatment group receiving the "new treatment" and a control group receiving no treatment are compared at the beginning of the experiment by means of pretests and are later compared at the end of the experimental period by means of posttests. The statistical analysis reveals that the treatment group scores are higher than the control group scores in the posttests.

Random assignment (see Figure 6.4) ensures that participants have an equal chance to be assigned to groups. In quasi-experimental and truly experimental designs a comparison is made between two or more groups. There are two types of group comparison: two or more groups receiving different treatments; two or more groups receiving different treatments and one of them receiving no treatment (control group).

Example: A study intends to compare the relative effects of two different instructional interventions (independent variable) on the acquisition of English past-tense regular forms. Participants are randomly assigned to three groups. The first group receives an innovative instructional treatment and the second group a more traditional instructional treatment. A control group is also used. This group is not exposed to any treatment. Two tests (dependent variable) are developed and consist of an aural interpretation task and a written completion production task at sentence level. A pre-test/post-test design is adopted. The scores are measured with the use of statistical analysis procedures that reveal that participants in the innovative group perform better than participants in the traditional group and the control group in all measures.

Randomization → Groups → Pretests → Instructional period → Posttests

Figure 6.4. Visual representation of a truly experimental design

Tests are commonly used as an instrument to collect data about participants' knowledge and performance on several areas such as grammar, metalinguistic awareness, vocabulary, and overall proficiency (e.g., interpretation tests; recall and multiple choice tests; grammaticality judgment tests).

Exemplary Study

Benati, A., Lee, J. (2010). Exploring the effects of processing instruction on discourse-level interpretation tasks with English past tense. In A. Benati and J. Lee. *Processing Instruction and Discourse* (178–197). London: Bloomsbury.

Participants:

- Twenty-nine Chinese native speakers
- School-age learners
- All learning English in a primary school

Materials and procedure:

- Pre- and posttest procedure.
- Subjects were randomly assigned to one of the following three groups: processing instruction ($n = 10$), traditional grammar instruction ($n = 9$), and a control group ($n = 10$).
- The instructional treatment lasted approximately six hours for the two groups. During the treatment period, feedback on performance was limited to telling participants whether an answer was right or wrong.
- Tests consisted of two interpretation tests: sentence level and discourse level.
- Statistical analysis was used to analyze data.

Results:

- The results of the statistical analysis clearly indicate that the processing instruction group improved from pretest to posttest on the interpretation of the sentence-level interpretation test. The performance of the processing instruction group was statistically significant and superior to the performance of the traditional and control groups.
- The results of the statistical analysis have clearly shown that the processing instruction treatment made significant improvement from pretest to posttest as measured by the discourse-level interpretation task. The performance of the processing instruction group was statistically significantly to the performance of the traditional and the control groups.

Conclusion:

- The results in this experimental research have confirmed the overall findings obtained by all studies investigating the effects of processing instruction at the sentence level. These studies have unanimously indicated that processing instruction is a very effective instructional treatment. In addition to that, this study provides additional support for the view that processing instruction is an effective instructional treatment in enhancing learners' ability to interpret a target form when it is embedded in discourse.

Consider this ...

Read the article written by A. Benati and J. Lee, 2010. (Exploring the Effects of Processing Instruction on Discourse-level Interpretation Tasks with English Past Tense. In A. Benati and J. Lee. *Processing Instruction and Discourse*, 178–197. London: Bloomsbury) in full and answer these questions:

What was the purpose of the study (academic importance)?
What was the research framework used?
What were the main findings and their significance?
What are the main implications?
What are the limitations of the study?

Observation Design

Observation has been one of the main research designs for observing classroom behaviors (through watching, listening, and recording) and it has provided important answers and insights into key questions/issues in second language acquisition. In second language research, observation is frequently used as an alternative to a formal experiment. An observation documents life inside the classroom; however, an observation study is different from an experimental study on three counts: assumptions, methods/procedures, and attitudes to evidence. In an experimental study the researcher investigates the possible relationship between an independent and a dependent variable. Experiments are analytical and hypothesis driven. They tend to investigate individual pieces of the language learning puzzle and are informed by specific questions and hypotheses formulated based on previous empirical research findings and the review of theoretical accounts.

Classroom observation is the main research design to observe classroom behavior in a natural context.

Observations are synthetic and data-driven approaches to second language research. In an observation study, a researcher will investigate a phenomenon in its entirety, the whole of the language learning puzzle. In other words, this research framework is data driven as the observer needs to collect enough data to be able to formulate a hypothesis or a question as a result of the analysis of the data collected.

Classroom observation belongs to the naturalistic tradition in its attempt to investigate language behavior in the natural context in which it occurs. It involves the study of the characteristics of a group in the real world, and the researcher makes no attempt to isolate or manipulate a phenomenon under investigation. Insights and generalizations emerge from close contact with the data rather than from a theory of language learning and use. In an observation the observer must consider three issues:

1. How the observation takes place (role of the observer and/or teacher). The main question is: Is the researcher planning to observe another teacher's class or observing his/her own class?
2. What observation items the research adopts (open or closed items). Using open items means that the observer has not determined exactly what she/he

is looking for. With the use of closed items, the observer has decided what he/she is looking for. The main question is: Does the observer know what he/she would like to observe? (The observer should develop and make use of closed items.) Or, is the observer starting with no predetermined categories? (The observer develops and makes use of open items.)

3. How the data are collected and analyzed. The data gathered may be quantitative; for example, frequency counts, or qualitative; for example, verbal descriptions. The main question is: Is the observer planning to collect data in numbers or words?

To summarize, the main principles of the observation research framework are:

–   Observation studies are normally conducted in the context in which the participants study and/or work;
–   Observation studies allow the observer to study a behavior in its natural context;
–   The observer tends to avoid any manipulations of the phenomena under investigation;
–   Generalizations and hypotheses usually emerge during data collection and interpretation (data-driven approach); and
–   It is a qualitative and process-oriented research framework, but more quantitative element (product component) can be incorporated.

Exemplary Study

Gurzynski-Weiss, L., Révész, A. 2012. Tasks, Teacher Feedback, and Learner Modified Output in Naturally Occurring Classroom Interaction. *Language Learning*, 62, 851–879.

Participants:

•   University students who were studying Spanish.
•   Intermediate students of Spanish between the ages of eighteen and twenty-two.
•   Nine classes comprised of an average of sixteen students each.
•   Of the nine teachers observed, five were native speakers of Spanish and four were nonnative.

Materials and procedure:

•   The authors videotaped the nine classes twenty-three times over a period of four days.

- The twenty-three fifty-minute classroom recordings were transcribed and coded by both researchers to ensure transcriptions and coding reliability.
- Data were collected for task-related variables, feedback, and modified output.
- Based on these variables, frequencies and percentages were calculated in relation to three main predictors (task, task focus, task phase).
  - Statistical analysis (chi-square tests, logistic regression) were used to establish possible associations and to measure the relationships between the dependent and independent factors

Results:

- The key findings indicated the following patterns:

- During nontasks work teacher feedback was twice as likely to be provided;
- During nontasks learners had more opportunity for output modifications;
- In unfocused tasks teachers were 60 percent more likely to provide feedback;
- In focused tasks more than unfocused tasks, teachers' corrections entailed an opportunity for learners to modify their production;
- Teachers preferred to provide feedback in the posttask phase and use implicit techniques such as recast and overt corrections as supposed to explicit ones.

Conclusion:

- The results clearly indicated that nontasks generated more feedback from the teachers and opportunities for learner output modifications.
- Language teachers tend to use the posttask phase as a forum for focus on form to a greater extent than the during-task stage. Task factors may be significant moderator variables of the incidence and use of interactional feedback.

Case Study Design

A case study is a detailed, often longitudinal investigation of a single individual or entity or a few individuals or entities. A case study is an intensive empirical enquiry that investigates a contemporary phenomenon within its real-life context. It can be longitudinal as it sometimes spreads over a long period. A researcher observes the characteristics of an individual or a unit (e.g., class or school), with the intent to generalize about the

> Case study is considered a naturalistic and qualitative research framework with no manipulation of subjects, and no specific treatment.

wider population to which the unit belongs. Case study is considered a naturalistic and qualitative research framework with no manipulation of subjects and no specific treatment.

A case study is not a standard methodological package like an observational study or an experimental study. It is rather an instance in action, and the researcher investigates the way that his instance functions in a specific context. Case studies normally consider data from different sources, examine an issue/problem in real life, and use theory to generalize the main findings. Key components in a case study are research questions, proposition/s, analysis, linking of data to proposition/s, and criteria for interpreting the main findings.

In a case study, questions are raised about a specific object (proposition) that needs to be studied in the case. The unit of analysis can be an individual or a unit (a group of students, a school, etc.). Data collection instruments normally include questionnaires and interviews, but in a case study the researcher can use multiple procedures (both qualitative and quantitative). The data analysis is linked to the case the researcher is trying to demonstrate and/or prove.

The steps within this framework: (1) the researcher defines the object of study before the study begins; (2) the researcher selects the case study and grounds his case on a clear theoretical background; (3) the researcher decides on the data collection procedures to use; (4) the researcher provides an interpretation of the data collected and analyzed; (5) the researcher develops an explanation of the findings; and (6) the researcher aims at generalizing the findings.

Exemplary Study

Farrell, Thomas & Choo Patricia. 2005. Conceptions of Grammar Teaching: A Case Study of Teachers' Beliefs and Classroom Practices. *TESL-EJ* 9, 1–13.

Participants:

- Two experienced English primary school teachers.
- The two teachers of this case study were both very experienced English language teachers.
- The teaching of grammar in Singapore.

Materials and procedure:

- The researcher adopted a case study methodological framework to investigate the two questions. Data were collection over a period of two months and consisted of the following instruments:

- – A prestudy interview with the two teachers (this was piloted);
- – Two observations of the teachers' classes (audio recording and fields notes);
- – Pre- and postclass interviews; and
- – Random samples collection of students' written work.

Results:

- Overall, both teachers adopted a traditional approach to grammar teaching. The observed lessons indicated that the teaching approach was teacher centered, with both teachers providing explanations and instructions, and asking questions and eliciting responses from the students on their knowledge of grammar items.

- The findings indicated that the two teachers had slightly different beliefs and classroom practices in terms of grammar teaching. For one teacher there was a clear convergence between beliefs (partly influenced by their own learning and teaching experience) and actual classroom practices. This teacher believed that learners can benefit from an explicit and deductive and traditional approach to grammar teaching. The classroom practices of this teacher reflected this belief. For the other teacher instead, there was less convergence between beliefs and actual practices. The teacher expressed the belief that grammar teaching should be integrated into the practice of other language skills such as speaking, writing, and reading. However, the classroom practices of this teacher were mixed using only a few activities where learners were involved in grammar practice or where grammar was contextualized into meaningful communicative situations. Most of the grammar was explicitly taught and grammar practice was mainly structured and prescriptive.

Conclusion:

- The main findings of this study suggest that teachers have a set of beliefs that are sometimes not reflected in their classroom practices. There are several reasons that explain this divergence: (1) time seems to be a constraint for both teachers. They both argued that most of their classroom instructional decisions were directly influenced by the syllabus and the lack of time; and (2) teachers' reverence for traditional grammar instruction was another key factor. Both teachers expressed some enthusiasm for deductive approaches of grammar teaching. However, they continued to employ a traditional approach to grammar teaching as they believed that traditional grammar teaching would result in more accurate use of the target language.

What Are the Main Instruments to Collect Data?

The main collection instruments in second language research are observation schemes, questionnaires, tests, and interviews.

Observation Schemes

Observation schemes, as a data collection research tool, are perhaps one of the oldest methods used to collect data in the language classroom. The rationale behind the use of this instrument to collect data is to provide detailed and precise information about what goes on in the language classroom and how it is used in second language research for various purposes.

Observation is the act of watching something and recording the results in a way that produces data that can be analyzed and interpreted. Observation approaches can be open or closed. Open observations do not require observers to specify in advance what they intend to look at or record. "Open" means that the observers are interested in what is happening, but they have not determined exactly what they intend to observe. The observer writes in-class observation notes. "Closed observation" means that the observers have decided what they intend to observe. The data gathered may be quantitative, for example, frequency counts, or qualitative, for example, verbal descriptions. A type of closed observation is a checklist (see example in the following text) that is a form with predetermined or closed categories, usually listed down one side of the page. Space is provided (often in little boxes) to mark the presence or absence of the predetermined category. The resulting data are frequency data. Structured observation is another form of closed classroom observation using previously defined categories. In some cases, an observation form is given to the observer with instructions to note when, how often, or examples of classroom activities that in the observer's opinion exemplify the category.

Check whether the student performed the following: YES NO

1. Asked for translation of unknown words
2. Used L1 in conversation with teachers
3. Used L2 in conversation with teacher
4. Used L2 in conversation with peers
5. Referred to textbook for unknown words
6. Asked for grammatical explanations

Although it was always considered a major way of collecting qualitative data, it has also been used in quantitative and more experimental research study. This is the case of a structured observation scheme called COLT (Communicative Orientation of Language Teaching). COLT (see Figure 6.5 COLT part A), which was developed to measure the communicative orientation of language classrooms, captures the main characteristics of the communicative language teaching approach. COLT has two parts: part A describes classroom events at the level of classroom tasks and activities, and part B analyzes the communicative features of verbal interactions between instructors and students in classroom activities. This observation scheme includes five major categories: activity type (type of tasks learner is required to do); participant organization (type of interaction); content (type of instruction, meaning based or form based in its orientation); student modality (time spent on developing the four skills); and materials (type, length, and source of materials used). Each of these categories is divided into subcategories designed to describe categories of classroom procedures based on the communicative language teaching theoretical and pedagogical approach. COLT describes differences in the kind of instruction students receive in the language classroom. The classroom is observed

TIME	ACTIVITIES	PARTIC. ORGANIZATION							CONTENT							
		Class			Group		Indiv		MAN		LANGUAGE				OTHER TOPICS	
		T s/c	S s/c	Choral	Same	Different	Same	Different	Procedure	Discipline	Form	Function	Discourse	Socioling.	Narrow	Broad

CONTENT CONTROL			STUDENT MODALITY					MATERIAL							
								Type				Source			
Teacher	Teacher/Stud.	Student	Listening	Speaking	Reading	Writing	Other	Minimal	Extended	Audio	Visual	L2-NNS	L2-NS	L2-NSA	Student-made

Figure 6.5. COLT Part A (adapted from Spada 1990)

by an investigator and all the activities are coded and subsequently analyzed. To establish differences among groups in the categories considered, the analysis involves the calculation of the amount of time spent by teachers and students on the various categories and subcategories of the observation scheme. By following this analysis procedure, percentages are obtained for the various categories of the scheme.

Example: An experiment is conducted to establish possible instructional differences among three groups learning Japanese at an intermediate level. The three groups have been instructed using the same communicative program. The data are collected by an observer using COLT part A in three classrooms for four weeks. The results of the analysis indicate that the three classes are similar in most features. For example, in the case of the participant organization category, the analysis shows that instruction is teacher centered for 50 percent of the time for all classes. Similarly, in terms of the student modality category, the three classes spend most of their time primarily listening to the teacher or other students (45 percent of the time). However, some of the results of the data analysis show some important instructional differences among the three groups. For instance, in the case of the content category, although the three classes spent most of the time (50 percent) focusing exclusively on meaning-based activities and less time on form-based activities, the analysis shows that there are some individual group differences in the amount of time spent on form-based instruction (group one 32 percent; group two 22 percent; group three 9 percent). Based on these findings, the researcher hypothesized that this particular instructional difference might have a direct effect on the three groups' learning outcomes.

The analysis can be qualitative or quantitative as in the case of structured observation schemes. Observations are often recorded. Observation schemes and techniques are presented and discussed in more detail in Chapter 4 of this book.

Questionnaires

Questionnaires are often used to collect data on phenomena not easily observed such as attitudes or motivation. They are more generally used to collect data on all processes involved in learning and using languages, and also to obtain background information (see Figure 6.6). Background questionnaires could provide information on the following: (a) background information; (b) quality and quantity of the learner's previous exposure to different types of foreign language learning; (c) learner's attitudes to the different language-teaching methods already experienced; and (d) learner's expectations, attitudes, and degree of motivation to learn a language.

1) Name: 2) Nationality:

3) Mother Tongue: 4) Age:

5) Sex: 6) Degree course:

7) Previous study or knowledge of Italian: yes   no

    If yes, what kind?

8) Do you use Italian in any way with someone outside the classroom?

9) Do you have any contact with native speakers outside the classroom?

10) Have you ever visited Italy?

    If yes, for how long?

Figure 6.6. Background questionnaire

A questionnaire is often seen as several questions related to a specific area of enquiry. A questionnaire can be administered in different ways: pencil-and-paper form, online form, e-mail form, and or telephone form. Questionnaires are often paper- or computer-based instruments asking respondents for their opinions, as opposed to measuring learning performance. Questionnaires comprise three sections: demographics, close-ended items, and open-ended items. At the beginning, the researcher needs to develop a section that contains the title of the questionnaire, the date, the name, and other general information about the respondent. Typically, a questionnaire is then formatted following two options: closed-ended and open-ended. A closed-ended questionnaire either asks the questionnaire-taker, called a *respondent*, to make a choice between two options; or alternatively it asks the respondent to choose an option that in some way produces a number. As a result, closed-ended items are often easier and faster to answer than open-ended items. Examples might include true or false and Likert scale items (see Figure 6.7).

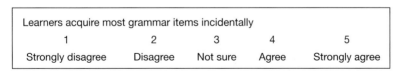

Figure 6.7. Questionnaire using Likert scale

An open-ended item is one that requires the respondent to express an opinion about a topic in direct response to a question (Figure 6.8). Questionnaire designers must decide which type of items to include.

> What do you think would be the best way to teach grammar?
>
> Write your answer here.
>
> _____

Figure 6.8. Open-ended item

Data from closed-ended items are usually drawn from a scale that quantifies the data. Depending on the scale used, this can mean frequency data (how many or how often); dichotomous data (true or false); ordinal data (ranking); or continuous data (e.g., from Likert scales) often on a one-to-five scale. Numerical data can be analyzed statistically to show trends or patterns ranging from simple percentages, descriptive statistics including mean, and standard deviation. Data from open-ended items are qualitative (words). Researchers take many steps to analyze this type of data. Firstly, they transcribe the data, probably into a document for easy manipulation. Secondly, they think about how they intend to use the data, and they group them accordingly. For example, if they posed their open-ended items to investigate A, B, and C, then they group the transcribed data responses into three groups named A, B, and C. Thirdly, they read what they have grouped together, looking for key ideas (patterns, common views, etc.). Fourthly, they read the key ideas/opinions again to see if they can identify reoccurring themes. Finally, for each theme they select a response that exemplifies the theme. More detailed information and discussion about questionnaires are provided in Chapter 5 of this book.

Tests

Tests are an instrument used to collect data about the subject's knowledge of a second language in areas such as vocabulary, grammar, language skills, metalinguistic awareness, and general proficiency. Tests are considered dependent factors in second language research and are often used to measure the effects of an independent factor that is usually a teaching method or a teaching technique.

Example: An experiment is carried out to investigate the effects of two different instructional grammar techniques (innovative vs. traditional) in the acquisition of English past forms. Two tests are developed for this study (listening test and writing tests). The listening test is constructed as a comprehension test as it consists of ten sentences (five target forms – present-tense third person, and five off-target forms – in the present tense – another person). Test takers would need to establish whether the sentence refers to an action in the past or in the present by relying on the verb ending. If they are not sure, they could tick the option "not sure" (see Figure 6.9). The scoring is calculated as follows: incorrect response = zero points, and correct response = one point.

The writing test is constructed as a sentence-completion production test to measure the learner's ability to produce correct forms in the past tense (see Figure 6.10), which test takers need to complete. The scoring procedure is the same as the listening test. Based on the statistical analysis of the two groups' scores, the researchers conclude that the innovative approach is more effective than the traditional approach in improving learners' performance on both interpretation and production of sentences containing the target feature.

You will hear twenty sentences. For each sentence you hear, decide who is doing the action or to whom the verb is referring. To Michael or his cousins:

	Michael	His Cousins	Not Sure	[Sentences heard by students)
(1)	____	____	____	plays the piano every day
(2)	____	____	____	visits the zoo three days a week
(3)	____	____	____	hates Coca Cola
(4)	____	____	____	lives in France
(5)	____	____	____	speaks Italian and Spanish

Figure 6.9. Interpretation test

You should fill the gaps with the right verb endings (ten gaps)

Sarah is a teacher. She 1.____ (works) in the local primary school. She 2. ____ (lives) five miles away from the school so she 3.____ (gets) up at 8 am 4.____ (eats) her breakfast 5.____ (gets) dressed and 6.____ (walks) to school. Sarah 7.____ (arrives) to school around 8.45 am and 8.____ (drinks) coffee before her lessons. At 9.15 am she 9.____ (starts) her first lesson and 10.____ (finishes) at 10 am.

Figure 6.10. Production test

Statistical analysis is used to compare the performance of two groups in a test (T-test).

Statistical analysis helps to determine that the difference between two or more groups is not due to chance. Two types of analysis are normally used: descriptive and parametric. Descriptive statistics is used to calculate the average (mean) and range (standard deviation) of the score for each group under investigation. Parametric statistics consists of several procedures to measure statistical relevance between and within a dependent and an independent factor. It is called *t-test*, the procedure used to compare two groups. It is called ANOVA, the statistical procedure used to compare more than two groups.

All tests need to be thoroughly evaluated before they are used. The discussion of tasks and criteria for assessment is in fact a key contribution to achieve a valid and reliable testing procedure. Reliability can be defined as consistency of measurement and is a measure of the degree to which a test gives the same results when it is given on different occasions or when different people use it.

Interviews

In an interview the researcher asks several questions to collect the views and opinions of the interviewee. A so-called open interview allows the respondent wide latitude in how to answer. An example is: *What is your view about grammar instruction?* Open interviews are normally used when the approach to the research is qualitative and the research's intention is to explore more general phenomena. A closed interview asks all respondents the same factual questions, in the same order, using the same words. Closed interviews are normally used in quantitative studies when researchers have developed a number of hypotheses they want to confirm or reject. To develop an interview, there are various issues that need to be considered. First, the type of interview that best suits the purpose of the research project should be chosen. Secondly, the audience/population to interview should be selected and considerations should be given on how many respondents should be interviewed. Thirdly, the questions should be formulated. There are a number of questions that can be asked in an interview: questions to cater to people's previous experience; questions to elicit opinions about a particular issue; questions to find out what people know; background questions such as gender, age, previous knowledge about something; and so forth. Fourthly, how the data should be collected and analyzed should be decided. There are two main approaches: extrapolating categories from the data as the researcher becomes familiar with the data and there is an attempt to interpret what the respondent is talking about. Categories emerge from the data and reflect the data. The researcher does not impose anything but lets the data speak to him, creating categories before the interview takes place. The researcher does not ask questions randomly; rather he has a clear idea of why he is asking certain questions. There are a number of steps that need to be taken to analyze an interview (see Figure 6.11).

Self-Paced Reading/Listening

Self-paced reading and self-paced listening are both implemented using computerized online software responsible for recording, listening, and reading time. Learners read a word or a phrase at their own speed. They are asked to push a button to bring up the next word or phrase once they have managed to process the information required. They keep repeating the procedure until they have processed all the input set by the researcher for the experiment. Response to online real-time processing is recorded by the experimental software. In most cases a

Step 1.	Listen to the recording and transcribe the interview.
Step 2.	Read the transcripts several times to familiarize yourself with what is being said.
Step 3.	Code the interview. Coding entails reading the transcript until certain themes become apparent. Identify each theme with a short word or phrase. This word or short phrase is the code. After you have your codes, define them so you can be consistent in coding across multiple interviews.
Step 4.	Write a summary of the coded data. For example, on a piece of paper (or word-processing document), write the code, and under each code list what the respondent said. For example, under the code "grammar" you put two comments, one of which was "Grammar is the main context of the course." Under the code block you put seven comments, one of which was "Course grammar book not related to academic writing." We then had reduced several pages of transcribed interview data down to one and a half pages of comments under various codes.
Step 5.	Write a memo to yourself that not only summarizes but also ties together.

Figure 6.11. Steps used to analyze interviews

noncumulative technique is used. In this technique only one segment (word or phrase) is visible to the learner at a time. When the next one is revealed, the previous one is masked. A self-paced technique provides the researcher with a measure of real-time processing and comprehension. Most studies, using this technique, investigate specific issues in second language acquisition such as violations and ambiguity. It is an effective online method to for sentence processing research.

Cross-Modal Priming

Cross-modal priming is an effective method to investigate moment-by-moment sentence comprehension. Learners are asked to process the input, and make a response (make a binary option, name a picture or word, etc.) as quickly as possible to a target stimulus. The stimulus is presented on a screen and comparisons are made in response times between target and nontarget stimuli. Faster response times reflect greater activation levels; thus, the researcher can examine what linguistic items are more or less activated in the learner's mind. Psycholinguistic studies often employ priming paradigms to address issues of whether and when certain representations are active in the course of language processing. In priming studies, researchers typically examine changes compared to a baseline level of performance in responding to a "target" stimulus when the target is preceded by a "prime" stimulus. This method is very natural as it allows for the stimulus materials to be presented uninterrupted and at a normal speech rate. It is used for studies related to lexical and grammatical online processing.

Eye-Tracking with Text

Eye-tracking is a method used to monitor, examine, and record learners' visual attention, visual search, and language processing during spoken or reading language processing. Eye-tracking is a method used to inform researchers with regard to eye movement behaviors. For example, it records where and for how long a participant is looking at an element in a sentence and/or where his/her eyes move next. The movement of the eyes across a sentence is not a straight line from left to right; it is much more turbulent. The eyes move in a series of jumps called *saccades*. Saccades are separated by short periods during which the eyes remain relatively still, called *fixations*. During reading, saccades move the eyes across the text to process particular words. Participants then spend most of the time, when reading a text, in fixations. This method is useful for detecting readers' sensitivity to ungrammaticalities, the interpretation of ambiguous grammatical features, and investigating online parsing procedures. This method gives researchers the opportunity to examine the moment-by-moment comprehension processes in a more natural way than, for instances, self-paced reading. Furthermore, it provides and records a more fine-grained reading profile of the different processing stages in reading: the so-called first fixations, which is the first time the eyes fixate on the region of interest (e.g., a particular word, sentence segments); the "first-pass" times, which sum up the time spent reading the region of interest from the first fixation until the eyes exit to the right or to the left; and how often the word was returned to for rereading (regressions).

Event-Related Potentials

Event-Related Potentials (ERPs) is a method used for exploring human cognitive language processing. ERPs reflect the real-time electrophysiological brain activity of cognitive processes that are time-locked to the presentation of target stimuli. Language-related ERPs research often employs a violation paradigm for presenting linguistic stimuli. In this paradigm, the ERPs' response to a linguistic violation (e.g., lexical, syntactic, morphosyntactic) is compared to the ERPs' response to a matched control word or structure. Data provides information related to timing effects (responses to a stimulus), effect polarity (positive or negative waive from a manipulation), and scalp distribution making use of electrodes across the scalp. Various types of violations (also called difficulties, disruptions, anomalies, etc.) have been shown to elicit particular ERP components in the L1. The ERPs technique allows the researcher to take the electrical activity recorded from the brain and use it to investigate cognitive processing. Researchers can record participants while they perform a task designed to elicit the proper cognitive response (e.g., attending to a specific linguistics property). To accomplish this, participants are asked to wear a mesh cap embedded with electrodes that record brain activity. In addition, electrodes can be used in the face to monitor eye movements.

What Are the Main Procedures?

Developing a question, problem, or hypothesis involves the developing of a good idea. We should never assume that, if we notice that two things usually happen together, there is a clear relationship between them. This is not always the case, as an observable phenomenon may be the result of other factors that have not been considered. Good ideas can certainly generate from intuitions and observations but at the same time must be grounded in theory and empirical research. You can develop an interest for a topic such as "the role of grammar teaching in second language learning." Through your reading and review of the relevant literature (theory and empirical evidence) you manage to focus your original interest/idea (research area) and narrow down the topic of your study (see example in Figure 6.12) to formulate researchable questions.

Good and researchable ideas come from many sources and activities. Reading published and unpublished material will help you to establish what we know and do not know about a phenomenon, a theory, and/or the key issue. It will help you to identify a gap in the existing knowledge (one issue is chosen). It will help you to make a case. WHY, now, I am the one who is going to embark in this research. Talking to people and experts will help to clarify issues, identifying gaps in the knowledge and evaluating what is already taking place. Attending conferences will help you to discover the direction of

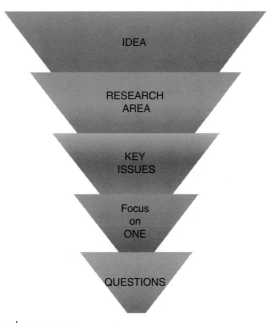

Figure 6.12. Narrowing down process

new developments and find out what is going on. In your journey to develop an idea for a study, you need to clarify WHAT specific aspects of a particular field are of most concern to you. You need to think about what the purpose of your investigation might be. Why you are interested in finding out more about the issue. This process will help you identify a list of priorities and then decide what is the most important.

Very often, whatever is the question a researcher comes to formulate, it is possible that the topic proposed has been addressed by other researchers before. This is very good news! Creating a research question is a considerable task. You start with what interests you, and you gradually refine the question until it is important and workable. There are some good tips about what a good question should look like: it should be relevant, manageable, clear, simple, and interesting. The question will be of academic, intellectual interest and relevance to your peers in the field. Questions arise from issues raised in the literature review. The first step in any investigation is to find out what other people have discovered about the topic. The literature review will provide you with the platform to discuss and cite the relevant published material. It is an opportunity to show the reader how you have managed to critically analyze what you have read. The literature review is the theoretical background underpinning your study. It provides the motivation for the study and leads to the main questions you are planning to investigate. There is a strong connection between the review/analysis of what other researchers have done and discovered about the questions in your study. The reader must be able to read the literature review and almost be in the position to anticipate the research questions you are planning to address. The questions set out what you hope to learn about the topic. The question, together with your methodological framework, will guide the choice of data collection and analysis. Some research questions focus your attention onto the relationship of particular theories and constructs: Does this theory/construct/approach affect the acquisition of English morphology? Some research questions aim to open an area to let possible new theories emerge: What is going on here?

You should be able to establish a clear purpose for your research in relation to the chosen field such as filling a gap in the existing theories, analyzing teaching practices, and comparing different approaches or testing theories within a specific population characteristic (age, gender, background, first language, motivation, etc.).

You need to be realistic about the main purpose and scale of the study you are proposing to undertake. Are you in the position to access population, specific tools from which to collect the data you need to fully address your questions? Are you able to access this data within the limited time and resources you have available to you? You need to work out how you can have access to the resources and tools you need to complete the study. Complex and unclear questions can sometimes lead to a confused research process. Questions must be clear and simple! The question also needs to intrigue you and maintain your passion throughout your study. Make sure that you have a grounded and motivated interest in your research questions!

The literature review (background section) is difficult to write! It is easy to write a summary, a descriptive account of what other researchers have said and done, but it is quite a challenge to produce a critical and analytical account of what they have said and done about a specific topic. The literature review is an in-depth synthesis of what (main purpose of the study) and how (methodological research framework) has been done in a particular field of research. To successfully review the relevant literature about a specific topic you need to apply certain categories to act as a filter in your reading. Each study you review (e.g., paper, article, chapter in book, research account) must be analyzed in terms of certain categories: motivation; research framework; what the results say and do not say; and the significance and limitations of the study. You should then provide a synthesis of each category across the relevant studies reviewed. This analysis will reveal gaps in the knowledge, contrast of opinions and findings, agreements and disagreements about theory and research, and indications for further research (see example in Table 6.1).

Once you have formulated your questions you need to think about HOW you are going to conduct your research to provide possible answers. How are you going to do it? The methodology (e.g., experiment, observation, case study, psycholinguistics methods, mixed research framework) you will select is the operating model that will provide you with the tools to conduct the study (see Table 6.2 for description of characteristics of main research frameworks).

The methodological research framework you choose will depend on the purpose and the research questions of the study. Don't think about the HOW before you

Table 6.1 Key Points for Literature Review Analysis

Author Date	Topic Questions	Theoretical Model	Research Design	Context and Setting	Findings	Limitations Gaps

Table 6.2 Research Designs

Research Designs	Type	Main Collection Instruments	Analysis Procedures
Case Study	Qualitative	Interviews Questionnaires Diaries	Content
Observation	Qualitative Quantitative	Observation Schemes Tests	Content Statistical
Experimental	Quantitative	Tests Questionnaires	Statistical
Action Research	Qualitative Quantitative	Tests Questionnaire	Content Statistical

have established the WHAT and WHY. Very often we use the one we already know as it has been used in the research papers we have read. It is important that we choose the one that can provide the better answer to our research questions.

As you review each research methodological framework to consider whether the description fits the way you envisioned your research investigation, you need to determine how the data collection and analysis will be conducted. This will help you to make very important decisions for your own study. The experimental framework will be drawing on previous studies to test or confirm hypotheses. The data collection is quantitative in nature and statistical techniques are usually used to summarize the information. Descriptive frameworks describe phenomena as they occur. It is used to identify and obtain information on the characteristics of a particular issue and in some cases to analyze and explain why or how something is happening. The data collected are often qualitative in nature. There is no consensus about how to undertake most research. Data collection procedures can supply quantitative data (numbers and statistics) or qualitative data (usually words or text). Quantitative data includes tests and surveys and attempts to test hypotheses or statements with a view to generalizing from the specific data that you have collected. This approach typically concentrates on measuring or counting and involves collecting and analyzing numerical data and applying statistical tests. Qualitative data use data instruments such as interviews, diaries, and questionnaires to generate hypotheses from the data collection rather than testing a hypothesis. Qualitative and quantitative data are not clear-cut or mutually exclusive. More recent research frameworks make use of both quantitative and qualitative data. The difference between qualitative and quantitative research in second language acquisition is based on the overall approach to research (process vs. product oriented) and on the emphasis and main objectives of the study (data driven vs. hypothesis driven).

There are three possible models of integrating methodology for second language research: in the first model, a qualitative research framework contributes to the development of quantitative instruments (e.g., questionnaire construction). The second model consists of a primarily quantitative study that uses qualitative results to help interpret or explain the quantitative findings. In the third model, the two frameworks and data instruments are used equally and in parallel to cross-validate and build upon each other's results. A mixed research framework that uses both qualitative and quantitative measures can be ideal and useful to help us to increase research validity and reliability.

Data are the main component of research. Data provide a connection between a theory and the application of the theory to the real world. Data make our research scientific and provides us with the empirical evidence to answer the questions raised. No data, no party! In a quantitative and experimental research framework, data collection instruments will mainly include tests and questionnaires. In a qualitative approach (case study and observation framework, for instance), data collection will mainly include questionnaires, interviews, diaries, and various observation techniques. You choose a particular instrument or instruments because they are considered the best way of providing empirical evidence to address the questions you have raised in the study (see Table 3.9). Whether you decide to use existing data-collection instruments, to adapt them, or to design completely new ones, the first attempt nearly always reveals unexpected difficulties. These may require the revision and refinement of the instrument to ensure validity and reliability. Validity in research is achieved when we have successfully measured what was originally planned. Reliability is related to whether our research is repeatable. The adoption of a particular data collection instrument determines the type of analysis: qualitative (descriptive) or quantitative (statistical), all depending on the data available (numbers, words, etc.).

Data obtained must be interpreted and discussed in relation to the literature you have reviewed at the beginning of this journey. Your discussion will include a reflection on the significance of the results and the possible multiple implications for research theory, methodology, and practice. You will need to indicate limitations of the study and areas for further research that should be explored by other researchers.

When you write the conclusion of your paper/dissertation, you need to remind the reader of the main thesis/objectives of the paper, so he is reminded of the argument and solutions you proposed. The conclusion is where the main points as puzzle pieces fit all together to create a bigger picture. The reader should walk away with the bigger picture in mind! No new ideas are introduced in the conclusion. The only new idea would be the suggesting of a direction for future research.

You should describe and explain your research methods, and justify your decision to use them, in the main body. Your appendices should contain blank copies of all your research instruments (questionnaires, observation sheets, etc.), together with translations into English if necessary. You should provide samples of completed questionnaires and so forth, and tables of the information that you have obtained. Very often these tables can be based on the research instrument – for example, you can replace individual responses to a questionnaire item or test score with an average of all the responses or scores. In other cases, it may be more sensible to construct new tables, for example with one row for each of your students and one column for each observed activity, questionnaire item, or whatever you wish to present. You should also include sample photocopies of students' work, if this helps to illustrate your findings, as well as transcripts (and translations) of relevant interview data and so forth. Raw data materials can also be presented in the appendix. In reporting a study and its results, whether it is in the format of a paper or a dissertation the following headings should be used: Introduction; Background (Literature Review); Motivation and Purpose of the Study; Design; Results; and Interpretation, Discussion, and Conclusion.

REFERENCES AND READINGS

- Benati, A. (2015). *Key Methods in Second Language Acquisition Research*. Bristol, CT: Equinox Publishing.
- Benati, A., Lee, J. (2010). Exploring the effects of processing instruction on discourse-level interpretation tasks with English past tense. In A. Benati and J. Lee. *Processing Instruction and Discourse* (178–197). London: Bloomsbury.
- Burns, A. (2010). *Doing Action Research in English Language Teaching: A Guide to Practitioners*. New York: Routledge.
- Dörnyei, Z. (2007). *Research Methods in Applied Linguistics*. New York: Oxford University Press.
- Farrell, T., Choo, P. (2005). Conceptions of Grammar Teaching: A Case Study of Teachers' Beliefs and Classroom/Practices. *TESL-EJ* 9, 1–13.
- Gass, S., Mackey, A. (2005). *Second Language Research: Methodology and Design*. Mahwah, NJ: Lawrence Erlbaum Associates.
- Gurzynski-Weiss, L., Révész, A. (2012). Tasks, Teacher Feedback, and Learner Modified Output in Naturally Occurring Classroom Interaction. *Language Learning* 62, 851–879.
- Jegerski, J., VanPatten, B. (2014). *Research Methods in Second Language Psycholinguistics*. New York: Routledge.
- Mackey, A., Gass, S. (eds.). (2012). *Research Methods in Second Language Acquisition: A Practical Guide*. Malden, MA: Wiley–Blackwell.

- McDonough, J., McDonough, S. (2016). *Research Methods for English Language Teachers* (3rd ed.). New York: Hodder Arnold Publication.
- McKay, S. (2006). *Research Second Language Classrooms*. Mahwah, NJ: Lawrence Erlbaum Associates.
- Nunan, D. (1992). *Research Methods in Language Learning*. Cambridge: Cambridge Language Teaching Library.
- Nunan, D. (1989). *Understanding Language Classrooms: A Guide for Instructors Initiated Action*. New York: Prentice-Hall.
- Sampson, R. (2012). The Language-Learning Self, Self-Enhancement Activities, and Self-Perceptual Change. *Language Teaching Research*, 16, 317–335.
- Seliger, H., Shohany, E. (1989). *Second Language Research Methods*. Oxford: Oxford University Press.

DISCUSSION AND QUESTIONS

1. Read the following article and fill these gaps: Benati, A. (2015). The effects of re-exposure to instruction and the use of discourse-level interpretation tasks on processing instruction and the Japanese passive. *IRAL*, 53, 2.

   Background

   Motivation and Q/H

   Methodology

   Results

   Significance of findings

   Implications

   Limitations and further research

2. Choose a couple of studies in second language research and identify the following:
   - Research questions/hypotheses
   - Research approach
   - Design
   - Data collection procedures and analysis
   - Results

3. Read these two studies and complete the following table.
   (a) Benati, A. (2005). The effects of PI, TI and MOI in the acquisition of English simple past tense. *Language Teaching Research* 9, 67–113.
   (b) Farley, A. (2004). The relative effects of processing instruction and meaning-based output instruction. In VanPatten B. (ed.) *Processing Instruction: Theory, Research, and Commentary* (143–168). Mahwah, NJ: Erlbaum.

Author Date	Topic Questions	Theoretical Model	Research Design	Context and Setting	Findings	Limitations Gaps

Please Answer the Following Questions:

What are the main findings? Are they different?

Do the authors have contrasting views?

What is/are the next step/s for further research?

7 An Overall Evaluation of the Key Questions in This Book

This book has addressed a number of key questions in language teaching. To provide an evaluation of what has been said in this book, a brief summary of the responses to these questions is given in the following text.

What Do We Know about Second Language Acquisition That Is Useful for Language Teachers and Teaching?

The perspective we embraced in this book is that language is not like learning any other skills such as driving a car or playing tennis. Language is special, abstract, and complex and humans have specific mechanisms specifically designed to deal with language. Mental representation (internal language system) and skill are distinct constructs. Mental representation represents our language competence; it is multicomponential (e.g., syntax, lexicon, universal features), implicit in nature, and abstract. L2 learners have cognitive mechanisms responsible for how they learn a language. Skill refers to our ability to use language in real time. The main implication for language teachers and teaching is that mental representation and skill do respond to different instructional treatments. Traditional practice may help to develop a so-called language-like behavior and not acquisition.

L2 learners' internal language system does not consist of rules. Their internal system looks more like a network of words connected to specific meanings and grammatical information. As we said, language is complex, implicit, and abstract. It is the result of complex interactions and emerges from what learners manage to internalize from the exposure to input. Acquisition is input dependent as it provides the main ingredient for our internal mechanisms to develop our internal system. The main implication for language teachers and teaching is that L2 learners should be exposed to input that is meaningful and comprehensible to ensure that it is appropriately processed.

Acquisition is processing dependent as not all the input we are exposed to is processed. L2 learners have processing strategies that select the information that they process, and universal principles that filter what is processed by our mind/brain. The main implication for language teachers and teaching is that successful instructional interventions must consider these processing problems. Instruction should be less about the teaching of rules and more about the exposure to form (focus on form through input manipulations/modifications). Pedagogical interventions to grammar instruction for instance should move from input (e.g., textual enhancement, structured input) to output practice (e.g., structured output, collaborative tasks).

Language production is internally constrained. L2 learners use output processing procedures to access the information in the internal language system for speech production. However, they access information in stages (due to the specific output processing procedures). The main implication for language teachers and teaching is that they should not push L2 learners through output practice too prematurely. When L2 learners are exposed to output, they should be exposed to meaningful exposure. Language interactive tasks provide L2 learners with the opportunity to interpret input, interact with others, exchange information, negotiate meaning, and eventually produce new language at the appropriate time. In effective language tasks, the role of the teacher is to set up language tasks and ensure that language learners have considerable exposure to language input and the opportunity to interpret, negotiate meaning, and produce language for a specific purpose. The role of L2 learners is to take responsibility in communicating information to others.

Is There a Particular Language Teaching Method or Approach Better Than Others?

There is not a direct answer to this question. Language teachers always expect to know what the best way is to teach languages. The language teaching field has witnessed a variety of methods or approaches in language teaching (e.g., Grammar-Translation, Audio-lingual Method, the Natural Approach, Communicative Language Teaching, Task-Based Language Teaching), highlighting advantages and disadvantages in using a particular method or approach. Language teachers should not look at the "right method" to teach languages, as there is not a single effective one. We should consider a principled and evidence-based approach to language teaching. One that is grounded and drawn from principles, theories, and research in second language acquisition, instructed second language acquisition, language use, and communication.

Language teachers are encouraged to take suggestions from here and there when it comes to pedagogical issues (teaching grammar, correct errors, developing an effective speaking activity, etc.) if their choices are guided and informed by theory and empirical research in language learning and teaching.

In this book, it has been argued for a learner-centered type of instruction, where L2 learners engage in communicative and effective tasks that involve group work and interaction with other learners. A teaching environment in which learners are exposed to tasks for a specific purpose and where the instructor is in the position to give the students many opportunities for spontaneous production, interaction, and negotiation of meaning should be achieved. A language classroom where learners should receive comprehensible input and be given opportunities to interact with their peers. Comprehensible, simplified, and message-based input is provided using contextual props, cues, and gestures rather than structural grading. A different role for the language instructor has been proposed, one that creates the opportunity and the conditions in the classroom for L2 learners to coparticipate and take responsibility for their learning. In this new environment learning can take place naturally and teaching can be more effective. In this teaching and learning environment, meaning is emphasized over form, the amount of correction is kept to a minimum, letting the students express themselves and self-repair.

An interactive classroom where L2 learners are exposed to tasks in which they engage in the interpretation, expression, and negotiation of meaning.

Based on our discussion in this book, teachers should go beyond methods and approaches and embrace a principled and evidence-based approach to second language teaching. Teachers should:

(1) Ensure they have a clear understanding of the nature and role of language to promote acquisition and not a language-like behavior;
(2) Ensure that learners are exposed to extensive "good quality" input. Input that is comprehensible and message oriented;
(3) Ensure that they develop a clear understanding of the nature and role of communication so as to develop tasks that encourage learners' interpretation, negotiation, and expressing of meaning in a given context and for a specific purpose;
(4) Ensure that language learners engage with effective language tasks (for speaking, writing, listening, and reading) where they can interact with each other and where meaning is emphasized over form;
(5) Ensure that there is also a focus on form component in their teaching and this type of practice moves from input to output;
(6) Ensure language learners are given opportunities for output practice but not through mechanical practice or the use of the Q/A paradigm. Interactive tasks (e.g., exchange information tasks, reading, and comprehension interactive tasks) should be used instead;
(7) Ensure that the amount of error correction is kept to a minimum, and learners are encouraged to self-repair; and
(8) Ensure that learners play an active role during language tasks.

Is There a Particular Type of Speaking Task Better Than Others?

Communication is the interpretation, expression, and negotiation of meaning for a specific purpose and in a given context. Output is the language produced by learners that has a communicative purpose. Oral communicative practice is in antithesis with traditional oral practice largely used in traditional textbooks. In traditional oral tasks learners are asked, for example, to look at some pictures or a dialogue and then perform that dialogue following a specific pattern. Another form of traditional oral task that is normally found in language textbooks is to ask L2 learners to talk about a topic (e.g., talk about your weekend) without taking into consideration the main principles of the communication act.

The concept of "task" is becoming quite key to ensure we adhere to the main principles of communication. Speaking tasks with a focus on meaning should be designed to allow language instructors and learners to interact with each other. The role of the instructor is to design the task and encourage participation and contribution from learners. The learner's role is to share responsibility in interaction and task completion. By providing a series of tasks to complete we encourage learners to take responsibility for generating the information themselves rather than just receiving it. Language teachers should develop speaking tasks in which learners are provided with opportunities to speak the target language and share knowledge by interacting with each other. The ability to communicate in a second language clearly and efficiently contributes to the overall success in the acquisition of a second language. Therefore, it is crucial that language instructors pay greater attention to the development of speaking skills. Rather than using mechanical practice or Q/A paradigm and leading learners to pure memorization, they should provide L2 learners with speaking tasks such as exchange information tasks and information-gap tasks that can greatly contribute in developing learners' communicative skills necessary to acquire a second language.

A task is a language-learning endeavor that requires students to (a) comprehend, (b) manipulate, and (c) produce the target language as they perform some set of work plans.

In structuring the so-called information exchange tasks, language teachers should adopt the following criteria:

- They should identify a desired information outcome;
- They should identify information sources;
- They should break down the topic into subtopics;
- They should create and sequence concrete tasks for learners to complete; and
- They should build in linguistic support.

Is There a Particular Type of Writing Interactive Task Better Than Others?

Writing is a cognitive process that involves a series of subprocesses. The same definition used for communication is applicable to the written language. Traditional writing tasks do not achieve this. Developing writing is a key component in developing learners' ability to communicate in a second language.

- Communicative composing-oriented tasks can enhance writing skills and provide L2 learners with various options about the content of what they can write.
- This approach should consider the various cognitive processes and principles responsible for developing writing skills.
  - Defining the rhetorical problem (goal/purpose and audience);
  - Planning (generating ideas, organizing them, setting goals); and
  - Reviewing (evaluation and review).

Using communicative composing-oriented written tasks that engage learners in authentic and interactive writing activities is desirable. These types of tasks aim at improving learners' writing skills and consist of three phases:

- Prewriting phase in which L2 learners are given different options so that they can make choices and decide in which direction to develop their composition;
- Writing stage that begins immediately after the previous phase and during which L2 learners become aware of the elements of good writing; and
- Language focus.

Is There a Particular Type of Listening Comprehension Task Better Than Others?

The role of comprehensible input and conversational interaction has grown important in second language teaching as learners benefit a great deal from exposure to comprehensible input, conversational interaction, and opportunities for negotiation of meaning. Listening is not just a bottom-up process where learners hear sounds and need to decode those sounds from the smaller units to large texts, but it is also a top-down process where learners reconstruct the original meaning of the speaker using incoming sounds as clues. In this reconstruction process, the listener uses prior knowledge of the context and situation within which the listening takes place to make sense of what he or she hears. Listeners use a series of mental processes and prior knowledge sources to understand and interpret what they hear. Listening is a very active skill given that learners are actively engaged in different processes while they are exposed to aural stimuli. In traditional listening comprehension practice, learners listen to a passage and answer questions or fill gaps. In a more communicative approach to listening comprehension, a three-stage approach has been proposed:

(1) In the prelistening stage, language instructors should set the context, create motivation, and activate learners' prior knowledge through cooperative learning tasks (e.g., brainstorming, think-pair-share). Prelistening tasks include vocabulary learning and/or identifying key ideas contained in the upcoming input.

(2) In the while-listening stage, tasks require learners to listen for main ideas to establish the context and transfer information. Learners are exposed to listening bottom-up tasks (e.g., word sentence recognition, listening for different morphological ending), top-down tasks (identifying the topic, understanding meaning of sentence), and interactive tasks (e.g., listening to a list and categorizing the words, following directions). Main listening tasks at this stage include guided note taking, completion of a picture, or schematic diagram or table.

(3) In the postlistening stage learners examine the functional language and infer the meaning of vocabulary (e.g., guess the meaning of unknown vocabulary, analyze the success of communication in the script, brainstorm alternative ways of expression). In the final stage of a listening comprehension task, language learners are given postlistening tasks that involve additional reading, writing, speaking, and interaction activities. Postlistening activities are both oral and written and allow teachers to bring together some of the key topics and areas of language that learners have been working on in the previous stage.

Listening comprehension tasks of this kind are preferable and more effective than traditional practice in teaching listening, which is based on merely the Q/A paradigm.

Is There a Particular Type of Reading Comprehension Task Better Than Others?

Reading/comprehension task is also an important component of a communicative classroom. Reading activities in traditional textbooks consist mainly of two types: translation tasks (read a passage and translate it) and answer questions from a text (a typical task/exercise is: Read the dialogue/text and answer the following questions). Reading should be viewed as "reading in another language rather than as an exercise in translation." The fact that language learners do not necessarily have the verbal virtuosity of a native reader means instructors need to use some strategies to help them. The framework presented here takes into consideration the need to guide learners in their comprehension of a text. Developing reading comprehension skills involves the interaction of a variety of knowledge sources. We propose an interactive model to develop L2 learners' reading skills. Specific guidelines have been suggested for second language instructors. Reading comprehension tasks should be developed to stimulate learners' motivation and should have specific communicative purposes and goals. A five-stage approach should be followed in designing reading comprehension tasks.

(1) The prereading stage is to prepare students for reading and activating their background knowledge.
(2) The reading stage is to help learners to read the text and scan for specific information or meanings.
(3) The text-interaction reading task stage is to gradually bridge the gap between the text and the reader.
(4) The postreading stage is to check and verify learners' comprehension.
(5) The personalization stage is to help learners to exploit the communicative function of the text with the use of various tasks (e.g., solve a problem, create a poster, apply main concepts to another context, relate key issues to a different context).

Is There a Particular Type of Explicit Information (Rules Explanation) Better Than Others?

The view is that we normally believe that learning rules is the main factor in the acquisition of a language. However, providing explicit information and giving rules might help in terms of developing a language-like behavior but not in fostering language acquisition. Acquisition is not driven by explicit rules but by interaction with input data and other universal language factors. Input must be comprehensible and message oriented to have an effect on our internal acquisition mechanisms. The internal language developing system is built up through the regular channels of acquisition and it is not affected by learning the explicit rules of a target language.

Is There a Particular Pedagogical Intervention to Grammar Instruction More Effective Than Others?

In traditional grammar practice, L2 learners are provided with long and elaborate grammatical explanations of target language grammatical rules (paradigms). This explicit information is normally followed by mechanical output drill practice. Drill practice usually moves from mechanical to communicative drills practice. In traditional instruction, real-life situations are completely ignored, and practice is implemented in a completely decontextualized way. A more effective and communicative way to incorporate a grammar component in language teaching is key. Although "one size does not fit all," there are some principles teachers should keep in mind when developing effective grammar tasks. (1) Incorporating grammar in a more communicative framework of language teaching by devising grammar tasks that enhance the grammatical features in the input. (2) Effective pedagogical interventions aim at manipulating the input (e.g., textual enhancement, input flood, structured input tasks) L2 learners receive. Input is grammatically manipulated to facilitate language processing and grammar acquisition. Output grammar-based tasks (e.g., structured output tasks, collaborative tasks such as dictogloss) can follow input practice and exposure. Vocabulary can be learned and practiced through language tasks where words are enhanced in a comprehensible and meaning-bearing input.

Is There a Particular Type of Error Correction Better Than Others?

The role of error correction (corrective feedback) in language teaching is not completely clear yet. Traditional explicit corrective feedback provides L2 learners with a meta-linguistic explanation about a form or structure or explicit error correction. This kind of direct error correction might have a temporary effect (improve performance) but does little good in the long run. A more implicit type of error correction has been proposed, one that might inform L2 learners of their nontargetlike use of certain linguistic features. Recasts, confirmation checks, clarification requests, repetitions, and even paralinguistic signs such as facial expressions can all constitute indirect correction options. These options mainly aim to offer the opportunity to identify contrasts between correct forms and incorrect forms and subsequently to promote "noticing." Through output (reformulating their initial utterances) they might be able to notice the gap between their current language and the target language. Repair can assist L2 learners in actively confronting errors in ways that may lead to revisions of their hypotheses about the target language. Recast might enable L2 learners to be exposed to target forms and elicit repetition, and this repetition may, in turn, enhance salience. Enhanced input may contribute to the acquisition of new linguistic forms.

Epilogue

The existence of this variety of methods and approaches in language teaching does not mean that we should necessarily adopt one of them, or attempt to develop a new one that has characteristics derived from them. Instead, the suggestion in this book is that we should consider a principled and evidence-based approach to language teaching. One that draws from theories and empirical research in second language learning and provides some effective options for teachers and teaching. This approach to language teaching should address some of the main pedagogical questions, and it should be guided and informed by theory and the findings from empirical research in language learning and teaching. It is not what we think might work but what works (based on evidence) and is effective in the language classroom that we need to consider. A principled and evidence-based approach will have the following characteristics:

- The language input provided in the classroom will be comprehensible and meaningful. Learners must be given the opportunity to interact and to be exposed to meaningful input;
- Grammar is not explained through rules or paradigms but it is embedded in the input (manipulated input) and language learners should be engaged with grammar tasks moving from input to output practice. It is paramount to have a good understanding of the role and nature of language to approach the teaching of grammar;
- Vocabulary is practiced taking into consideration the following: present new words repeatedly and frequently in the input; use meaning-bearing comprehensible input when processing new words; present words in an enhanced manner;
- Tasks become the main type of activities in the classroom and are based on a specific definition of communication. During language interactive tasks (e.g., information-exchange tasks, problem-solving tasks), learners have the opportunity to interpret input, interact with others, exchange information, negotiate meaning, and produce new language;
- Error correction is kept to a minimum. Teachers provide more exposure to correct input through recasts and language learners are encouraged to self-repair;
- The role of the teachers is the one who sets up language tasks and ensures that language learners have considerable exposure to language input and the

opportunity to interpret, negotiate meaning, and produce language for a specific purpose;

–   Listening, reading, writing, and listening skills are better developed using a pre-while-post task approach.

Teachers must be encouraged to actively conduct their own investigations in the language classroom to test the effectiveness of all these options and pedagogical interventions in language teaching.

As we look at the future, language scientists need to continue to conduct research looking into how language is represented in the mind/brain, how it is comprehended and produced, and how universals and bilingualism affect the human mind-brain. The mission of researchers and practitioners is to change the idea that language is a list of rules, that a paradigm is the way language is represented in the mind/brain, that communication can be reduced to the Q/A paradigm, that explicitly teaching grammar and vocabulary is necessary or even beneficial, that practice makes perfect, that first-language transfer is the source of all learning problems, and that adults learn languages differently from children.

'The way forward is to provide appropriate language teachers training for TESOL and modern language teachers; to change practices and policies as far as language curriculum and language testing in schools and universities. Curriculum or language teaching materials must be genuinely informed by what we know about language and language acquisition. Language scientists have the responsibility to carry out appropriate and sound empirical research. Language scientists have started to investigate the brain signatures of second language acquisition by comparing different groups of learners undergoing different kinds of language instructions. They have been using machines and lab equipment (eye-tracking, self-paced tests, and EEG systems) to test what happens to students' brains in real teaching/acquisition contexts. Very soon we will be in the position in which we can predict whether acquisition of a second language is really taking place when using specific pedagogical interventions.

We should continue to conduct neurolinguistics and psycholinguistic longitudinal and cross-sectional experiments in real language classes with real learners. Neuro-/psycholinguistic-teaching research is the new quest for the "Holy Grail." We can now track the internalization and development of language competence. This would widen the horizons of second language acquisition research to an extent that cannot be predicted now.

Glossary

Action Research Action research is a research design used in second language research to undertake a small-scale investigation by teachers in the classroom.

Audio-Lingual Method The Audio-Lingual Method is a teaching method based on the behaviorist theory and structural linguistics. The main tenets for this method include the use of paradigms, repetition, and mechanical drill practice.

Behaviorism The theory of behaviorism attempts to explain human behavior without reference to thinking or mental processes. At the heart of this theory is the belief that language is a set of patterns or habits.

Case Study Case study is a research design often used to conduct a detailed longitudinal investigation of a single identity or a group.

Clarification Request/Confirmation Check The two terms refer to a series of conversational and interaction devices used by both learners and instructors to require more information when there is a breakdown in communication. Learners and instructors sometimes request clarifications (e.g., what did you say?) and/or confirmations (e.g., did you say ...?) if they do not comprehend language input.

CLIL This is a method to language teaching that uses the L2 as the medium of instruction to teach other subject matters such as chemistry or philosophy.

Communication Communication is defined as the interpretation, expression, and negotiation of meaning in a given context and for a specific purpose.

Communicative Competence Communicative competence comprises different competences: Grammatical Competence, Pragmatic Competence, Sociolinguistic Competence, and Strategic Competence.

Communicative Language Teaching Communicative Language Teaching is an approach to language teaching that views language as an act of communication. The main goal is to ensure L2 learners develop communicative competence.

Complexity Theory Complexity Theory views second language acquisition as the result of the interaction of various components.

Comprehensible Input This term refers to simplified and modified input that learners need to acquire a second language. Input is an effective tool for acquisition, if it contains a message that can be comprehended by L2 learners. Features in language (e.g., vocabulary, grammar pronunciation) make their way into the learner's language system only if they are linked to some kind of meaning and are comprehensible to L2 learners.

Consciousness Raising This term refers to a particular pedagogical intervention to grammar instruction that intends to raise learners' consciousness on a specific grammatical form/structure in a targeted L2 while it provides the opportunity to engage in meaningful interaction. Consciousness-raising tasks can be inductive or deductive. In the case of an inductive task learners are provided with some language data and are required to provide an explicit representation of the target linguistic feature. In the case of a deductive task learners are given a description of the target linguistic feature and are required to use that description to apply it to L2 data.

Corrective Feedback This term refers to a series of techniques that involve drawing learners' attention to an error in their input. Corrective feedback techniques are used by teachers to provide feedback to L2 learners about the incorrectness of utterances.

Declarative/Procedural Model The Declarative/Procedural Model is unlike other second language acquisition theories in that its roots lie in neuroscience and the structure of the brain. Fundamental to the model is that there are two memory systems served by different parts of the brain.

Dictogloss This term refers to a type of collaborative output tasks that aims at helping L2 learners to elicit output and use their grammar resources to reconstruct a text. Dictogloss tasks are designed to draw learners' attention to language forms/structures while promoting negotiation of meaning.

Direct Method This is a method of language teaching based on principles of L1 child language acquisition. In this method the teacher encourages learners to make associations between a grammatical form of a target language with the meaning that form encodes.

Drills A drill is a classroom technique used to practice new language. It involves the teacher modeling a word or a sentence and the learners repeating it or substituting a word in a sentence using the correct form.

Elicitation Elicitation is a correction technique that prompts the L2 learner to self-correct. Learners are asked to produce the correct form either by completing the teacher's own restatement, asking learners questions about how something should be said, or asking learners to repeat utterances in a reformulated version.

Emergentism Emergentism is cognitive psychology theory that attempts to account for human learning and knowledge. The main claim of this theory is that language acquisition makes use of the same general architecture for knowledge and performance as any other form of learning (e.g., how to learn to play football).

Experimental Study Experimental study is a research design where two main variables are controlled and manipulated: the independent (teaching method) and the dependent (language tests). The main objective of this methodology is to establish a relationship between the two variables.

Exchange Information Tasks This term refers to pedagogical tasks where L2 learners engage in oral communication and use the information they have gathered to accomplish a task. In structuring the so-called information exchange task, language teachers should adopt the following criteria: identify a desired information outcome; identify information sources; create and sequence concrete tasks for learners to complete; and build in linguistic support.

Explicit Corrective Feedback Explicit corrective feedback is characterized by an overt and clear indication of the existence of an error and the provision of the targetlike reformulation and can take two forms: explicit correction and metalinguistic feedback.

Focus on Form This term refers to any pedagogical attempts to draw learners' attention to linguistics properties of a target second language in the language input. Focus on form is learner centered.

Focus on Forms Focus on forms refers to teaching discrete linguistic structures in separate lessons based on structural syllabus. Focus on forms instruction is teacher centered.

Form–Meaning Connections This term refers to the connections made between a form (-*ed*) and the meaning that that from encodes (in this case, pastness).

Input This term refers to the language learners hear or read and has a communicative intent. Many scholars have agreed that input is the main ingredient for the acquisition of a second language. Two main characteristics make input useful for the learner: input must be message oriented and comprehensible.

Input Enhancement This term refers to a particular pedagogical intervention that attempts to bring a particular form/

structure to L2 learners' focal attention by enhancing the input through the use of various devices such as textual enhancement. In textual enhancement activities the target form is enhanced, visually altering its appearance in the text (i.e., the form can be italicized, bolded, visually altered with a different color, or underlined). The form/structure is highlighted in a text/dialogue with the hope that learners will notice it.

Input Flood This term refers to a pedagogical intervention where L2 learners are exposed to many instances of the same form/structure in the input. The form is not usually highlighted, and the instructor does not draw learners' attention to it. The purpose of designing/using input flood activities is to help learners to be exposed to a greater amount of input containing the target form, which hopefully will allow learners to notice and subsequently acquire this form.

Input Processing For the Input Processing Theory L2 learners bring processing strategies for making form-meaning connections to the task of comprehension. As L2 learners attempt to comprehend what they hear, they encode linguistic features in the input for use by the internal mechanisms responsible for the developing of mental representation.

Interaction This term refers to conversations between native speakers and nonnative speakers that might affect acquisition. The importance of interaction (both input modifications and feedback) is that it can bring something in the input into the learner's focal attention at a given moment, offering an opportunity to perceive and process some piece of language the learner might miss otherwise.

Interaction Hypothesis The Interaction Hypothesis makes a number of claims in terms of the role of input, interactional modifications, feedback, and output in second language acquisition. Input plays a crucial role in second language acquisition. Interaction also plays a key role. Output is necessary for the development of language. Negative feedback obtained during negotiation of meaning might facilitate the acquisition of vocabulary, morphology, syntax, and pronunciation.

Jigsaw Task This term refers to a collaborative output task where L2 learners can work in pairs or in small groups. Each pair or group has different information and they have to exchange their information to complete the task. Each individual or pair must give and receive information, and therefore opportunities for negotiation of meaning are promoted during jigsaw tasks.

Language Language can be described as an abstract and complex construct. Language acquisition is not like learning how to drive a car or play tennis. Language acquisition is different than the concept of skills. Another concept related to language is the one about mental representation.

Listening Comprehension Tasks Listening is one of the language skills most frequently used. L2 learners receive a great amount of information through listening from instructors and other interlocutors. Listening can be defined as an "active skill." Listeners are actively involved in interpreting what they hear by bringing to a listening task their own background knowledge and linguistic knowledge to be able to process and understand the information contained in what they hear. In a listening comprehension task, a prelistening task stage is developed to enable students to activate what they already know, predict information, and/or to deal with problematic vocabulary and structures. During the listening stage, language instructors can develop tasks in which L2 learners are asked to match short phrases with a list of dates and/or identify specific sentences in the passage. In the postlistening task stage learners are asked to articulate their ideas and clarify meanings. Learners are given the opportunity to "personalize" their understanding of the passage and monitor their own progress.

Mental Representation This term refers to the abstract, complex, and implicit system in learners' mind/brain.

Metalinguistic Feedback In metalinguistic feedback the focus of conversation with the language learner is diverted toward rules or features of the target language. Metalinguistic feedback is divided into three subcategories: metalinguistic comments, metalinguistic information, and metalinguistic questions.

Natural Approach The main principles of this approach to language teaching are that language instructors should provide good comprehensible and message-oriented input for acquisition. They should create a good classroom atmosphere in which there is low filter for learning and orchestrate a wide range of classroom activities.

Negotiation of Meaning This term refers to interactional modifications such as comprehension checks or requests for clarification between an instructor and a learner or between a learner and another learner during communication. Negotiation of meaning is triggered when there is a communication breakdown between two or more interlocutors. The purpose of negotiation is to resolve the communication breakdown and can occur in just about any kind of interaction.

Nonverbal Feedback Nonverbal feedback is also another form of corrective feedback. Body movements and signals such as gestures, facial expressions, rolling your eyes, crossing your arms, and head, hand, and finger movements are all different forms of feedback. Nonverbal feedback is feedback that the teacher provides to students with their actions (e.g., smiling, patting a student's shoulder).

Observation Study This is a research design making use of both qualitative and quantitative procedures to measure a number of behaviors in the classroom.

Output This term refers to the language that learners produce. Language production (oral and written) can help learners to generate new knowledge and consolidate or modify their existing knowledge. Output has several roles in second language acquisition: output practice helps learners to improve fluency, check comprehension and linguistic correctness, focus on form, and realize that the developing system is faulty and therefore notice a gap in their system.

Paradigm This term refers to the use of tables to introduce and explain to learners the rules and grammatical structures of a target language.

Processability Theory Processability theory's main concern is to investigate the constraints on learner production of formal features during real-time communication.

Processing Instruction This term refers to a pedagogical intervention of grammar instruction whose main aim is to help L2 learners to accurately and appropriately process grammatical forms/structures in the input. It is a type of focus on form that draws on the principles of the input processing model. Processing Instruction seeks to intervene in the processes learners use to get data from the input. Research on input processing has attempted to describe what linguistic data learners attend to during comprehension and which data they do not attend to; for example, what grammatical roles learners assign to nouns or how to position in an utterance influences what gets processed. Processing Instruction guides and focuses learners' attention when they process input. Processing Instruction consists of three main components: learners are given explicit information about a linguistic structure or form; learners are given information on a particular processing principle that may negatively affect their picking up of the form or structure during comprehension; and learners are pushed to process the form or structure during structured input activities in which the input is manipulated in particular ways to push learners to become dependent on form to get meaning. Structured input activities can be of two types: referential and affective.

Prompt Prompt consists of four prompting moves: elicitation, metalinguistic clue, clarification request, and repetition. All these moves offer learners a chance to self-repair by withholding the correct form.

Reading Comprehension Tasks Developing reading skills is seen as developing the ability to read in another language. L2 learners read texts in another language for a specific purpose. They read to gain specific information. The purpose of the reading comprehension tasks is to bridge the gap between the reader and the information contained in the text. The tasks follow a five-stage approach with a prereading stage, a reading stage, a text-interaction stage, a postreading stage, and a personalization stage.

Recast This term refers to a type of corrective feedback in which language instructors provide a correct version of an incorrect utterance. Recasts are restatements of a learner's utterance that occur naturally in interactions. They usually occur when the L2 learners have produced some kind of nonnativelike utterance and the other interlocutor is confirming what the learner intended to say, as a kind of confirmation check.

Repetition This form of corrective feedback is simply the teachers or interlocutors' repetition of the ill-formed part of the student's utterance, usually with a change in intonation.

Sociocultural Theory Sociocultural Theory argues that the development of human cognitive functions derives from social interactions and that through participation in social activities individuals are drawn into the use of these functions.

Skill This term refers to the ability to perform in the target language accurately and fluently. *Accuracy* refers to the ability to do something correctly. *Fluently* refers to the speed and confidence of the learner to perform an activity.

Skill Acquisition Theory Skill Acquisition Theory is a theory in cognitive psychology centered around three stages of development: cognitive, associative, and autonomous. The three stages are distinguished by major differences in the nature of knowledge, usage, and behavior.

Structured Input Tasks Structured input practice is one of the components of the pedagogical intervention called processing instruction.

Structured Output Tasks This term refers to a type of form-focused task that involves the exchange of previously unknown information and requires learners to access a particular form of structure to express meaning. James Lee and Bill VanPatten have provided some guidelines to develop structured input activities: present one thing at a time; keep meaning in focus; move from sentences to connected discourse; use both written and oral output; and others must respond to the content of the output.

Task A task is a language-learning endeavor that requires students to (1) comprehend, (2) manipulate, and (3) produce the target language as they perform some set of work plans. Tasks provide learners with a purpose for language use and make language teaching more communicative.

Task-Based Language Teaching Task-Based Language Teaching refers to a type of language teaching that takes "tasks" as its key units for designing and implementing language instruction.

Textual Enhancement It refers to a type of focus on form used to make particular features of written input more salient with the scope to help learners notice these forms. The target form is enhanced by visually altering its appearance in the text (italicized, bolded, underlined). Oral input enhancement can also be provided by using special stress, intonation, and gestures in spoken input.

Total Physical Response Method Total Physical Response Method is a comprehension-based method to language teaching. The method assumes that language learning should start with understanding the language we hear or read before we proceed to production. It is a method of language teaching that makes use of physical movements to react to verbal input.

Traditional Grammar Instruction Traditional grammar instruction refers to the paradigmatic presentation of rules followed by mechanical drill practice.

Traditional grammar instruction fosters a language-like behavior in L2 learners but it does not lead to acquisition.

Translation Translation was initially considered as a subcategory of recast, but what distinguishes it from recast is that the former is generated in response to a learner's ill-formed utterance in the target language while the latter is generated in response to a learner's well-formed utterance in a language other than the target language.

Universal Grammar Theory Universal Grammar Theory sees language as mental representation. That is, it is an abstract and complex system residing in the mind/brain of a human. An important aspect of this theory is what is called the poverty of the stimulus. The poverty of the stimulus is based on the observation that people come to know more about language than what they have been exposed to.

Writing Tasks Writing tasks refers to communicative composing-oriented written tasks that engage learners in authentic and interactive writing activities. These types of tasks aim at improving learners' writing skills and consist of three phases: prewriting phase, writing phase, and focus on language phase. Writing tasks would need to reflect authentic purposes. Writing tasks should have clear guidance and a scaffolding approach.

References and Readings

Ahmed, R. Z., Bidin, S. J. B. (2016). The Effect of Task Based Language Teaching on Writing Skills of EFL Learners in Malaysia. *Open Journal of Modern Linguistics* 6, 207–218.

Asher, J. (1977). *Learning Another Language through Actions: The Complete Teacher's Guide Book.* Los Gatos, CA: Sky Oaks Productions.

Azizeh, C. (2016). The Effects of Task-Based Instruction on Reading Comprehension among Iranian Intermediate EFL Learners. *Applied Research English Language* 4, 19–29.

Barcroft, J. (2018). *Vocabulary in Language Teaching.* New York: Routledge

Benati, A. (2015). *Key Methods in Second Language Acquisition Research.* London: Equinox Publishing.

(2013). *Issues in Second Language Teaching.* London: Equinox.

(2005). The Effects of Processing Instruction, Traditional Instruction and Meaning-Output Instruction on the Acquisition of the English Past Simple Tense. *Language Teaching Research* 9, 87–113.

Benati, A., Angelovska, T. (2016). *Second Language Acquisition: A Theoretical Introduction to Real World Application.* Bloomsbury: London.

Benati, A., Batziou, M. (2019). The Effects of Structured-Input and Structured-Output Tasks on the Acquisition of English Causative, *IRAL*, 57 (3), 265–288.

Benati, A., Lee, J. (2010). Exploring the effects of processing instruction on discourse-level interpretation tasks with English Past Tense. In A. Benati and J. Lee. *Processing Instruction and Discourse* (178–197). London: Bloomsbury.

(2008). *Grammar Acquisition and Processing Instruction.* Clevedon: Multilingual Matters.

Benati, A., Rastelli, S. (2018). Special Issue: Perspectives in the Neurocognition of the Second Language Teaching-Acquisition Interface. *Second Language Research*, 34.

Benati, A., Schwieter, J. (2019). Pedagogical interventions to L2 grammar instruction. In J. Schwieter and A. Benati (ed.). *The Cambridge Handbook of Language Learning* (475–499). Cambridge: Cambridge University Press.

Bernhardt, E. (1991). *Reading Development in a Second Language.* Norwood, NJ: Ablex.

Brown, S. (2011). *Listening Myths.* Ann Arbor: University of Michigan Press.

Burns, A. (2010). *Doing Action Research in English Language Teaching: A Guide to Practitioners.* New York: Routledge.

Chomsky, N. (1965). *Aspects of the Theory of Syntax.* Cambridge, MA: MIT Press.

Corder, S. Pit. (1981). *Error Analysis and Interlanguage.* Oxford: Oxford University Press.

Dave, W., Willis, J. (2007). *Doing Task-Based Teaching.* Oxford: Oxford University Press.

DeKeyser, R. M. (ed.) (2007). *Practice in a Second Language: Perspectives from Applied Linguistics and Cognitive Psychology.* Cambridge: Cambridge University Press.

Dörnyei, Z. (2007). *Research Methods in Applied Linguistics.* New York: Oxford University Press.

Doughty, C., Pica, T. (1986). Information Gap Tasks: Do They Facilitate Second Language Acquisition?, *TESOL Quarterly* 20, 305–325.

Doughty C., Williams, J. (eds.) (1998). *Focus on Form in Classroom Second Language Acquisition.* New York: Cambridge University Press.

Ellis, N. (2007). The associative-cognitive CREED. In B. VanPatten and J. Williams (eds.) *Theories in Second Language Acquisition* (77–95). Mahwah, NJ: Lawrence Erlbaum.

Ellis, R. (2003). *Task-Based Language Learning and Teaching.* Oxford: Oxford University Press.

Ellis, R., Shintani, N. (2014). *Exploring Language Pedagogy through Second Language Acquisition.* London: Routledge.

Farley, A. (2004). The relative effects of processing instruction and meaning-based output instruction. In VanPatten B. (ed.) *Processing Instruction: Theory, Research, and Commentary* (143–168). Mahwah, NJ: Erlbaum.

Farrell, T., Choo, P. (2005). Conceptions of Grammar Teaching: A Case Study of Teachers' Beliefs and Classroom/Practices. *TESL-EJ* 9, 1–13.

Field, J. (2008). *Listening in the Language Classroom.* Cambridge: Cambridge University Press.

Gass, S., Mackey, A. (2005). *Second Language Research: Methodology and Design.* Mahwah, NJ: Lawrence Erlbaum Associates.

Gass, S. M., Behney, J., Plonsky, L. (2013). *Second Language Acquisition: An Introductory Course.* New York: Routledge.

Grabe, W. (2009). *Reading in a Second Language: Moving from Theory to Practice.* New York: Cambridge University Press.

Gurzynski-Weiss, L., Révész, A. (2012). Tasks, Teacher Feedback, and Learner Modified Output in Naturally Occurring Classroom Interaction. *Language Learning* 62, 851–879.

Hinkel, E. (2005). (ed.) *Handbook of Research in Second Language Teaching and Learning.* Mahwah, NJ: Lawrence Erlbaum Associates.

Housen, A., Pierrard, M. (2005). *Investigations in Instructed Second Language Acquisition.* New York: Mouton de Gruyter.

Keating, G. (2018). *Second Language Acquisition: The Basics.* New York: Routledge.

Krashen, S. (1985). *The Input Hypothesis: Issues and Implications.* New York: Longman.

(1982). *Principles and Practice in Second Language Acquisition.* Oxford: Pergamon.

Krashen, S., Terrell, T. (1983). *The Natural Approach: Language Acquisition in the Classroom.* Hayward, CA: Alemany Press.

Jegerski, J., VanPatten, B. (2014). *Research Methods in Second Language Psycholinguistics*. New York: Routledge.

Larsen-Freeman, D. (2000). *Techniques and Principles in Language Teaching*. Oxford: Oxford University Press.

Lee, J. (2000). *Tasks and Communicating in Language Classrooms*. New York: McGraw-Hill.

Lee, J., VanPatten, B. (2003). *Making Communicative Classroom Happens*. New York: McGraw-Hill.

Lightbown, P., Spada, N. (2013). *How Languages Are Learned* (4th ed.). Oxford: Oxford University Press.

Loewen, S., Sato, M. (eds.) (2017). *The Routledge Handbook of Instructed Second Language Acquisition*. New York: Routledge.

Long, H. M. et al. (2018). A Micro Process-Product Study of CLIL Lesson: Linguistic Modifications, Content Dilution and Vocabulary Knowledge. *Instructed Second Language Acquisition* 2, 3–38.

Long, M. (2015). *Second Language Acquisition and Task-Based Language Teaching*. Malden, MA: Wiley-Blackwell.

(2007). *Problems in SLA*. Mahwah, NJ: Erlbaum.

Long, M., Doughty, C. (2009). (eds.) *The Handbook of Language Teaching*. Oxford: Wiley-Blackwell.

Lyster, R., Ranta, L. (1997). Corrective Feedback and Learner Uptake: Negotiation of Form in Communicative Classrooms. *Studies in Second Language Acquisition* 19, 37–66.

Mackey, A. (2002). Beyond Production: Learners' Perceptions about Interactional Processes. *IRAL* 37, 379–394.

Mackey, A., Philip, J. (1998). Conversational Interaction on Second Language Development: Recasts, Responses, and Red Herrings? *Modern Language Journal* 82, 338–356.

Mackey, A., Gass, S. (eds.) (2012). *Research Methods in Second Language Acquisition: A Practical Guide*. Malden, MA: Wiley-Blackwell.

MacWhinney, B., Bates, E. (eds.) (1989). *The Cross-Linguistic Study of Sentence Processing*. Cambridge: Cambridge University Press.

McDonough, J., McDonough, S. (2016). *Research Methods for English Language Teachers* (3rd ed.). New York: Hodder Arnold Publication.

McKay, S. (2006). *Research Second Language Classrooms*. Mahwah, NJ: Lawrence Erlbaum Associates.

Motallebzadeh, K. (2013). The Effects of Task-Based Listening Activities on Improvement of Listening Self-Efficacy among Iranian Intermediate EFL Learner. *International Journal of Linguistics* 5, 24–34.

Nassaji, H. (2015). *The Interactional Feedback Dimension in Instructed Second Language Learning*. London: Bloomsbury.

Nassaji, H., Fotos, S. (2011). *Teaching Grammar in Second Language Classrooms*. New York: Routledge.

Nation, I. S. P. (2001). *Learning Vocabulary in Another Language*. Cambridge: Cambridge University Press.

Nunan, D. (2004). *Task-Based Language Teaching*. Cambridge: Cambridge University Press.

Nunan, D. (1992). *Research Methods in Language Learning*. Cambridge: Cambridge Language Teaching Library.

(1989). *Understanding Language Classrooms: A Guide for Instructors Initiated Action.* New York: Prentice-Hall.

Ortega, L. (2010). Exploring interfaces between second language writing and second language acquisition. Paper presented at the Symposium on Second Language Writing, Murcia, Spain. Oxford: Oxford University Press.

Pienemann, M. (1998). *Language Processing and L2 Development.* Amsterdam: John Benjamins.

Polio, C. (2018). *Teaching Second Language Writing.* New York: Routledge.

Qin, J. (2008). The Effect of Processing Instruction and Dictogloss Tasks on Acquisition of the English Passive Voice. *Language Teaching Research* 12, 61–82.

Richards, J. C. (2012). *Tips for Teaching Listening.* London: Pearson.

Richards, J. C., Rodgers, T. S. (2001). *Approaches and Methods in Language Teaching.* Cambridge: Cambridge University Press.

Robinson, P. (ed.) (2012). *Routledge Encyclopedia of Second Language Acquisition.* New York: Routledge.

Rost, M. (2002). *Teaching and Researching Listening: Applied Linguistics in Applied Linguistics in Action.* London: Longman.

Rost, M., Wilson, J. (2013). *Active Listening.* London: Pearson.

Sampson, R. (2012). The Language-Learning Self, Self-Enhancement Activities, and Self-Perceptual Change. *Language Teaching Research* 16, 317–335.

Savignon, S. (2005). *Communicative Competence: Theory and Classroom Practice.* New York: McGraw-Hill.

Savignon, S. J. (1983). *Communicative Competence: Theory and Classroom Practice.* Reading, MA: Addison-Wesley.

Saville-Troike, M., Barto, K. (2017). *Introducing Second Language Acquisition.* Cambridge: Cambridge University Press.

Schmidt, R. (ed.) (1995). *Attention and Awareness in Foreign Language Learning.* Honolulu: University of Hawai'i, National Foreign Language Center.

Schwieter, J., Benati, A. (2019). *The Cambridge Handbook of Language Learning.* Cambridge: Cambridge University Press.

Seliger, H., Shohany, E. (1989). *Second Language Research Methods.* Oxford: Oxford University Press.

Selinker, L. (1972). Interlanguage. *International Review of Applied Linguistics* 10, 209–231.

Sheen, Y. (2011). *Corrective Feedback, Individual Differences and Second Language Learning.* New York: Springer.

Slabakova, R. (2016). *Second Language Acquisition.* Oxford: Oxford University Press.

Swain, M. (1995). Three functions of output in second language learning. In G. Cook, and B. Seidlhofer (eds.), *Principles and Practice in Applied Linguistics* (125–144). Oxford: Oxford University Press.

VanPatten, B. (2007). *While We're on the Topic: BVP on Language, Acquisition and Classroom Practice.* Alexandria, VA: American Council on the Teaching of Foreign Languages.

(2003). *From Input to Output.* Hightstown, NJ: McGraw-Hill.

VanPatten, B., Benati, A. (2015). *Key Terms in Second Language Acquisition.* London: Bloomsbury.

VanPatten, B., Rothman, J. (2014). Against rules. In A. Benati, C. Laval, and M. Arche. *The Grammar Dimension in Instructed Second Language Learning* (15–35). London: Bloomsbury.

VanPatten, B., Smith, M., Benati, A. (2019). *Key Questions in Second Language Acquisition: An Introduction.* Cambridge: Cambridge University Press.

Williams, J. (2005). *Teaching Writing in Second and Foreign Language Classrooms.* Hightstown, NJ: McGraw-Hill.

Willis, D., Willis, J. (2007). *Doing Task-Based Teaching.* Oxford: Oxford University Press.

Wilson, J. J. (2008). *How to Teach Listening.* London: Pearson Longman.

Wong, W. (2005). *Input Enhancement: From Theory and Research to the Classroom.* New York: McGraw-Hill.

Wong, W., Simard, D. (2018). *Focusing on Form in Language Instruction.* New York: Routledge.

Wong, W., VanPatten, B. (2003). The Evidence in IN: Drills Are Out. *Foreign Language Annals* 36, 403–423.

Zhao, H. H., Anderson, N. J. (2009). *Second Language Reading Research and Instruction: Crossing the Boundaries.* Ann Arbor: University of Michigan Press.

Index